CONGREGATIONS:

Their Power to Form and Transform

C. Ellis Nelson

Editor

John Knox Press
ATLANTA

Acknowledgment is made for permission to quote from the following sources:

To Anthony Clarke for material from *Spiritual Direction and Meditation*. Reprinted by permission of Anthony Clarke from *Spiritual Direction and Meditation* by Thomas Merton. Copyright 1975 by Anthony Clarke.

To Hodder and Stoughton, Ltd. for material from *Fire in Coventry*. Reprinted by permission of Hodder and Stoughton, Ltd. from *Fire in Coventry* by Stephen Verney, copyright 1965.

To Turret Books and Christopher Logue for material from *Ode to the Dodo, Poems 1953–1987*.

Library of Congress Cataloging-in-Publication Data

Congregations : their power to form and transform.

    Includes bibliographies.
    1. Church.   2. Mission of the church.   3. Pastoral theology.   4. Christian education—Philosophy.
I. Nelson, Carl Ellis, 1916-
BV600.2.C64   1988   250   87-35252
ISBN 0-8042-1601-0

Preface

This book is just one of many projects which have been conceived or encouraged by the Lilly Endowment, Inc., to help congregations achieve their potential for spiritual and moral leadership. I want to thank the Lilly Endowment for a grant to cover most of the expenses related to developing this book and Robert W. Lynn for his personal interest in the project.

When Carl Dudley, Janet Fishburn, and Mary Elizabeth Moore met with me in Chicago to design this book, we planned a consultation between the writers and a group of ministers and lay leaders. The purpose was to give the writers a chance to see how the intended audience for this book understood what had been written and to hear an evaluation of its usefulness. In the light of this two-day consultation, the writers modified their essays in order more clearly to communicate their ideas to the people who are responsible for the worship and work of congregations.

I want to thank the following ministers and lay leaders for reading the chapters and taking two days to share their responses with the writers. The following persons participated in this consultation: Constancio Amen, Ora Baker, John R. Braulick, Mary Currie, Faye Lee Decker, E. B. Elswick, Pamela Engler, David Evans, Marian Fielder, R. Douglas Hester, Ken Jatko, Richard Johnson, Eula Rae McCown, Susan McKeegan-Guinn, David J. McNitzky, Laura Mendenhall, Nancy Moss-man, Warren J. Muller, Michael G. Renquist, Ronald Paul Salfen, Ray Schroeder, J. Allen Smith, Robert C. Walker, Jr., and C. Keith Wright. In addition, Professors Laura Lewis and David Hester helped plan and participated in the Austin consultation.

I want to express appreciation to Austin Presbyterian Theological Seminary and to its president, Dr. Jack L. Stotts, for providing student assistance, administrative services, a congenial place for the consultation to be held, and for the secretarial services of Dorothy Andrews and Laura Black.

Also, appreciation is expressed to Dr. John Spangler for his careful and helpful editorial work in preparing this volume.

C. Ellis Nelson

Contents

Why This Book on Congregations?

C. ELLIS NELSON

Austin Presbyterian Theological Seminary

The reason for publishing a book on *congregations* is the easiest part of the question to answer. The Christian faith is rooted in congregations. The books of the New Testament were letters to congregations, about congregational life, or, possibly, composed by congregations. Individuals are urged to repent, to believe, and to conduct themselves as persons who acknowledge Jesus Christ as their Lord and Savior. But individuals are always in congregations or, according to the New Testament, are expected to join a congregation. Individual Christians, apart from a community meeting for worship and for a sharing of life's experiences in the light of their faith, are unknown in Scripture.

The reason for *this* book on congregations requires a more involved answer. There are many books, written from a theological perspective, on what congregations ought to be, how they ought to worship, or what they ought to do. There are helpful books for ministers on how they can improve some aspects of congregational work such as stewardship, evangelism, social action, or education. Few existing books have the purpose of this one, namely: *to help ministers, Christian educators, and lay leaders explore the major factors which create, sustain, critique, and transform the unique characteristics of congregations and to propose ways they can influence the character and mission of the congregations in which they have a leadership role.*

Process

In order to achieve this purpose, a meeting was convened for a small group of persons who have special interests in and concerns for congregations. They met to work out plans for this book and to select writers who have given special attention to different phases of congregational life. As a part of the design, it was decided to submit the chapters to a group of ministers and lay leaders ("responders") for their critical review. The writers and the responders met in Austin, Texas for a two-day consultation. During that time, each writer had his or her chapter critiqued by a cross section of the people for whom the book is written. As a result of that consultation, writers revised their essays and the nature of the book was modified to make it more usable.

This book is suitable for study by groups of officers or lay leaders in congregations. However, it is not a "how to do it" book, nor is it a manual that takes people by the hand and leads them through a simplified version of congregation improvement. Rather, it is an attempt to deal with the complexities of ten major factors affecting congregational life in such a way that church leaders can apply them to their situation. If we had suggested that changes in congregational life were easy, we would have been false to what we know about churches. On the other hand, congregations can change when some leaders become serious about their leadership, their life together, and their mission to the community in which they are located. If such concern were to lead to a study of the nature of their congregation in order to help it to become a more faithful demonstration of Christian faith and life, then this book is a guide they can use to develop an understanding of congregational life and to suggest ways of changing. Exactly how a congregation should attempt to change is something that each group must work out for itself or the change will not be authentic; that is, it must be something the members desire to do because they believe it to be their response to the guidance of the Spirit of God.

Special Features

We believe ministers, Christian educators, and lay leaders know a lot about congregations. Their knowledge comes from experience in different congregations in diverse locations. When I talk with these leaders in informal situations, such as while standing in the hall, sitting in an office, or even in a home, I find a great deal of savvy—"street smarts," so to speak— that comes directly from experience or from being close to a people struggling to make congregational life more significant. But these same leaders, when they speak in official places, such as in congregational officer meetings or in the higher governing bodies of a denomination, suppress their experiential knowledge of congregations and shift to theological language reflecting what a congregation ought to be.

This suppression of the experiential knowledge of congregations and the substitution of theological language would have surprised the first Christian theologian, the Apostle Paul. Paul was realistic about humankind. He named his competitors in the church at Corinth, he cited persons engaged in immoral practices, he protested selfishness and drunkenness in people who gathered for the Lord's Supper, and he condemned other congregational practices which were out of harmony with the spirit of Christ. In fact it was the sinful human conditions in the congregation that persuaded Paul to write the letter in order to relate theology to their condition. When properly related to Christian belief, therefore, experience is the way we develop our understanding of congregational life.

It may be that ministers often suppress their experiential knowledge of congregations because it is related only to a few congregations or because it is about conditions they think were peculiar to a certain time and place. Therefore, they think their experience cannot be generalized into "rules" or "principles" which would be of interest to others or could be transferable to other situations. That judgment may be true, but experience is valuable if it is reflected upon and if it is placed in a larger perspective where it has a rightful place. It is hoped that, as church leaders use this book in a study class context, they will find opportunities to use their experiences to give personal meaning to the range of congregational situations discussed in this book.

1. The focus is on the congregation as a whole. This is easy to say but difficult to comprehend. We think of a congregation as a whole when it needs to make decisions such as approval of a budget, or when assembled for worship, or when it calls a new minister. Otherwise, we think of a congregation in terms of groups, such as the choir, the officers, youth groups, or Bible study classes. That kind of thinking is what this book is trying to change—namely, the idea that music is done by the choir, decisions are made by officers, education takes place in classes, and our responsibility to youth is to provide a group to which they can belong. As right and necessary as it is to have groups within a congregation, it is wrong and unnecessary to look on these groups as anything more than a practical way to have something special for the edification and enrichment of all parts of the whole congregation. The idea of this book is that music, for example, is something in which the choir may have a special competence but that music as a companion of the soul is for the whole community of believers.

It is our contention that the congregation is more than— and different from—the sum of its groups. It is *more* because the whole includes all ages and conditions of members; therefore, it represents the body of Christ and reminds us of our obligation to each other. It is *different* because the promise of God's Spirit is to be present in the community of believers; therefore, there is a need to search for God's will for the *whole* congregation. (See Matt. 18:15–22 for one example.) All of the chapters in this book were written from the standpoint that the *whole* congregation should be the reality about which we must think if we are to bring about significant change.

   2. It provides a Christian interpretation of individualism. The previous point about the whole congregation as the reality about which we are writing raises the question of the place of individuals within the collective. The individual is the basic reality of our conscious life, but as already affirmed, the Christian faith is rooted in a local community where people share the meaning of faith and organize to do God's will in the world. The congregation is thus perceived to be, in a sense, superior to the individuals who make up the congregation. Such an affirmation is offensive to many people, especially Americans, so we must pause for a few paragraphs to put the matter in perspective.

   The individualism so dear to Americans is relatively new. It had its origin in the Enlightenment which started in England in the seventeenth century and spread to France and other Western countries. The political form of this American individualism is enshrined in the Declaration of Independence: "We hold these truths to be self-evident, that all men are created equal, that they are endowed by their Creator with certain unalienable Rights, that among these are Life, Liberty, and the Pursuit of Happiness. . . ." These "Rights" plus others that have been picked up along the way are often referred to nowadays as individual freedom.

   Robert Bellah and his colleagues have pointed out that earlier—in our colonial period—such individualism was relatively unknown. In that earlier era individuals covenanted together to make a society which would provide security and help for all people. Thus individuals owed allegiance and service to society for the common good. But much of this earlier sense of obligation for society has been eroded away as people today seek "utilitarian" or "expressive" individualism. That is, they are busy feathering their own nests or seeking ways to enjoy life with little regard for the common good or for future generations. These forms of individualism, according to Bellah and his associates, lack commitment to the welfare of society. Their study ends with a call to transform American culture by a variety of means so that individuals will once again understand responsibility for the commonwealth.[1]

Such a transformation will be difficult, for there are other factors that enforce the radical individualism of the Declaration of Independence. One is our fairly recent history of western expansion. As the nation moved west, independence and self-confidence were the most prized qualities for Indian-fighting, for cutting down forests to build log cabins and to create farm land, for a lonely existence in isolated regions, and for living in a territory without customs or laws except what the settlers brought with them. Much of this period is celebrated in the "Lone Ranger," a cowboy type who appears in conflict situations, makes things "right," and then moves on in the setting sun to straighten things out somewhere else. It is unfortunate and unhistorical to exclude women from this past. A literature is now developing which shows that women were as heroic in the realm to which society assigned them as were the men.[2] However, leaving gender aside, traits of self-confidence, self-assertiveness, and self-reliance and a willingness to struggle against nature and hostile Indians created a special brand of American individualism.

The Christian interpretation of individualism underlying these chapters emphasizes the responsibility and the accountability of individuals but always in a context of commitment to being the body of Christ—the church—in the community in which we live. This allegiance to a community of believers is not an assignment that must be carried out, nor is it something that one can elect to accept or reject. Rather, a congregation is the place where the Christian faith is communicated from past to present, where the faith is interpreted for the needs of the day, and where the faith might grow stronger by exercising it with people who share the faith. This corporate nature of Christianity is stressed in the following chapters to help counteract the excessive individualism that Americans have absorbed from our society.

Assumptions

Those two special features (the congregation as a whole and a Christian form of individualism) are augmented by the following assumptions about congregations.

First, the congregation is a unique social institution. Congregations are not clubs, yet friendships generated within a congregation are often the best human relationships we know. They are not established to reform or rule society, yet many changes in our social life are rooted in the life and witness of Christians. They certainly are not business enterprises, yet congregations, through their members, are related to much commercial activity. They are not interest groups for the arts, yet no other institution has supported the arts over a longer period of time or provided more inspiration for music and architecture than have congregations. They are not schools, yet congregations probably spend more time and money on education than any other single activity. Congregations are unique because they are a gathering of people who share beliefs and seek to understand and do God's will in the circumstances of their lives. Their constant reference to God—who is in but also beyond life—is what gives congregations a unique status among all groups to which a person belongs.

Second, congregations have a corporate personality created by their history, location, size, beliefs, and leadership. This corporate personality has a mental image and a momentum. The mental image lies in what most members believe is its place and mission. Thus, some congregations in small communities are self-consciously the community at prayer. Some see themselves as having a mission to a racial or ethnic group. Other congregations think of themselves as a "cathedral," that is, the dominant church in town with the self-assigned duty of organ recitals and other activities attractive to the public. Moreover, the image members carry around in their heads has a momentum. The image is transmitted to new members, and children accept it as a given, just as they accept the church building as the proper kind of building for religious activities.

This momentum of the mental image can be good or bad, depending on what it is. But regardless of quality, the writers have assumed that efforts to change an image are difficult and can be made only at a slow pace.

Congregational personality also embraces a style of life which characterizes the people. Thus some congregations are "friendly," others "cold," "indifferent," "enthusiastic," or "conventional." Moreover, the mood of the people may be experimental—they'll try new ideas and programs. Or, the congregation may be against anything that breaks with past traditions. Where the congregation is in its life cycle affects its action. A newly formed congregation is full of expectation and discusses the kind of activities they desire in their developing program. Older congregations in older neighborhoods may be facing an identity crisis. It is not difficult to identify and describe a congregation's personality. All one has to do is to answer questions such as, "What do the members spend their time doing?" "What does the congregation spend its money for?" "What is the nature of the decisions made by the officers for the past five years?"

Third, the dynamic element in congregations is the interaction of its members. One demonstration of this power is in governance—the way the community makes corporate decisions. All congregations have rules—written or commonly accepted—to guide the conduct of their business. The rules are about procedures, not about the decisions to be made. So what we see in congregational decisions is the outcome of the interaction of members. If, for example, most members want to start a youth program, they will talk about it until a way is found to begin some activity toward that end.

This dynamic element is related to leadership. In several chapters there is reference to the central role of leaders in setting goals and shaping the outlook of the congregation, which can only be done within boundaries in which leaders may operate. Otherwise their suggestions will be thwarted or rejected. The interaction of members is a normal and natural aspect of human associations. Such interaction is not to be feared, but it must be recognized; nor can it be commanded, but it can be influenced. Ministers and lay leaders can provide style and substance for this ongoing interaction through worship, careful committee work on matters going to the congregation (or governing body) for decision, and classroom teaching.

Another demonstration of the power of congregational interaction is in education. Notice that in the sentence about places where influence could be exercised I used the term "classroom teaching." Important differences exist between teaching and learning, between education and schooling. This book assumes education to be extremely important and closely related to the dynamic interaction that goes on incessantly in congregations. Some of the most significant things about Christian faith are learned from members talking to each other about moral choices they have made in particular circumstances, about prayers that were answered, about things that were included or excluded from their religious outlook, about the "right" attitude toward economic and political issues, or about the truth of a certain doctrine. This condition has great potential for shaping the life of a congregation. If, for example, many adults become interested in Bible study and begin to read the Bible with the same seriousness they use to examine important documents, then that concern will slowly permeate the whole congregation.

Contrasted with education, schooling is an organized effort to teach, usually in a classroom. In American Protestantism, schooling is considered to be the "Sunday school." As long as the Sunday school is seen as an effort to instruct, it is properly perceived and will have a rightful place along with all other efforts to teach the Christian faith. Unfortunately, however, Sunday school is thought to be the principal agency of education—something that cannot be true. The principal agencies of education are the family, the congregation, the peer group and, for adults, their work situation.

The Sunday school is often equated with education because of its history. When the Sunday school movement spread to America from England in the early 1800s, it changed in order to fit a different environment. The United States at that time was struggling to separate religion from the public school and to establish a public school system. The two leaders in this enterprise, Horace Mann and Henry Barnard, who became the first United States Commissioner of Education in 1867, never tired of saying the public schools should not teach religion, for the churches could do that in their Sunday school. At that time (during the 1830s) and throughout the rest of the 1800s several realities predominated: (1) a general Protestant ethos in the nation, (2) the family as a close unit with strong parental leadership, and (3) the enormous influence of the church in the community, partly because many ministers had educations superior to community leaders. In that setting, the Sunday school for a few hours each week could explain the Christian faith and enlarge people's knowledge of what they already knew in a general way from many other sources.[3] That setting is not our situation today because (1) the Protestant ethos—in fact, the whole Judaeo-Christian tradition—is no longer a force that formulates issues and offers solutions from a religious perspective; (2) the nuclear family (in the sense of parents with their biological children and the mother working in the home), although idealized as normative, is not the experience of half our people; and (3) the church, though present nearly everywhere, does not shape public opinion in the decisive way it did in the nineteenth and at the beginning of the twentieth century. Today, without this supporting environment, the Sunday school cannot be the chief educational agency of the church.

If the Sunday school as a strategy for communicating Christian faith will no longer be sufficient because times have changed, what should our strategy be? This book is an attempt to answer such a question by saying that the congregation is the agency for interpreting the faith by the way it fashions its life and work. The congregation with a comprehensive education program for adults, plus classes for all ages, can effectively communicate faith and the meaning of faith to all of its members. This congregational strategy requires that we understand the power of the community as members interact with each other. Each of the chapters in this book starts with the congregation and then relates the whole to the parts. The Sunday school, or any other effort to instruct, is important; but it is the whole congregation which sets the interpretive pattern for understanding the Bible and supplies the motive for worshiping God and seeking God's will in the changing circumstances of life. Unless readers understand this primacy of the congregation, they will not be able to appreciate why the writers discuss their subjects in a special way.

Fourth, congregations can change. This was assumed by all the writers, and in some chapters they indicated how changes could be inspired. Even chapter three (concerning how the present situation of a congregation tends to supply a way to interpret the past in order to support its current interests) affirms that congregations can change and suggests how leaders can bring about change. Other chapters are more specific in this regard. However, the reader should not expect to find a set of rules or steps that should be taken to bring about change. Rather, this is an effort to focus attention on the centrality of the congregation and then to help the reader begin an analysis of a congregation so that program and planning will be rooted in the total life of the community. To be specific, little will be accomplished if a congregation tries to improve its Sunday school by selecting a different printed curriculum. However, much will be accomplished if a congregation instructs adults in the faith and maintains a worship and communal life which enriches the spiritual life and broadens the mental perspective of adults, since all the Sunday school teachers and youth leaders come from the adult members.

Reader's Guide

What follows is a brief statement about each of the chapters. The purpose is to show why the chapter was written and to relate it to the purpose of the book.

Memory in Congregational Life. We start with the biblical understanding of faith rooted in congregational life. This fact, made especially clear in the New Testament, turns our attention to those events in the past that have established the nature and substance of our Christian faith. We also notice

that congregations formed soon after the crucifixion of Christ
had tensions within them as they sought to reconcile their
situation with their image of what God expected them to be
and do.

The chapter, however, does not leave us with this dilemma. Bruce Birch concludes with some suggestions as to how
congregations today can refresh their memory of the Christian
tradition, especially the Bible, in order to develop their vision
of what their mission should be in the community in which
they are located.

**The Congregation as Chameleon: How the Present
Interprets the Past.**   For many congregations, however, the
present is so powerful that it obscures or distorts the past so that
the past does not provide the guidance needed for the present.
This comes about rather easily if people in a congregation make
their current interests the basis of their church life. The result
will be congregations that are primarily social clubs, political
associations, or societies for civic betterment. If such interests
become the spectacles through which the past is viewed, then
the past is used to support whatever the congregation wants to
be. The church that takes on the coloration of the present becomes indistinguishable from other good organizations in the
community just as a lizard (chameleon) can turn whatever color
is necessary to look like the branch it is on.

Jackson Carroll knows the power of the present and
how wrong it can be, yet he resists the temptation to condemn
it or to propose a simple formula of going back to the past to
get our bearings and then applying that knowledge to the
present. Rather, he proposes that congregations *learn* to be
open to the present. This means congregations must appropriate the past for the present. They do so by being aware of
human needs in the community and the positions their denomination has taken in national and world issues. Leadership—lay as well as professional—is essential for the process
of congregational self-analysis to be effective. Usually this
means that the minister must have a vision of what the rule

of God in contemporary life should be in order to help church members move toward a proper openness to the world. If a congregation understands the present this way, it will become a good chameleon because it will have a mission to the world of which it is a part.

Why Do People Congregate? In keeping with the purpose of this book, we started with the congregation and noted how the past should influence the present and how the present tends to interpret the past. Now we need to think about the individuals who make up the congregations. A congregation cannot be formed, grow, or change unless we know why people come together and what holds them in fellowship.

David Steward begins his answer by showing how unique our American situation is. The Europe from which many Americans came originally had state churches into which one was born, so that the meaning of membership was already defined. In America the church became separated from the state and people could choose to join, not join, or drop out of congregations. Thus, today an individual participates in a church only if the congregation offers something of value. Theologically speaking, what should be valued is the opportunity to worship God and to serve God's concern for the world about us. Unfortunately, not all church members have that motivation, or perhaps the congregations they have been in do not live up to their expectations. Steward, therefore, reviews studies of why people leave the church on the assumption that, if we knew why they left, congregations would know what they should be like in order to retain their members. In order that this evaluation from drop-outs not be negative, Steward ends his chapter with three good reasons why people congregate.

Using Church Images for Commitment, Conflict, and Renewal. As soon as we think of particular congregations, we begin to have mental images of the church building, of the minister, of certain things that the congregation has done, or of the denomination of which it is a part. Also, images are derived from the Bible or from the church's membership, such

as being a "society church" or being made up of a certain racial/
ethnic group. Those images are in a sense stereotypes and do
not accurately describe a congregation, but they do represent
a mental effort to grasp the significant features of a congregation so that we can appraise its significance.

Carl Dudley uses this image-making propensity of the
mind to create eight types of congregations. These eight categories are descriptive of different ways the congregations might
be faithful to their mission. The categories are not designed to
be critical of any particular style unless a congregation carries
its uniqueness to excess. No congregation, according to Dudley,
is exclusively one type. Rather, a congregation reflects several
types as it goes about its activities. Moreover, as a congregation
goes through stages of development, it will probably change
from one image to another. From a practical perspective, this
understanding of images is useful in conflict situations, for if
advocates of contrary positions understand the image that inspires them, then the controversy can be turned to a discussion
of what ought to be rather than of what individuals desire.

Centers of Vision and Energy. We now move directly
to a particular congregation in order to review the way people
interact with each other and their environment as they work
out their common purposes. The sum of all these activities over
time produces an ongoing story which explains its continuity
with the past and the changes which have taken place.

Donald Miller uses a congregation's story as the way to
open up a discussion of where they are and where they want
to go. He then offers a six-step method by which a congregation
can examine some aspect of its life with a view to making
appropriate changes. How to bring about changes in a congregation so that the congregation itself grows and becomes more
effective is a complex matter. Miller develops this complexity
by noting that congregations have special characteristics which
predispose them to change. The liturgical type will be open to
events that tie congregational changes with worship; the management type will respond to projects that are problem-

centered; the primary group type picks up readily on people-problems; the growth and development type is concerned for well-planned programs; the prophetic type is sensitive to injustice; while the interpretation type is alert to events as they happen. Miller's use of congregational types is not really an effort to classify (as Dudley has done in the previous chapter). Rather, it is a way to find an entry point in the ongoing life of a congregation so that significant changes might be made.

Meeting in the Silence: Meditation as the Center of Congregational Life. Another way of fostering change in a congregation is to give serious and careful attention to contemplation. This form of meditation is characterized by silence in which an individual or group seeks to relate to God. The circumstances of life surround the enterprise, for we know ourselves in terms of gender, age, responsibilities, hopes, fears, and other conditions which shape our self-knowledge. In the midst of all this, the purpose is to "draw near to God," not simply to pray for answers or instruction on how to solve pressing problems. Such silence is almost unknown in American Protestant congregations, intent as we are on doing things.

Mary Elizabeth Moore writes that "listening for God is an art to be cultivated." She discusses meditation, prayer, and contemplation along with study and reflection, receptivity, and awe and reverence as disciplines that can be learned. Moreover, she maintains that through these disciplines the congregation will not only learn but also be led into actions guided by its listening to God. Moore has been supervising seminary students as they participate in congregations, studying how these congregations relate to God in their congregational life. From these experiences she describes six practical aspects of an educational ministry based on listening.

Belonging: A Sacramental Approach to Inclusion and Depth of Commitment. The theme of spiritual formation is continued in this chapter as such formation relates to noteworthy turning points in a person's pilgrimage. Congregations with easy standards for membership and, perhaps, with few ceremonies related to significant points in one's life cycle, have only a small percentage of the members participating in the work and worship of the congregation. Congregations with high standards for membership tend to be smaller but with a higher percentage of the members participating.

Robert Browning analyzes this situation in terms of what membership in a church should mean. The clue he offers is an inward commitment based on self-understanding. Such belonging needs to have a back-and-forth relationship between the major points in one's growth and a recognition of that point's spiritual significance, such as: birth/baptism, coming of age/confirmation, need for communion/Lord's Supper or Eucharist, vocation/ordination of clergy or consecration of laity. Other significant points in the life cycle are discussed and all are related to how these developmental stages provide opportunities for recognizing God's grace, which is always present. To belong to a congregation that celebrates these occasions properly is to experience the meaning of the Christian faith in the changing circumstances of one's life.

Leading: Paideia in a New Key. Leadership is recognized almost everywhere as the key to a properly functioning congregation. Two major questions arise when we focus attention on leadership. One is "Who leads—ministers or lay people?" The other is "What is the nature of leadership in a congregation?"

Janet Fishburn does not accept the easy answer to the first question by affirming the leadership of both ministers and lay people. Rather, she describes how in former times the Sunday school as a semi-autonomous lay movement generated its own leadership. In recent times, the Sunday school has been taken over as a part of the congregation's work, but the congregation has not always accepted responsibility for training leaders for the Sunday school or any other church activities. Thus lay people function more as "members" than as leaders of congregations.

Fishburn answers the second question by saying ministers will need to recall the theology of congregations as found in Ephesians 4 and then share that vision with the congregation. A nurturing ministry—that is, people taking responsibility to care for each other's needs—is a spiritual venture involving visitation and sharing of mutual concerns. It can never be reduced to a course in "leadership." She concludes her essay with practical suggestions about how a congregation can be mobilized for spiritual formation and, as a by-product, produce leaders of the type appropriate to Christian congregations.

Communicating: Informal Conversation in the Congregation's Education.   Beneath the surface of the program and worship life of the congregation, a dynamic set of informal structures and processes exists. One of the most obvious elements in this undercurrent of activity in a congregation's life is the constant informal conversation among church members. Although it has content, it is usually considered unofficial or unimportant. It certainly does not have the status of official Sunday school curriculum, important announcements of the congregation, or sermons.

Charles Foster, however, takes the position that informal conversation between church members is about important personal or congregational matters. It has power to enrich, diminish, distort, or reinforce whatever is said in Bible classes or sermons. It can also promote and secure change in congregational activities or schedules. Thus, conversation must be considered educational, for it is a deliberate effort to transmit information, attitudes, and desires. Having shown how hidden curriculum can be discovered, Foster proceeds to suggest three ways to facilitate conversation so it can enhance and improve congregational life.

Teaching: Forming and Transforming Grace.   Teaching is almost always defined as deliberate activity toward rather clear goals. Learning is usually considered to be what people appropriate from teachers or from experience. This distinction has value but is probably too tidy because life is not lived with such clear boundaries. Life is much more cluttered with teaching and learning intermingled in many activities.

Maria Harris, therefore, starts this concluding chapter

with a conception of the Christian life as a response to God. Thus, her idea of teaching is not first how to do it or even how to set a goal. Rather, she says we must first ask "Who calls us to teach?" That question focuses attention on the self in relation to God and leads naturally to a sharing of our knowledge about God. After that question is answered Harris then points out that teachers are able to decide what should be taught, understand and use the influence of the congregation as context, identify sources of inspiration and help, and, finally, understand what can be done to make teaching an activity that involves all our senses around units of work that are reasonable and fun to accomplish.

Postscript

As indicated at the beginning of this introduction, the purpose of this book is to help church leaders see congregational life as the place where individuals may "grow in the grace and knowledge of our Lord and Savior Jesus Christ" (2 Peter 3:18). Such understanding will, we hope, cause church leaders to take a fresh look at all of the opportunities for making their congregation a better learning community.[4]

We who have worked on this project were tempted to propose a set of specific things congregations could do in order to have a better learning environment. We resisted that temptation because we know that no set of suggestions would fit a particular congregation. What you will find in the following chapters will be a discussion of some major factors you need to consider as you work through the specific circumstances of your congregation. Many of the writers also have suggested principles by which a group of church leaders could develop programs to make congregational life more meaningful.[5] We wanted to emphasize over and over and over again that the *particular* congregation is the community in which persons experience the meaning of the Christian faith and the community to which they refer mentally as they make decisions in all the circumstances of their lives. Thus, we hope this book will be used by church leaders to open up specific things they can do in their situation to become more like the body of Christ, always looking, as the Apostle Paul did, to Christ as the source of direction and inspiration. In the language of the Gospel writer John, the congregation needs to seek the guidance of the Holy Spirit, for we have the promise that the Spirit will not only comfort us, but also will lead us to the truth we need for our lives today (John 14:15–17, 25–27).

Memory
in
Congregational
Life

BRUCE C. BIRCH
Wesley Theological Seminary

A few years ago an active member of our congregation objected to one part of a litany being written for the reception of new members. It was a segment giving thanks to all of those faithful women and men who had labored in the communities of faith that went before us. It remembered with gratitude our ancestors in the biblical communities and those who carried the work of the church through subsequent history. This man objected because he said that he felt little or no tie to those people. For him the church was important because of the support and witness of this congregation in the immediate present. He participated because of what he found there and not because of what the past had been.

A bit later on the same evening, older members were sharing with new members the aspects of life in that congregation that meant the most to them. The man who objected earlier shared as his most cherished moments in the life of the congregation the oneness of community he felt in those times when we gathered around the table for the passing of bread and wine in Holy Communion. Someone immediately challenged him, "Dave, did you think the sacraments were originated by our worship committee?" He and every member of a Christian congregation owe a great debt to our past, but most church members are not very conscious of that debt.

How are congregations influenced by the past? Why is awareness of that past important? How do we bring that past to greater consciousness in the life of the congregation? How do we draw on the resources of our past to enable our mission as the church in the present? Those are questions we hope to bring into focus by looking at the role of memory in the life of the congregation. It is in the activity of remembering that our past as the church becomes a source of power for the present and for the future. A central role for memory in congregational life was present from the very beginnings of faith communities in the biblical tradition.

The Formation of Congregational Life

When they were first called into being the communities of faith in the Old and New Testaments were individual congregations. The "congregation of Israel" at Mt. Sinai where the covenant was formed could be addressed by Moses in a single assembly. The early church, empowered by the Spirit at Pentecost, consisted of the apostles and those people converted by Peter's preaching on that day. They organized themselves as a single congregation. Soon the people of God in Israel, and in the early church, grew too large for the gathering of a single congregation. Yet many understandings of faith community had become fixed in the life of the congregation which continued to be important for the extended life of the people of God into many congregations. Because of those beginnings as congregation, our biblical faith is strongly insistent on a faith that has meaning in the life of local communities seeking to live in relationship to God. Attempts to focus faith on the larger trans-congregational institutions of religious life always have met with a challenge from prophets or apostles who called for expressions of faith that included and addressed the needs of local communities of faith (e.g., Hosea's concern for the people of the land while kings and priests focus on the needs of palace and temple, or Paul's letters to struggling young churches in spite of conflicts with the authorities in Jerusalem).

Several features are clear in the biblical formation of congregational life. These features deserve renewed attention in our assessment of the ways in which the past addresses modern congregational life.

1. A congregation is formed in response to God's initiative of grace. In the Old Testament Israel was brought into being as the people of God by God's deliverance of the Hebrews from bondage in Egypt (Exod. 14—15). In that Exodus event God freely entered human history in an act of grace to slaves with no worldly standing, and that graceful act was motivated by love alone (Deut. 7:7–8). That Exodus experience became for Israel a model throughout succeeding generations for the way in which God's saving grace is experienced. As with Israel at the Red Sea those who trust in God's grace can experience hope out of despair and life out of death. The future is opened up by God in unexpected ways.

At Mt. Sinai the congregation came into being as a covenant community in response to God's salvation. Exodus created a delivered people but it was with the covenant at Sinai that Israel became an organized congregation of response to God's saving action. In the covenant accounts we see Israel struggling to give concrete expression to its life as a delivered people. Faith cannot exist in the abstract. It must issue forth in how people live as community in the world. The congregation must give form to its faith in worship, in relationship to the neighbor, and in faithful life in the world.

In the New Testament the dynamic is virtually the same. It is God's grace in Jesus Christ which initiates and calls us to response as the church. In crucifixion and resurrection we see once again the drama of God's salvation. Death becomes life. Despair turns to hope. It is this resurrection faith that is experienced as God's grace generation after generation in the church. When Pentecost comes and the church is born, it is in response to God's grace and made possible by God's Spirit (Acts 2). The earliest Christian congregation in Jerusalem immediately set to work organizing its life in patterns consistent with the grace they had come to know in Jesus Christ. Concrete patterns of worship, sharing of resources, and missional activity in the world came into being (Acts 2:43–47; 4:32–37).

It is important in the modern church's congregational life to see faithful community as a response to the grace which comes from God, and not as the source of God's grace itself. Thus, the agenda for congregational life is always set by God's will, prayerfully and reflectively considered, rather than the congregation's own self-interest. Such self-interest was also a temptation for the biblical communities of faith; but when the priority of God's grace and the community's stance of response to God's initiative in the world was lost from view, the result was judged in biblical tradition to be broken covenant and sinful exercise of self-interest.

2. A congregation is formed around the qualities of memory and vision. Memory is oriented to activities of remembering what God has done and how faithful response has been made to God's action. Vision is oriented to activities of anticipating what God is yet doing in the world and aligning congregational life to serve that action of God's grace. The cultivation of memory and vision issues forth in the congregation's *identity and mission*. The community of faith stands with one foot rooted in a historic tradition from which it draws its identity as God's covenant people. Its other foot is firmly planted in a future, God's future, toward which it lives in anticipation of the fulfillment of God's desire for love, justice, and wholeness.[1]

In the covenant-making at Mt. Sinai God's first words call the people to an act of historical remembering. "I am the LORD your God, who brought you out of the land of Egypt, out of the house of bondage" (Exod. 20:2). The words of Peter's sermon at Pentecost are a summons to historical memory. "Men of Israel, hear these words: Jesus of Nazareth, a man attested

to you by God with mighty works and wonders and signs which
God did through him in your midst, as you yourselves know . . ."
(Acts 2:22). The faith community in our tradition was not organized around abstract philosophical principle or socio-political
theory. It was organized around historical particularity maintained in the act of remembering. Out of this remembering
comes the vision of what God's community is called to be. This
is immediately expressed in the Sinai setting by the Decalogue
and the Covenant Code which follows it. This quality of antic-
ipatory vision which marks the mission of the congregation can
be seen more broadly in the theme of the "land to which I (God)
am bringing you." The challenge to "choose life and good" over
"death and evil" (Deut. 30) in that land stands as an admonition
to congregations of all generations as they approach the new
horizons of their futures.

   Throughout the Old and New Testaments the necessary
interrelation of memory and vision can be seen grounding community identity and empowering community mission. As Israel
struggled with the new vision of nation-building, the people
were admonished to "remember that you were a slave in the
land of Egypt, and the LORD your God redeemed you"
(Deut. 15:15). Memory reminded a young nation, tempted to
pride because of its roots among the dispossessed, about the
humility which comes from recognizing its life as the gift of
God. Alongside such calls to memory came the proclaiming of
new visions: blessing to all the families of the earth (Gen. 12:3);
swords beaten into plowshares (Isa. 2:4); covenant written on
the heart (Jer. 31:33); the day when "steadfast love and faithfulness will meet; righteousness and peace will kiss each other"
(Ps. 85:10). The dramatic power of memory and vision to bring
hope and to empower community is perhaps seen best in the
preaching of Second Isaiah in response to the despair of the
Babylonian exile. On the one hand, he calls those mired in
hopelessness to "look to the rock from which you were hewn,
and to the quarry from which you were digged. Look to Abraham your father and to Sarah who bore you" (Isa. 51:1b–2a).
This very same prophet says to those same exiles: "Behold, I

[God] am doing a new thing; now it springs forth, do you not perceive it?" (Isa. 43:19). Memory of what God has done and vision of what God yet will do enables hope in the midst of crisis.

In the New Testament the Gospels themselves are a unique witness to the early church's understanding of its life as lived between memory and vision. The Gospels are unique forms of remembering Jesus and embodying that memory for use in the life of the church. But while the Gospels reminded the church of the kingdom already broken into their midst, they simultaneously called the church to a life of discipleship in the service of the kingdom yet to come. Even before the Gospels were written, the Apostle Paul could draw strength and identity from his and others' experience of the resurrected Christ and see a new vision of mission even to the Gentile nations. That new mission would clearly not have been possible apart from the remembering of the historical particularity of God in Jesus Christ. It is in Jesus Christ that there is neither Jew nor Greek, slave nor free, male nor female (Gal. 3:28).

As in the biblical communities, memory and vision and identity and mission are necessary and interrelated in the life of modern congregations. Those two aspects of congregational life are frequently treated as an either-or. Overemphasis on either pole distorts the life of the church. Those who stress memory and identity exclusively (e.g., Bible reading as a devotional end in itself apart from mission) run the risk of becoming the fossil church. A fossil is an extraordinarily faithful witness to the past, but it is incapable of responding to the present or the future. Those who stress vision and mission without maintaining a rootedness in faith memory run the risk of becoming the chameleon church. Having no identity of its own, it is likely to take on the coloration of whatever ideology, cultural context, or fad happens to surround it.[2]

Both memory and vision are necessary to an adequate theology of the church for every congregation. Rootedness in our past tradition and trust in God's future is what frees us from the tyranny of the present. Too many congregations are so overwhelmed by the challenges of their present (budgets, membership decline, complex societal issues) that they become cut off from their past and incapable of seeing visions. (The same dynamic can apply to the lives of individuals.) They become tyrannized by the present. It is instructive that in biblical Hebrew verbs do not have past, present, and future. They have only completed actions and incompleted actions. In the Old Testament the present exists only as that invisible instant when what has been gives way to what is to be. Thus, a congregation seeking to be faithful cannot wallow in its present. It must draw on its memory and move into the future.

Much of the modern literature on church renewal has focused on the renewal of the church's mission. It seeks to rekindle vision and challenge churches to move courageously toward such visions. If the biblical understanding sketched above is correct, this cannot happen apart from renewal of the church's memory as well. Since this essay focuses on the congregation's use of the past, it is on renewal of the memory pole of this dynamic that I will focus much of the remainder of this article.

It is clear biblically that the congregation is the chief agent of memory in the life of faith. Primarily in its local congregational form, the church is the bearer of biblical and historical tradition. The canon of Scripture itself grew out of materials that became authoritative in the life of local congregations and only later were recognized by wider "official" forums of church life. Thus, congregations must become self-conscious about the continuation of this important task of passing on the church's memory. We shall have more to say later about the role and enhancement of memory in congregational life.

3. *The biblical congregations formed around memory and vision have a distinctive character.* In both Old and New Testaments, congregations are called to model life as *alternative communities in the midst of their prevailing cultural settings.*[3] Those who had received and acknowledged the gift of God's grace could not simply reflect the patterns of life in the surrounding cultures. To know God's grace made a difference in

relationship to God, to other persons of faith, and to one's neighbors in the world. Faith congregations were to be "in but not of the world," called to alternative community for the sake of God's grace in the world.

In the Old Testament *covenant* was the term applied by the congregation to its model of alternative life. The covenant model set forth a vision of community that intimately tied relationship with God to relationship with the neighbor. From the very beginning one's neighbor included not only other believers but also sojourners, strangers at the gate and aliens in their midst. In the early period the scale of relation to the neighbor was local and tribal; but as Israel became a nation among nations the tradition, especially the prophets, expanded the concept of covenant relatedness to include relationship among the nations.

Within the covenant model, congregations are called to live out different understandings of religion, economics, and politics. The religious focus of covenant community is on relationship to a radically free God. In the Exodus deliverance from Egypt, Israel had experienced the free gift of God's grace. This was a God free from the state triumphalism seen in Egypt and Mesopotamia where the gods' fortunes were tied to those of the kings. This was a God free from the manipulations of magic and divination which characterized ancient religions of the Near East. This was a God whom Israel came to understand as creator of all things and sovereign over all history. Israel's religion was oriented not to the control of God, but to the acknowledgment of a God who had claimed them.

Relationship to a God of freely given grace required graceful living toward the neighbor. In covenant congregational life this issued forth in an economics of equality and in a politics of justice. The community sought to make the resources necessary for meeting basic human needs available to all on the basis of need. Such equal access to basic resources is seen in concrete embodiment in the law codes and practices of early covenant community. In the political sphere the making of decisions and the exercise of power was distributed from the grass roots up through families, clans, tribes, and federation. Justice was to guard the integrity of the political order so that the worth of all persons was insured and those more vulnerable than others could not be exploited.

Eventually in Israel some desired to have a king and be "like all the nations" (1 Sam. 8:5, 20). Under the kings the economics of privilege and the politics of oppression replaced the covenant calling to equity and justice. Great gulfs grew between rich and poor, and hierarchical power centered in the king and crowded justice from the spotlight. In religion the relationship to a free God was replaced by relationship to a domesticated God. Idolatry and nationalized religion became the chief marks of this domesticated religion. In this context of royal community the prophets called for the renewal of covenant life and challenged congregations to repentance and hope. Much of the Old Testament story is one of struggle between covenant vision and the temptations of privilege, oppressive power, and domesticated religion.

In the New Testament the pattern of calling to alternative community and of temptation to worldly accommodation is remarkably similar to what we see in Israel's story. The early church established itself in response to a free act of God's grace in Jesus Christ and resisted the notion that one could be justified by righteous works. This led the early church to organize its life in ways that were radically different from those of the Hellenistic world. The earliest Christians forsook ownership of goods and shared economic resources on the basis of need. They ignored the political boundaries of their world and converted women and slaves and persons of all economic and social classes or nationalities. The politics of the early church were based on servanthood and not power, on community and not status.

This has been but the briefest survey of the content of biblical understandings of the vocation of faith congregations as alternative communities in the world. What is important to note here is that in biblical remembering within the life of modern congregations there will be a constant calling to a life lived not only in tension with the patterns of the world but also for the sake of the world. Memory in the life of the congregation is never limited to the comfort of discovering one's historic identity. The very content of that biblical identity is discomforting since it calls us to the difficult task of alternative life amidst the constant cultural pressures on the church to conform. It is, however, the biblical understanding that this tension is the creative one from which the church's mission arises and is empowered. That mission is to mediate the grace of God we have already experienced to a broken world in need of healing grace. The model of the congregation's own life as an alternative community in the covenant model is one of the significant ways in which that mission is carried forward.

The Role of Memory in Congregational Life

Recognizing that congregational remembering is never an end in itself but must be balanced by enactment of the church's vision for mission, we can now focus particular attention on several aspects important in understanding the role of memory in congregational life.

1. The most important function of memory in the congregation is in the *formation of identity and character*. We are shaped as community by what we call to memory from our biblical and historic tradition. The importance of congregational activities of remembering is often underestimated. Many of those most committed to the renewal and effectiveness of the church in the world have focused almost entirely on the question: "What is the church to do?" The concern for the church's "doing" ranges from needs for spiritual wholeness, to the formation of supportive community, to the witness of reconciliation in a world still divided by poverty, injustice, and oppression. But since Scripture and tradition (the sources of the church's memory) seldom tell us precisely what decisions to make or actions to take, many people in active congregations treat Scripture and tradition as little more than distant historical background.

Alongside the concern for congregational "doing" must be concern for the congregation's "being" ("Who are we to be?"). Activities which enhance the congregation's remembering of its own biblical and historic heritage make available resources which shape us individually and corporately. Memory plays a primary role in forming our identity, values, perceptions, dispositions, and intentions. The character of Christians and Christian congregations becomes as important as their conduct.[4] When we come to know and internalize the Hebrew affirmation that creation is good or the Pauline insight into the universality of the Gospel, "all are one in Christ Jesus," then we are shaped in our basic identity and character in ways that affect our "doing" as congregations.

Although memory's primary congregational role is in shaping our being, it can play a limited role in situations where the congregation's mission is being acted out. Sermons preached or statements made, which draw upon biblical and historic images and insights, can empower us in mission whether that mission is expressed in the support of a grieving family or a struggle for justice in the public arena. Still, these appropriations of faith memory are effective only to the extent that the inheritance of our faith has already been cultivated and made available within individuals and congregations. When a beloved member of a congregational family dies, our grief must draw on the images of hope and life which have already been implanted in our being. If they are not there, then even the most eloquent memorial sermon will be limited in the comfort and hope it can bring. Likewise, an effort to mobilize church concern for homeless people left on the streets will bear less fruit if admonitions to care for the poor do not find resonance from a congregation's encounters with that fundamental biblical concern as a part of the identity of the people of God.

This means that the role of memory in the formation of congregational identity and character is a long-term and ongoing task. Without long-term cultivation in the life of the congregation, references to the Bible or to a particular historic tradition will only be sprinkled into the church's activities to lend justification to priorities already determined on other grounds. On the other hand, nurtured over the course of a congregation's ongoing life, the images and insights of biblical and historical memory will be available as part of the identity that the church carries with it into every decision on priorities or action in behalf of missional calling. Congregations which do not know something of their biblical and historic roots will have little of their own to offer the world. Such congregations can seldom do more than reflect their own cultural context in the world.

2. In order for memory to play its role in congregational life we must understand the *locus and dynamics of congregational remembering*. Although faith memory can be drawn upon as a resource in the life of the scattered church in the world, it is as the gathered community of faith that we primarily nurture the congregation's memory.

The *sources of congregational remembering are the Bible and tradition*. A congregation's memory must reach back to find its roots in the biblical communities of faith or it will lose touch with those traditions that make the church Christian and not just one of many volunteer associations in society. The Bible contains the record of the origin of the church and witnesses to the God who called that church into being. All that we know of God rests on scriptural foundations, for even our discernment of divine activity in our own time is dependent on knowing who God revealed the divine Self to be in biblical tradition. In fact, sharpening our understanding of the God who called Israel and the church into life can give us new eyes to see the grace of God in our midst.

In particular, the Bible is the unique and authoritative witness to the person and work of Jesus Christ who stands as the central focus for our faith. No Christian identity is possible apart from some relation, acknowledgment, and appropriation of relationship to Jesus. That, of course, may take place in different ways as reflected in the many different denominational traditions of which congregations are a part. Thus, we relate to biblical memory not simply by leaping back from our moment to biblical times and experiences. We have access to

biblical memory through the mediation of historic faith tradition, and that tradition is also a part of congregational
remembering.

Some churches vest a great deal of authority in tradition
alongside of Scripture (e.g., Roman Catholic), and others want
to claim the Bible alone as a source of faith. In spite of these
differences, it must be said emphatically that all congregations
are a part of some historic tradition that has mediated the
witness of Scripture to them, and it is important to be conscious
of that tradition and to acknowledge the shaping power of that
tradition memory.

The influence of tradition as an aspect of congregational
memory may find its most powerful expression for many congregations in the ongoing influence of local history. The continuing effect of a previous pastor, the local conflicts and issues
that have affected the community, or a special mission focus
that led to the founding of a congregation are examples of
powerful local memory which can shape congregations in important ways. These must be acknowledged and understood as
a part of our remembering which needs critical reflection as
surely as does Scripture or denominational tradition.

Questions of authority related to Scripture and tradition
are among the most vexing in many modern churches. It is
well to remember that whatever authority is to be ascribed to
the Bible or to the tradition is authority *derived* from God who
is truly absolute. Authority refers to the revealing of God's
disclosure of the divine Self through the witness of the Bible
and the historic traditions of faith. Thus, any form of dogmatic
biblicism or denominational elitism is to be avoided as a denial
of God's freedom. Such responses worship the witness itself
rather than the God to whom witness is offered.[5]

The *arenas of congregational remembering are worship,
religious education, and the life of the congregation as a community.* We can look briefly at the dynamics of memory in each
of these arenas.

In many ways Christian *worship* can be considered a
ritual act of congregational remembering. Although its central

purpose is celebration, it is celebration based on the remembrance of what God has done in Jesus Christ and on the remembrance of who we are called to be as God's people, Christ's church.

In every aspect of Christian worship, we are surrounded by signs and symbols which evoke congregational memory. The physical settings of worship include architectural designs, objects of art, and furnishings which speak to the congregation out of the remembering of particular biblical or historic traditions. These may run the gamut from austere to ornate, but whether a meeting house or a cathedral, a simple cross or stained glass windows, every worship setting with its symbols speaks to the congregation of a particular pattern of faith memory.

It goes without saying that liturgy too is filled with word images which are rooted in and have meaning only in reference to our faith memory. Participation in Christian worship, whether simple in liturgy or more elaborate, is itself an exercise in Christian remembering. Such participation can, of course, become rote exercise with little depth of meaning. Efforts to broaden understanding of the images and traditions which are used in our liturgies can pay great dividends. By the same token, efforts to enrich the liturgies we use (within the bounds of practice and belief in our various denominations) can broaden the range of remembering to which congregations are exposed in worship. Finally, the sacraments are unique vehicles of congregational remembering since they not only speak God's Word but also re-enact it in our midst. In spite of the variety of sacramental theologies, sacraments in most Christian traditions have a unique capacity to make memory present in our midst in ways that renew and empower the congregation for its mission in the world.

Several elements within the liturgy are of special importance in the nurture of congregational memory. The reading of Scripture is for many church members the only regular, direct exposure to the Bible. The use of the historic creeds ties the gathered congregation to earlier central affirmations of the church. The sermon, of course, proclaims God's Word anew to the congregation, but not as an act only of the moment. In proclamation we lay claim anew to the memory of our faith in the confidence that it has a word to speak to us in our own moment. The preacher proclaims, not out of his or her authority alone, but on the basis of God's Word mediated in Scripture and tradition.

In the *educational life* of the church the nurture of congregational memory is a central task. Reflection on and study of the Bible and of our diverse historic traditions is an obvious part of the church's educational task. But it has not always been given the central attention it deserves because the nurture of congregational memory itself has been so often devalued. In many congregations Bible study is still primarily a matter of children's church school and not a high priority for active adult church members. Changing patterns of family and vocational life leave less time for study and reflection that enriches our faith memory. Even where active educational programs are in place, well-intentioned curricula actually screen people off from direct contact with the sources of congregational remembering. We study what someone else says about the Bible rather than learning to study the Bible itself. Many church members have become consumers of other persons' biblical reflection rather than producers of biblical reflection themselves.

Memory also is nurtured in the shape and quality of *congregational life*. Many congregations simply are shaped by the institutional structures which are dictated by a particular denominational polity. However, to be serious about Christian community as a calling and not simply as a part of institutional structures will require a drawing upon faith memory to choose with prayerfulness and commitment the images and understandings which will inform the life of the congregation. The life of any given congregation will model the memory images it has chosen to hold before its people. In mission has it chosen to consider "the least of these" as Jesus urged? In evangelism does it have genuine good news of the gospel to proclaim or is it simply seeking statistical growth? Does it encourage and enable the life of prayer and spiritual devotion with its personal dimensions of congregational remembering, or is it more interested in populating its committees? In pastoral care do we bear images of hope to one another drawn from the wellsprings of our faith or are we left with the hollow platitudes of secular life? These choices from faith memory for congregational modelling in its life will be affected by worship and study experiences, for all of these arenas interrelate.

3. Some special comments need to be made about the *importance of the whole canon* in the church's biblical remembering. Many church people have come to regard the existence of the biblical canon as problematic. They have correctly discerned that the texts and traditions of the Bible are not treated in the church as possessed of equal authority. We do not take dietary laws as seriously as the Ten Commandments. We do not treat prophetic utterances of judgment against the nations in the same way as we accept Jesus' admonition in the Sermon on the Mount to "love our enemies." This has led some to reject the authority of Scripture altogether and others to suggest selecting a "canon within the canon" of texts that we find acceptable and edifying. We want to suggest here the recovery of the importance of the whole canon, and also to make some suggestions on renewed ways in which the authority of the canon can be understood.[6]

A first observation is that the Christian canon should not be regarded as books which the church chose and granted authority. The church has always stressed that the complex process of the formation of the canon represented only the recognition by the church of authority from God already established in the life of the church. "The concept of canon was an attempt to *acknowledge* the divine authority of its writings and collections. . . . In speaking of canon the church testified that the authority of its Scriptures stemmed from God, not from human sanction."[7] These materials arose from within ancient faith communities and were preserved because those communities found in them the address of God's Word. This perspective provides a safeguard against the notion that the church, having made the canon, can therefore redo it, leaving out those portions which some regard as outdated or irrelevant. To do so would cut us off from a portion of memories that earlier communities thought it important for us to recall.

If the canon is thus understood as the product of actual faith communities then we also may see that it reflects all the gifts and failures of those communities. It is the record of obedience and disobedience, discernment of God's will and failure to discern God's will clearly. It records the enduring address of God's Word and the historical settings in which that Word was heard. Thus, Scriptures will not only reveal to us something of God's truth, but also something of the earthen vessels in which that truth is contained.

Such a canon, reflecting the realities of actual congregations, is necessarily pluralistic. The canon does not speak in a single voice. This is both a witness to the variety of experience with God and a corrective against absolutizing any selection of voices through which the Bible speaks. That the biblical communities themselves can be seen judging, reinterpreting, and measuring the tradition alongside their own experience of God can be read as a support for similar activity on our part.

God has continued to make the divine will known to the church in all succeeding ages, and God is present still, disclosing the divine will for the church and the world in our time. The task of authentic biblical interpretation for congregational life is to aid the community in discerning the divine will. This will require labor at the intersection of the biblical story with our story. What is authoritative in the biblical witness must be consistent with what the church knows from its experience with a living God.

The goal is a canon in truthful dialogue with our own experience of faith in particular congregations. The conversation will be as diverse as the canon itself, and to the degree that we can receive that diverse witness we will be enriched with new eyes and new ears for our own receiving of the biblical word. The dynamic relationship of canon and contemporary faith experience is two way. As we come to see the pluralism of the canon's own witness, we become more attentive and receptive to the diversity of modern witness to what God is doing to bring the power of divine grace into our own time.

Congregations are then empowered by the address of God's Word to align their life as communities with that grace-full activity of God.

The goal toward which we should strive is a de-absolutized canon which allows for the honoring of ancient witness to the degree that it reveals to us the basic truths of our faith, while at the same time honoring the power and authority of our own experience of God. Only such a goal can do justice to the notion of a living God who speaks to us through a living Word and an ongoing presence in the midst of our congregational life.

4. A final word must be said about *the social location of congregational memory.* The process of nurturing and appropriating faith memory in the life of a congregation does not go on in a vacuum. It is a dynamic process affected not only by what we find in the texts and traditions of biblical and historical witness but also by what we bring with us to the process of remembering. In particular the process is affected by our social location in the appropriation of the church's memory.

New awareness of the importance of this insight has come from the emergence of insistent and perceptive voices in feminist, ethnic, and Third World theologies. They have shown us how frequently a white, middle class, male social location is assumed as normative, and how often the process of congregational remembering has failed to see or hear texts and traditions that address the concerns of women, people of color, the poor, and the dispossessed. Congregations must be aware that within their own membership social location will cause different persons looking at the same biblical text to hear a different Word addressed to them, and they must be prepared to honor those perspectives as authentic encounter with God's Word. The task then becomes to hear and understand the different shape that our remembering takes because of social location, and to work toward finding with those differences ways of joining in the common work of the body of Christ.

Even where such differences are not apparent in a local congregation, awareness of those perspectives from social location in denominations and in the global church must be fostered. Use of resources that show us the view of Scripture or tradition through other eyes can be helpful. For example, *The Gospel in Solentiname*[8] simply records the discussions of Gospel passages by village folk in Nicaragua, but what they find in those texts is powerfully and movingly different because of the social location from which they hear the Scripture. The same experience of new eyes and new ears for congregational remembering can be found in resources that reflection women's experience, the Black experience, or the experience of any segment of the church which occupies a social location different from our own.

The Enhancement of Memory in Congregational Life

Since the role of memory is crucially important to the life of the local church, how can congregational memory be fostered and enhanced? We can offer only a few brief observations and suggestions. They are neither fully developed nor exhaustive of possibilities. They are offered in the hope of stimulating further creative efforts at enhancing congregational memory.

1. Serious attention must be paid to the empowerment of the laity for roles in nurturing congregational memory. Clergy are not the principle guardians of faith memory. Yet the feeling is widespread that serious appropriation of Scripture and tradition requires skills that are principally available to the pastor or other church professionals with seminary training. Clergy themselves too often foster or allow this attitude as a way of preserving clear-cut arenas of clerical authority. The pastor of a large and prosperous suburban church once told me that he objected to teaching laypersons the skills of exegesis because "next thing you know, they'll be wanting to preach." Laypersons with opportunity and training for leadership in all arenas of the church's life can be the needed leaven in the loaf for generating seriousness about the role of memory in congregational life. This will not happen if the role of the laity is seen primarily in terms of serving institutional structures or providing the personnel for various missional activities. They also must be intimately involved in knowing and articulating the faith vi-

sion that comes from our biblical and historical memory. Lay-persons must be involved in areas often left to the clergy alone (e.g., the teaching of adults, the shaping of congregational worship life, and the giving of pastoral care).

2. Since the arena of Christian education in the local congregation is perhaps the most crucial place for the deepening of faith memory there are numerous points at which some renewed effort can bring great dividends.

Although not advocated by any responsible voices of leadership there are still many congregations where sustained educational programming is available only to children. Adult education where it exists is often episodic and lacking in any long term strategy for the nurture of memory resources.

In children's education, programs and curricula for teaching the Bible to children are still dominated by the idea that the Bible is an adult book and only can be taught to children in the most watered down way.[9] Although demand for more biblical curricula has resulted in more explicit biblical material in children's lessons, this material still too often is pre-digested in ways that do violence to the biblical stories and their natural power. We need a recovery of appreciation for the simple power of biblical storytelling done with integrity and skill. The Christian faith is a predominantly story-oriented faith. Its real identity always has been in the narrative traditions from Genesis to Jesus. The steeping of children in the stories of the Bible for their own sake builds up a fund of faith memory, which does not need to be immediately tapped for the drawing of morals, the learning of lessons, or the immediate application to life experience. All of these things have their place, of course, but the stories have intrinsic value beyond conclusions that might be drawn from a day's lesson.

Both children and adults should be given more opportunities for learning basic skills and tools that make direct study and interpretation of the Bible possible. Too much of our educational efforts in building biblical memory involves teaching about the Bible and little contact with the Bible itself. Exegesis (the interpretation of biblical texts) sounds like a forbidding and complex process, but the fact is that some of its basic tools and methods are simple enough for children of upper elementary age to learn. Adolescents and adults can, of course, learn to use these tools and skills to even greater advantage if given the opportunity.[10]

Teacher training for congregational education programs should include opportunities for deepening knowledge and understanding of the Bible and our historic traditions for their own sake. Training events usually focus on help for the preparation and teaching of lessons in the classrooms. But those charged with deepening the faith memory of the congregation in study and reflection must have opportunities to deepen their own encounter with biblical and historical memory without having to immediately think in terms of application or use of that material in educational programs.

3. The depth of congregational memory can be greatly enhanced by the renewal and reformation of membership preparation. If membership in a congregation is to be meaningful, then it should be accompanied by some serious opportunity for renewing or building faith memory. This should apply not only to those entering congregations by profession of faith but also to those transferring membership. In our ecumenical age this often can mean a change in denominational tradition. Even if this is not the case the decision for membership should be accompanied by opportunities to reflect together on the faith with persons in the congregation, the pastor, and others seeking membership. Some of the most successful membership preparation processes involve study, reflection, and prayer by potential members with their sponsors from the membership of the congregation. Thus, every group of new members to enter the congregation provides an opportunity for renewal of faith memory by a group of those already members of the congregation. Over a period of years this can have a broad and profound effect on the availability of resources from the church's memory and on openness to new memory, thus enhancing aspects of the church's life.

4. Although there are notable exceptions, many congregations suffer from a poverty of visual image and symbol. We

should not think that enhancement of congregational memory is solely accomplished by words. Historically the church has a rich tradition of expression in the visual arts, but the close relationship of artistic expression with the life of the church in many earlier periods is not characteristic of ours. Many people regard visual expressions of the biblical and historical heritage which is ours as frills. Lack of such visual expressions of faith often is defended as making money available for urgent arenas of the congregation's missional program. The danger, however, is an impoverishment of the spirit that ultimately affects the energy and vision by which we pursue the mission of the church. I have seldom been in the sanctuary of a congregation well-known for its active program and outreach that I did not find color and form, sign and symbol, proclaiming the identity of that congregation in images drawn from the church's memory.

5. Many denominations are experiencing a renewal in exegetical preaching. This is encouraging and to be further encouraged. Nothing could be more helpful in encouraging congregations to attend to the role of memory in their life than to hear preaching which is itself rooted in that memory in ways that demonstrate its power to address our lives and inform our mission. Nothing could be more damaging to the nurture of congregational remembering than preaching drawn only from the preacher's resources. No matter how insightful, if a sermon does not draw on faith memory then there is little to distinguish it from speeches that might be heard in secular forums.

The renewal of lectionary preaching, especially in those denominations not traditionally accustomed to the use of the lectionary, has been an encouraging recent development and does much to enhance the role of memory in the congregation. In many instances it broadens the range of Scripture read in worship week to week, and it surely has deepened the biblical base of much preaching in our churches. One might, however, utter a word of caution. The lectionaries in use do not encompass the whole of Scripture. If one were to preach an entire ministry on the three-year lectionary cycle there would be huge portions of the Bible never used for preaching. In spite of the rewards of lectionary preaching, pastors should be encouraged to explore beyond the lectionary in their own Bible study and to depart from the lectionary from time to time in order to share the insights gained from that broader exploration of biblical memory.

There are surely many other areas and methods for the enhancement of memory in congregational life. As long as these efforts are seen in conjunction with the church's vision for mission and not as an end in themselves, this nurture of congregational memory can prove richly empowering to the life of a local church. "God heard their groaning, and God remembered his covenant . . ." (Exod. 2:24). In the hour of our need God always has remembered us. In the midst of the broken world to which the church is sent, let us remember God. Let us give thanks for the remembering of those who went before us, enabling us to know of the God who called us into being as a people and to recognize that same God present in our midst yet today.

The Congregation as Chameleon: How the Present Interprets the Past

JACKSON W. CARROLL
Hartford Seminary

Introduction

Tracing the history of his congregation in the course of a Doctor of Ministry project, a pastor described the church as a "chameleon." By this metaphor, he wished to make the point that a key to the congregation's survival for over a century was, similar to a chameleon, its capacity to adapt to its changing environment.[1] From one perspective, this is a positive image, and it was intended as such by the pastor. Adaptation to changing circumstances in its setting is a necessity for any congregation. Despite a fascination with the internal dynamics of congregations (encouraged in recent years by an emphasis on organizational development), congregations are decisively affected by their social external contexts. Such classic analyses as H. Paul Douglass and Edmund deS. Brunner's *The Protestant Church as a Social Institution* have made this point clear.

It is unlikely that a church will survive if it clings unbendingly to old patterns while the society around it changes. This is true not only for survival's sake but also if the congregation is going to be able to minister faithfully within its changing setting. In this sense it is a healthy situation, others things being equal, when a congregation's present is allowed to interpret its past.

At the same time (and in ways most likely not intended by the pastor's description of his congregation), the chameleon metaphor obviously points to a less positive, downright frustrating characteristic of congregations as human communities: their tendency to adapt so readily to their social contexts that they become indistinguishable from them. The transcendent power of the gospel is hidden, if not lost, in a congregation's earthiness. Social class, race, ethnicity, and gender create new walls of hostility that divide congregations from one another or members within the same congregation. Conflicts and rivalry among members, selfishness and vanity on the part of leaders, an emphasis on survival over service, lukewarmness about evangelization, timidity in the face of injustice, and support of class interests of members are additional examples of ways congregations reflect, chameleon-like, some of the characteristics of their social contexts.

This problem is an ancient one, at least as old as the eighth century B.C., when the prophet Amos (5:21–24) scathingly referred to Israel's "congregational" observances as the "noise of solemn assemblies"; and some more recent applications of sociological perspectives to congregations have also made us painfully aware of the negative effects of social factors on congregations. H. Richard Niebuhr's *The Social Sources of Denominationalism,* Robert S. and Helen Merrill Lynd's studies of Muncie, Indiana, *Middletown* and *Middletown in Transition,* and Liston Pope's penetrating analysis of the impact of social class on religion in Gastonia, North Carolina, *Millhands and Preachers,* are a few examples from earlier in this century which help to clarify the character of congregations as *social* organizations. In the 1960s, sociologist Peter Berger drew on many of these studies to describe what, after Amos, he called *The Noise of Solemn Assemblies.* By this, he meant that the churches were so captive to their social location and to the values and interests of their members that they primarily sanctified the status quo. Similarly, Pierre Berton wrote about *The Comfortable Pew,* and Gibson Winter analyzed *The Suburban Captivity of the Churches.* Winter and others like him were so discouraged about the possibility that traditional congregations could escape their captivity that they sought new missionary structures for the church.

The perspective on churches taken by these various authors and critics is now commonplace. We take for granted that social factors have an important effect on congregations and that many congregations are, in fact, chameleons in the more negative sense of the metaphor. But let me add a caution. Because the subject matter of the chapter is now commonplace, it will be tempting for some readers to dismiss the perspective of the chapter as "old hat," as repeating what one already knows. To do so, I believe, risks serious failure in faithfulness, not because I have some grandiose belief about the novelty or brilliance of what I have written, but because *it has been my experience that congregational leaders frequently ignore the character of the congregation's social context as they plan for their congregation's ministry and mission. And in ignoring their context, they not only fail to see how they are unwittingly conforming to it but also miss opportunities for faithful ministry and mission that the context provides.*

My purpose, therefore, in this chapter is to make yet another foray into the field of the interaction of congregations and their social contexts. My focus will be, on the one hand, on the power of the social context over congregations (in the double sense implied by the chameleon metaphor) and, on the other hand, on the capacities within congregations for making and maintaining responses to the gospel in their social location. Can the chameleon adapt to its surroundings without losing its identity and abandoning its calling? The answer I will give to this question is a qualified "yes." I will argue both that local churches are inevitably and profoundly affected by their social contexts and character as social institutions, and that there are limited but *crucial* possibilities for transcending, though

not escaping, those effects. I will also argue that the social
character and social location of congregations are not all negative in their influence. These social characteristics are the
media that help to transform possibilities for faithful and effective congregational ministry and mission.

An Open Systems Perspective on Congregations

One helpful way of thinking about congregations is an
"open systems" perspective. Such a perspective is a complex
one, and here I will necessarily be selective. To think of a
congregation as an open system calls attention both to its *systemic* character—that is, as an organization of identifiable, semi-
autonomous but interdependent parts that interact with one
another as the congregation pursues it mission—as well as to
its relative *openness*—that is, the congregation's interaction
and exchanges with elements in its environment.

Focusing on the systemic character of a congregation
leads in part to a consideration of the congregation's internal
structure and processes in the accomplishment of its purposes.
Thus, one considers the patterning of the various parts of the
congregation, their relationship to each other, the contribution
that each part makes to the functioning of the whole, and the
various processes that help or hinder that functioning. Such
processes include assessment and planning, communication,
agreement over roles, interpersonal and intergroup dynamics,
and the management of conflicts, to mention several of the more
important functions. Systemic thinking has been at the heart
of efforts in recent years to apply organization development
theories and techniques to congregations. Some aspects of it,
however, are hardly new in application to the church, as is
evident in St. Paul's metaphor of the church as the "body of
Christ," with various interdependent organs or parts, each necessary for the functioning of the whole.

My interest here, however, is not primarily with the
internal characteristics of congregations—although I take them
very seriously—but with congregations' systemic relationships
to their environments which are especially implied by the em-

phasis on congregations as *open* systems. In the broadest sense, a congregation's relevant environment includes not only its local neighborhood or community, but the regional, national and global context, and also the larger denominational and interdenominational systems of which it is a part. In this global village in which we live, a congregation is inevitably linked to national and global issues and events, whether it wishes it or not. Nonetheless, a congregation is related most immediately to its local context, be it neighborhood, town, rural district, or metropolitan area, which members define as the congregation's primary field of service. This local community context provides a mediating link between the congregation and the effects of many aspects of its larger extended environment. Thus, much of what follows focuses on the congregation's local community context.

The relationship of the congregation as a system to its local community context is a critical one. It is the most immediate arena in which the congregation seeks to carry out its ministry and mission in response to the gospel. Also, it is the locus of many of the resources needed for its survival and mission—for example, members' time, talent, and treasure; and also for information and feedback necessary for continued decision-making about its ministry and mission. Without regular replenishment of such resources, a congregation will not long survive. In systems language it will experience "entropy"; it will run down from lack of energy.

Open systems, which include all biological and social systems, are relatively permeable in relation to their environment. In contrast to closed systems that are relatively impervious to external influences (a mechanical system, such as an electric motor, is an example), open systems are not shut off from their environment but interact and carry on transactions or exchanges with it. In these exchanges, they can affect their environment as well as be affected by it. To be sure, some congregations are relatively closed in comparison to others. That is, they construct substantial "walls" or "boundaries" around themselves—doctrinally, behaviorally, organizationally—to shut themselves off from being affected by the "world" and its influences. And some also make no effort to affect their environment. Still, they are open systems—at least relatively so—and they cannot totally escape interaction and exchanges with their environment.

Open systems, such as congregations, have another important characteristic, which mechanical systems do not have. They can modify themselves structurally—or better, members can modify the structure of their congregation—as they carry on exchanges or transactions with their environment. As members gather information about their environment, they can use this information to compare what they are actually doing as a congregation with what they wish to do. Within limits, they also can make needed changes that allow them to be more faithful and effective in pursuing their mission.

To be sure, thinking about congregations as open systems is not the typical way that most members or their leaders think about them, nor does it by any means exhaust the reality of congregations. Nevertheless, when trying to understand how the congregation's social context affects its ministry and mission—how its present interprets its past—the open systems perspective can be a useful one. Let me try to make this clear by turning now to several implications of this perspective for understanding both the power of the social context over congregations and the crucial, if limited, capacities of congregations for transcending determination by their context.

Congregational Vulnerability to the Context

I begin with the vulnerability of congregations to their social contexts, concentrating primarily on the local community context. That vulnerability is two-fold: to changes in the context, especially the local area the congregation seeks to serve; and to the social characteristics, values, and interests which members bring to the congregation from their location and involvements in other aspects of society.

Because they are open systems at the local community level, congregations are vulnerable to changes that occur in their local community context. This is especially true for congregations that have as one of their primary goals to serve and/ or influence the quality of life in their local communities. For example: (1) A congregation that has developed an extensive ministry to youth in the community becomes aware that the program, which has been an important aspect of the congregation's identity, is floundering. Members blame the failure on lack of leadership. The primary cause, however, is the changing demographics of the community, since there are no longer many youth in the church's local community context. (2) A nursery school of recognized quality, through which one congregation has long met an important need in its local community, is hit by the sharply declining birthrate. The need for the school continues, but smaller enrollments lead to higher per-pupil costs and tuition increases, making it difficult for many moderate and low income children to attend the school. Can the congregation provide scholarship aid out of an already overtaxed budget? (3) Many suburban congregations flourished in the 1950s and early 1960s, partly because they provided important services in new suburbs which were institutionally underdeveloped in terms of an infrastructure of community services—nursery and kindergarten programs, scouting, adult education and social groups, personal and family counseling. As this infrastructure was subsequently developed by agencies outside the church, suburban congregations often found themselves floundering, in terms both of an understanding of their local mission and membership attrition. A somewhat opposite situation has occurred more recently as federal programs for the poor have been reduced and congregations and other agencies in the voluntary sector have found themselves confronted with massive needs for services in the community that seriously tax their financial and human resources.

But it is not only the congregations that seek to serve their community that are vulnerable to community changes. As noted in the discussion of open systems, all congregations are to some extent dependent on their local communities for needed resources—especially members and money. Effects of this dependence are most obvious for congregations located in communities which undergo transition, especially racial or ethnic transition, by a group different from that of a congregation's traditional membership. But dependence on the community for needed resources is evident even for congregations that are relatively closed systems and those that draw their members from a dispersed geographical area. Research about factors affecting church membership and income indicates that growth or decline in the population and total income in the ZIP code area in which a congregation is located are powerful predictors of membership and income changes in the congregation. Younger churches (10 years old or less) are more strongly affected than older churches, but all are influenced in significant ways. This is true, though to a lesser extent, even for congregations in which the majority of members live outside the immediate ZIP code area of the congregation. To be sure, the research found churches that are exceptions: some succeed when their context is declining, and some decline when their context is growing. It obviously is of considerable importance to understand the dynamics of these exceptions. The experience, however, of the majority in the study lends considerable weight to the old dictum, "as goes the neighborhood, so goes the church."[2] These findings are not novel. Rather, they confirm an observation made some fifty years earlier by pioneer sociologists H. Paul Douglass and Edmund deS. Brunner:

> The quality and changes of [a congregation's] environment are almost inevitably communicated to the church. Differences in human fortunes suffered by the church's immediate constituencies and changes in these fortunes due to changes in the environment largely control the institutional destinies of each particular church. Where the environment is prosperous and progressive the church can scarcely fail to "succeed." Where it is miserable and deteriorating the church can scarcely avoid failure.[3]

I do not share the strongly deterministic tone of Douglass and Brunner's statement. But I do believe that a congregation that fails to keep abreast of changes in its community context does so at great risk. While this seems so obvious, to repeat an earlier point, I am regularly surprised by how often congregational leaders do, in fact, ignore changes in their context as they evaluate and plan various aspects of their ministry and mission.

Congregations are vulnerable to being shaped by aspects of their local contexts in another important way. Members of a congregation, who are also community residents, contribute in important ways to a congregation's vulnerability. As community residents, members share in the culture and social life, not only of the congregation, but also of the local community and broader society. What some have called members' "social worlds"—the perceptions of reality and the values and interests that shape a people's daily life—are brought into the congregation.[4]

It is through their social worlds that individuals make sense of their lives, giving meaning and order to the diverse and often threatening experiences they face. How are social worlds shaped? They arise from the multiple experiences, groups, roles, and networks of relationships in which persons are involved. These include not only the church, but also family, racial or ethnic identity, gender, age, peer and friendship groups, and many others. An individual's social class position, reflecting especially educational background, occupation and income (or that of her or his family), plays a particularly important role in shaping one's social world. To be sure, the church also exerts some influence on the social worlds of its members. More likely than not, however, the stronger influence is in the opposite direction. That is, members' social worlds exert an influence on the church.

The members' extra-church identities and involvements often influence both their choice of a congregation and their pattern of involvement in its life. This is especially the case in American society where congregations are essentially voluntary associations and individuals are free to choose among them to find one that seems consistent with their own social world and lifestyle. As they try to find some sense of "ultimate meaning" behind their particular social world and lifestyle, individuals seek out religious organizations that seem supportive of them. And when people join together in a congregation with others who share similar social worlds and lifestyles, this in turn shapes to some degree the identity and religious style of the congregation itself. That action lends credence to the second meaning of the metaphor of the congregation as chameleon, namely, the tendency of congregations to adapt to their social contexts and to become indistinguishable from them.

Numerous studies have described the influence of a person's extra-congregational identities—for example, gender, age, ethnicity, and especially social class—on individual religiosity generally and on involvement in congregational life in particular. These findings are reasonably well-known and I will not repeat them here, especially since my primary interest is the effect of the social factors on the congregation rather than on the individual.[5] What I am concerned with is how a congregation's identity and style are shaped by the social worlds and other characteristics of its typical members.

I do not wish to suggest, in a kind of crude Marxist fashion, that congregational styles, like religious beliefs and practices generally, are nothing more than the reflection of class interests. Rather, I find Max Weber's concept of "elective affinity" helpful. Weber believed that the inherited traditions and beliefs of a religious group and its class interests interact to shape the beliefs and style of the group. Summarizing Weber's view, Hans Gerth and C. Wright Mills argued that "Ideas, selected and reinterpreted from the original doctrine, do gain an affinity with the interests of certain members of special strata; if they do not gain such an affinity, they are abandoned."[6] Thus, particular theological emphases and styles are "elected" or selected out for emphasis in particular groups or congregations because they have an affinity with what I have called the "social worlds" of congregational members. The theological themes and styles are not mere reflections of class interests or social worlds as an overstated Marxism might suggest, but there is an affinity between them that leads to selective emphasis. I will return to this important issue in the final section, where I consider the role of theology in providing leverage for transcending social determination.

The works of H. Richard Niebuhr, Liston Pope, and others I noted previously, provide ample documentation of the effects of social forces and class interest on religious life.[7] Even the New Testament churches, which are often turned to by reformers as models of church purity, were not exempt from conditioning by their social contexts. Recent studies of the congregations founded by the Apostle Paul make this clear. For instance, biblical scholar Wayne Meeks carefully assesses the social class and status characteristics of early converts to Christianity. In particular, many Pauline converts, especially the most active and prominent, were people of high status inconsistency. That is, their achieved status (for example, income, or freedom to travel within the Empire) was higher than other status attributes (such as being a woman or a Jew, or having a low-prestige occupation). Meeks shows the elective affinity of these characteristics with Pauline theological images and also with the ritual and symbols associated with baptism and the Lord's Supper. Baptism, for example, signalled not only a dying and rising with Christ, but also a putting off of one's old negative and inconsistent status attributes and assuming new and consistent ones in a community that supported the new definitions. Also, many of the conflicts experienced in the Pauline churches can be traced to class and status differences which members brought with them into the congregations and which persisted in spite of baptism into the new community.[8]

It is possible to see the same processes operative today. If people are attentive to the sermon themes, worship styles, hymns, and teachings of different congregations, they can discover a congregational language—both discursive and non-discursive—that speaks to and reflects the values and interests of a particular class, race, or ethnic group that is the congregation's primary constituency. A middle or upper middle class congregation, for example, is much more likely to sing such hymns as "Rise Up, O Men of God" or "I Sing a Song of the Saints of God," which express a confidence in life and our part in it (despite the ironical exclusion of women in the language of the first hymn). On the contrary, in a lower or working class congregation typical hymns very likely will depict the world as a place of suffering and hardship which can only be relieved by the action of God coming into this "vale of tears" from the outside. This contrast was dramatically illustrated for me in the world views and beliefs expressed in "back-to-back" televised services of Oral Roberts and Robert Schuller: the former making frequent references to the demonic power of Satan who has us in his grip, and whose bondage can be overcome by the power of God working through his (Oral Roberts') hand as it also did through the hand of the Apostle Paul; the latter preaching on "The Be-happy Attitudes" and prescribing a readjusted mental attitude as the solution to sin and unhappiness. When one considers the different audiences/congregations to which each is appealing and the different social worlds which the hearers bring to the experience, the contrast in the theologies becomes understandable. While this example is perhaps extreme and risks caricature, it is not difficult to find similar contrasts in typical congregations anywhere. Each has its own language that is drawn, in part at least, from the social worlds of its members. The importance of this kind of socially determined congregational language for the church's educational task is demonstrated in subsequent chapters of this volume, notably, in Charles Foster's discussion of the "hidden curriculum" by which a congregation educates, and in Maria Harris' comments about "implicit" and "null" curricula in a congregation's educational program.

The effects of social worlds on congregational language and style are especially critical for congregations in racially and ethnically mixed communities. I belong to a historically white, middle class congregation in a suburban community where the Black population is now 30 percent and growing. Most members and leaders want the church to be racially inclusive; however, very few Blacks are members or active participants. Instead, most belong to historically Black congregations in the neighboring city. While a number of issues are involved, a major one is that of worship style. If our congregation is really serious about wanting to be racially inclusive, what will it cost in the way of changes in our worship, the point at which most members most visibly participate in the congregation? Will we be able to continue our traditional, staid, rather formal and rational New England style of worship with which most members are comfortable? Or will we be willing to incorporate more "soul" into our services, honoring the Black religious experience in this and other important ways? It is not clear that we are yet willing to make such changes. Similar issues face the Black church that wishes to engage in the reverse process. In particular, many Black churches are experiencing this tension sharply, as Blacks of West Indian origin and American-born Blacks encounter each other's differing social worlds and traditions in congregations.

Catholics—once perceived to be monolithic in style and practice—are not immune from vulnerability to the social worlds of parishioners. The American Catholic population, historically immigrant and working class in character, has experienced considerable upward social mobility, especially since World War II, so that on the whole the majority equals or surpasses mainline Protestant members in occupational, educational, and income levels. This, coupled with the changes wrought by Vatican II, has had a radical effect on the traditionally hierarchical and clerically dominated style of many parishes, transforming them into a much more open and participatory approach. After describing changes in worship styles, adult education, and lay leadership roles typical of many parishes, researchers studying American Catholic parishes commented:

> Lifelong learning and serving are highly valued by middle-class Americans and that is what most non-Hispanic American Catholics are. Perhaps that is one reason why American Catholics are finding that they have so much in common with mainline confessional, sacramental, and even evangelical Protestant churches. When people are similar socially, their parish ministries and programs begin to resemble each other.[9]

The authors indicate, however, that these changes are far from universally accepted or shared. For many working class Catholics, "Their pieties, their devotions, their sense of the mystery in the Eucharist and Confession, their sense of the holiness and authority of the priest—all remain unshaken."[10] The pluralism of social worlds results not only in considerable heterogeneity between parishes, but also in many differences and conflicts within the same parish.

The social worlds and extra-congregational experiences of members also strongly influence the orientations that congregations hold towards mission, as a study which two colleagues and I undertook of Protestant, Catholic, and Jewish congregations in Hartford, Connecticut demonstrates.[11] Four orientations to mission in the community were examined, two which were this-worldly in focus (called activist and civic) and two which were other-worldly (evangelistic and sanctuary). In addition to the this-worldly and other-worldly emphases, the orientations also reflect an engaged versus withdrawing stance. Thus, activist congregations emphasize not only working for change in the world, but doing so actively as a congregation. Predominantly civic congregations, as I will note in more detail below, also give importance to the quality of life in this world, but they stress education and individual initiative rather than congregational action. Similarly, while both evangelistic and sanctuary orientations de-emphasize this world in favor of the world to come, the evangelistic congregations are actively concerned with witnessing and saving individuals from the sins of the world. In contrast, sanctuary-oriented congregations not only emphasize withdrawal from worldly involvement, but place little importance on active evangelistic efforts. Except for noting that most congregations are mixtures of the four orientations with one style usually dominant over the others, space here does not permit further discussion of these four orientations. Instead, let me just illustrate how the social worlds of members lead in some congregations to what is referred to as a civic orientation—the orientation typical of many mainline Protestant congregations. I might add that each of the other orientations is also related to members' social worlds.

In congregations whose orientation is civic, there is a belief that this world is the arena in which God calls persons to service and responsible action. Christians can make a difference in the quality of life in their community. Nevertheless, unlike their activist counterparts who also are this-worldly in focus, civic congregations do not believe that a congregation should take corporate action in challenging the community or broader society on behalf of justice. Rather, civic congregations are more likely to accept the existing social order than to challenge it publicly. Moreover, they are not very likely to engage in corporate action for change, whereas they are very likely to define the congregation's role in educational terms. The congregation's task is to provide discussion and clarification of public issues. Differing opinions are tolerated—indeed, tolerance of diversity seems to be an overriding value in civic congregations. And if members, including the pastor, choose to involve themselves in public issues—as they are encouraged to do—they do so as individuals, not as representatives of the congregation. As a result, it is often difficult to point to much of anything concrete that civic congregations do intentionally as congregations to influence their communities (except perhaps for relatively "safe" social service projects).

In speculating on why civic congregations place such a high value on tolerance of diversity that it cuts the nerve of social action, we must consider the effects on church involvement of members' social worlds and the roles and relationships which these social worlds reflect. Members experience cross-pressuring from their various roles, relationships, and the interest groups to which they belong: family, work organizations, political parties, friendships. If the civic congregation were to take an active stand on a controversial social or economic justice issue within the community, its members would quite likely experience internal conflict because of the cross-pressures from their other roles and relationships. These cross-pressures lead members to value discussion over action, and especially to emphasize tolerance of diverse opinions within the congregation. The net result is often support of the status quo, tacitly if not explicitly.[12] One way to avoid the effect of cross-pressuring, similar to methods in many sectarian groups, is to make involvement in the congregation so time consuming and demanding that a member's extra-congregational involvements

are severely curtailed. This can be further enhanced by a theology that defines the world, and involvement in it, in negative
terms—in other words the congregation becomes a closed system. One of the sanctuary-oriented churches described in the
study did just that. Neither of these strategies, however, is apt
to be readily acceptable to civic congregations or, more generally, to congregations with middle or upper middle class
constituency.

These various examples illustrate ways in which congregations, as open systems, are vulnerable to the influences
of their social contexts—both to changes in the context and to
the social worlds and class interests of their members. Of course,
the effects of other social factors on congregations could also
be cited: for example, the influence of social class and occupational characteristics on typical leadership styles within a
congregation; the influence of regional cultures which persist
in spite of the homogenizing effects of television and mobility;[13]
the age, marital, and family status of typical members; or simply the size of the congregation.[14] The point, however, should
be sufficiently clear. As they interact with their environments,
and as these environments enter the church through the characteristics and experiences of members, congregations are decisively influenced and shaped. The chameleon metaphor is an
apt one.

As noted in the Preface, the metaphor is partly positive.
Congregations do need to adapt to changes in their environment if they are to survive and be faithful to their calling.
However, it also is negative in implication. Are congregations
only reflections of their contexts? How can they be faithful to
the Gospel when they are so vulnerable to social conditioning?

Vulnerability and Faithfulness

I turn in this final section to a limited answer to these
important questions, recognizing that authors of other chapters
will be addressing such issues more fully. I begin, however,
with what may seem somewhat contradictory to developing
ways of transcending social conditioning.

I strongly believe that congregational vulnerability is not only not all bad, but also that it truly can be a positive characteristic of congregations. Congregations that try to reduce their vulnerability by "circling the wagons" and becoming closed systems are not, I believe, being faithful to the Christ whose body they are called to be.

As Christians, we owe our allegiance to an incarnate God, who became fully vulnerable to the world in Jesus of Nazareth, even to the point of death on a cross. When we affirm that the Word became flesh, we mean the Word's embodiment not only in a human body—Jesus, the son of Mary and Joseph—but also in a particular geographical, social, and cultural context at a particular moment in human history—Jesus of Nazareth in first-century Palestine during the reign of the Roman emperor, Caesar Augustus. Such embodiment, indeed enculturation, meant that Jesus, the Word, accepted the opportunities and limitations which those particularities of place, culture, language, and society imposed. It also meant that he became vulnerable to those particularities. At the same time, those limits and their attendant vulnerability made it possible for the Word to be experienced and acknowledged freely by men and women who encountered Jesus of Nazareth as one of their own, as one who made God present—transformingly so—in the midst of their social worlds and their ordinary experiences—joys, hopes, perplexity, suffering, and sorrow. As the early theologian Irenaeus wrote: "He was made what we are that He might make us what He is Himself."[15]

The resurrection, far from being a freeing of the Word from its vulnerability to time, place, and culture, was instead a freeing of it to become flesh—vulnerable—again and again as communities of believers embody Christ in the limits of their own times, places, and cultures. Thus, if a congregation takes seriously its calling to be the body of Christ in its particular setting, then it simply cannot avoid the vulnerability that is implied in that calling. In this sense, the social worlds that members "bring into" the church as a part of their humanness are not simply a weakness and limitation to be endured and/

or overcome. They are also important points of connection between the gospel and ordinary day-to-day experiences—joys,
hopes, perplexities, sufferings, and sorrows—of members of their
communities.

Andrew M. Greeley and Mary Greeley Durkin make this
incarnational point in a slightly different way, arguing against
a tendency which they perceive within contemporary Catholicism to de-emphasize the traditional Catholic parish's connectedness with its neighborhood and, frequently too, with a
particular ethnic tradition. They write:

> A parish was—and still is—successful if it is able to tell
> the religious stories that respond to the needs of the people, if
> it helps people appreciate the sacramental moments of life, and
> finally if it links its members with the world beyond. A successful
> parish is one in which laity and pastoral leaders (especially the
> pastor) share a vision of its meaning, when the community
> works together to continue God's presence in its time and place.[16]

Still, one might legitimately object that in affirming both
Jesus' and the church's vulnerability, I have neglected the issue
of faithfulness. Jesus was not only vulnerable unto death; he
was also faithful unto death. The liberating and transforming
vision of God's kingdom with which he identified himself at
the outset of his ministry (Luke 4:16–21) was the consistent
theme that made his life, ministry, and death a seamless whole.
Are not congregations, as the body of Christ, also called to
embody that vision with appropriate integrity and faithfulness? The answer is a qualified yes, qualified by the necessary
and crucial acknowledgment that congregations are earthen
vessels and exist as communities of forgiven sinners whom God
nevertheless calls to ministry and mission. As Bruce Birch
makes clear in the preceding chapter, there is a creative tension
in which congregations live as they seek to be alternative communities, bearing witness to their experience of God's grace,
while keenly aware of the cultural pressures to conform which
their humanity entails. It has been the repeated failures of
congregations to maintain this creative tension, and to be faithful in their humanness, that has led to the various criticisms
of congregations which were noted at the outset.

The failures and critics notwithstanding, I believe that it is possible to point to several ways for congregations to remain open and vulnerable to their contexts without losing their identity as the body of Christ and sacrificing the integrity of their calling. Let me note three ways by which congregations can reduce, if not avoid, being conditioned by the power of their contexts, or to put it positively, to remain faithful in their vulnerability. These possibilities reflect the capacity of congregations, as open systems, for self-modification and renewal. Let me emphasize, however, that none of these three possibilities is easily transformed into reality. There is no easy formula for faithfulness. Indeed, it is much easier to describe and acknowledge a congregation's vulnerability than it is to be faithful in the midst of it.

Developing a Strong and Positive Identity. Congregations, like individuals, have identities. When we speak of an individual's identity, we refer to the meaning(s) a person has come to attach to him or herself over time with the assistance of others with whom she or he has interacted. It is the "I" which persists through the various roles and relationships in which one engages. A person who has a strong identity about which he or she has positive feelings is quite likely to act with a degree of autonomy from immediate situational pressures to conform, to be "inner directed," true to his or her identity. We also speak of a person with a strong identity as having "character," implying that she or he acts with integrity. But a person who has no clear sense of identity is very likely to be an "outer directed" conformist who goes where he or she is "pushed" by social circumstances.

How does this apply to congregations? As with individuals, congregations develop and maintain identities. A congregation's identity reflects at "rock bottom" the basic assumptions that members hold about their particular congregation and its purpose. These basic assumptions in turn reflect the meanings that the congregation has developed over time, and they are the means by which members interpret the congregation to themselves and to others on the outside. Such meanings come from various sources. They come in part from the congregation's *past*—from these significant events and relationships in its unique history and heritage that have shaped the congregation and continue to be remembered and interpreted in the present. Sometimes this is referred to as its "little tradition," in contrast to its "great tradition"—the history and heritage that a congregation shares as a part of the church universal and of the particular denominational stream of which it is a part. Meanings from both of these traditions are available to the congregation in the shaping of its identity. The meanings also come from the congregation's *present*—both its relationships to its social context and the character and characteristics of its present members (including their social worlds). Additionally, the meanings out of which a congregation's identity is shaped may come from the *hopes* of its members—their images of the future of their congregation which play an important role in the interpretation of the congregation's present.

Over time, a congregation constructs out of these various sources of meaning an identity, an image (or images) of itself, which implicitly or explicitly interprets and guides its common life and which reflects its basic assumptions. Some congregational identities are clear and strong; others are diffuse and weak. Some are positive, and some are negative, leading to either good or bad feelings about a congregation's identity.[17] Furthermore, there is always the question about whether or not a congregation's identity is faithful to the gospel.

Much of the time congregations are not really aware of their identity; they simply give expression to it for better or worse. However, if a congregation's leadership wishes to avoid uncritical conditioning by the social context, and instead desires to be intentional about its ministry and mission, then it is necessary for them to develop clarity about the congregation's identity. What difference does this make? Sociologist Orrin Klapp, who has applied identity theory to organizational systems, writes that "only systems with identity can be autonomous, that is, act for themselves, decide on the basis of who they are or were, what to do and to be."[18] The clearer the meaning an organizational system has for its members, the greater its potential for self-direction. Further, Klapp notes that loss of meaning or weak identity increases entropy (the loss of energy) for the organizational system, just as it does for the individual. He cites both a closing of ranks against the stranger and a sense of nostalgia as several symptoms of entropy in an organization. The implications of this for congregations seem clear. Where leaders—lay and clergy—are aware of their congregation's identity and can affirm it positively, they will very likely be able to act "in character" as they make decisions and seek to shape their future. There will be an integrity about the decisions they make and the goals they pursue, even when those decisions are tough and the attainment of goals is uncertain. They will have a sense that some things—for example, particular programs, emphases, or ways of operating—are appropriate to their identity, and others are not.

The multiple sources of meanings from which congregational identities are constructed make it clear that a congregation need not simply be captive to its present circumstances, if it uses these sources to clarify and strengthen its identity. There are within the resources of every congregation, especially from the traditions (great and little) and its images of the future, elements that make it possible for a congregation to be "inner directed," shaping its relationship to its context even while it remains open and vulnerable to it. Earlier, I mentioned Max Weber's idea of the "elective affinity" between beliefs and class and status interests. However, as I noted, Weber, unlike Marx, did not believe that class and status totally determine beliefs. While class interests and experiences influence the selection of particular emphases from the inherited tradition, the tradition itself has a shaping influence on the direction that class interests take. Said Weber, "Not ideas, but material and ideal interests, directly govern men's conduct. Yet very frequently the 'world images' that have been created by 'ideas' have, like switchmen, determined the tracks along which action has been pushed by the dynamic of interest."[19] George A. Lindbeck's recent work on *The Nature of Doctrine* draws in part on a Weberian perspective and makes a similar point. He emphasizes the way that the cultural and linguistic forms of a religious tradition—for the Christian, the story of Israel and of Jesus—play a role in the shaping and molding of the self.[20] Consequently, it is through the regular telling of and reflecting on that story, in ways that connect with a congregation and its members' particular stories, that the congregation's identity—its basic assumptions about itself—is shaped and reshaped.

Such a consequence is not automatic. To be sure, a congregation's identity is to some degree unconsciously shaped and molded by the stories and symbols of the faith expressed in its rituals, creeds, hymns, sermons, and sacred spaces. But as I have emphasized earlier, a congregation's leaders, lay and clergy, must at times become intentional about the congregation's identity. How they do this, how they get a "fix" on its identity, and how they address the issue of faithfulness are very important questions which, unfortunately, are beyond the scope of this chapter. Fortunately, these questions have been dealt with in some detail elsewhere.[21] Also, in a subsequent chapter of this book, Carl Dudley explores various images of the congregation and their formative potential for a congregation's life. These images will assist congregational leaders who are trying to discern their congregation's identity. Suffice it to say here—appropriate to a book stressing the educational ministry of the congregation—that coming to understand and affirm one's identity as a congregation is a critical educational task.

Knowing Its Context. Developing a strong and positive identity is one way for a congregation to remain faithful within its vulnerability. But this must be supplemented by knowledge of its social context, the local and broader environment in which it is set. Here I will be brief, since much that I have emphasized previously makes this point. Particular reference is made to the discussion of congregations as open systems, emphasizing the importance of a congregation's context, both as the locus for important resources needed for its survival and as the setting given to it by God for carrying out its ministry and mission. I have also tried to show how vulnerable to social determination a congregation is, especially when it ignores its context.

Earlier students of congregations, following the lead of H. Paul Douglass whose contributions were mentioned earlier, placed heavy emphasis on the importance of knowing the congregation's context. And, indeed, much of their work was focused in this direction. There has been a countertendency in recent years, perhaps in reaction to what was perceived as an overemphasis on context, but also, as noted, as a consequence of the application of organization development theory and methods by congregational consultants. Many of the latter have focused primarily on internal dynamics of the congregational system (on programs, processes, and leadership issues) because organization development perspectives yielded new insights about how internal elements can function more effectively. But their inward look also probably reflected frustration over the seemingly complex and willful aspects of the congregation's context. For whatever reason, some consultants have come to view an understanding of the congregation's context as relatively unimportant.[22]

I do not wish to minimize the importance of the internal character and dynamics of a congregation. My emphasis on congregational identity should make this clear. I believe there probably was an overemphasis on adaptation to the context in some of their earlier work on congregations. However, I also believe that it is folly to overreact in the opposite direction and ignore the strategic importance of knowledge of a congregation's context for faithful ministry and mission. I emphasize *strategic* knowledge—that knowledge which enables an informed, intentional response to its situation in light of a congregation's understanding of its purpose. Such knowledge includes an understanding of

● the power of the context over members' own lives and the life of the congregation;

- important factors in the context—for example, its demography, its economy, its political structure—and how they may be changing in ways that will affect the congregation;
- the social worlds—members' own and those of prospective members—that help to shape their concerns and interests;
- broad regional, national, and global trends that have an impact on local affairs and on congregational life;
- the opportunities that exist within the context for ministry and mission.

While gaining such strategic knowledge requires intentionality and effort on the part of a congregation's leaders, there are resources that can assist in the task.[23] The more leaders and members know and understand, in a strategic sense, about these various aspects of their social context, the greater the likelihood that they will develop their congregation towards a more faithful and effective expression of their unique identity as part of the body of Christ. Or, to put it negatively, a failure of leaders and members to understand the context and take into account contextual implications for the congregation's ministry and mission is to be in the situation described by Carl Sandburg in *The People, Yes.*

> He took the wheel in a lashing roaring hurricane.
> And by what compass did he steer the cause of the ship?
> "My policy is to have no policy," he said in the early months,
> And three years later, "I have been controlled by events."[24]

Leadership.   Critical both for clarifying and strengthening congregational identity and for developing strategic knowledge of the context is effective congregational leadership, lay and clergy. In his monumental work on leadership, James MacGregor Burns defines leadership in relational terms. Leadership is

> leaders inducing followers to act for certain goals that represent the values and the motivations—the wants and needs, the aspirations and expectations—of *both leaders and followers.* And the genius of leadership lies in the manner in which leaders see and act on their own and their followers' values and motivations.[25]

For Burns, leadership becomes *transformational* when leaders and followers engage with one another in such a way that each raises the other to higher levels of morality and motivation.

It is this kind of transformational leadership that is essential if congregations are to transfrom their contexts and not vice versa. When Douglass and Brunner tried to account for congregations that had "risen above their environments and succeeded where most others had failed," they listed "exceptional leadership" as first among the attributes of these churches.[26] Study after study of effective (and ineffective) congregations, since Douglass and Brunner's early work, have confirmed their findings on the crucial importance of leadership. Such leadership, both lay and clergy, is critical for helping a congregation clarify and strengthen its identity and gain the strategic understanding necessary for choosing how, given its identity, the congregation will respond faithfully to the constraints and possibilities of its context.

In the previously cited study of congregations and public life in Hartford, evidence confirmed that clergy leadership is especially critical in "managing the interface between the congregation and the community" as this leadership task was called.[27] It includes assisting the congregation to be clear about its orientation to public life, helping to shape members' perceptions and understanding of the context and public issues, and functioning visibly within the community as representatives of the congregation.

But clergy leadership alone in these matters was insufficient. Very instructive was the contrast between two congregations in the study, whose primary orientation to public mission (which is one aspect of a congregation's identity) was designated "activist." Activist congregations are those that are committed to taking stands and engaging in action on public issues as congregations. Similar to the previously described "civic" congregations, activist congregations believe that Christians have a responsibility to engage in service and to work for justice in their communities. But, unlike civic congregations, they are willing to do so as congregations rather than leaving it to individual members. In one activist congregation, a Catholic parish, the key leader responsible for the parish's activist stance was the pastor. While a number of the younger members of the parish energetically supported his activist efforts, many members, perhaps the majority, were not highly involved in this activism. Rather, they held what has been designated "sanctuary" orientation. In contrast, another activist congregation, a downtown Baptist church, had a much broader ownership of its activist orientation. The congregation's core lay leadership, especially, was committed to the orientation, so much so that sympathy for activism was made an essential ingredient of the job description when a new pastor was called. In reflecting on these two congregations, we concluded that identity as an activist congregation was much more clearly institutionalized in the Baptist congregation than in the Catholic parish because of lay as well as clergy ownership of the orientation. We speculated that, should the present pastor leave the Catholic parish, it would quite likely shift rather quickly back to its more traditional "sanctuary" identity, whereas such a shift would not be very likely in the Baptist congregation. Since the study was completed that shift in orientation in the Catholic parish did happen, in fact, after the priest was transferred to another parish.

The point is that leadership, lay as well as clergy, is necessary for articulating a congregation's identity, developing strategic information about the context of the congregation, and, thus, helping to shape the congregation's programs and processes in ways that honor its identity as the body of Christ in its particular time and place. Elsewhere this has been referred to as "reflective leadership," the capacity to bring to bear faith commitments, theological and theoretical knowledge, analysis of the situation, and past experience on critical decisions facing congregations. In this reflective process, such leaders often discover new and creative opportunities to minister faithfully in the situation, enabling their congregation to be transformative within its context.[28]

Conclusion

The chameleon image, both in its negative and positive implications, is appropriate to describe congregations. Congregations cannot avoid adapting to their environments, not only for survival's sake but, more importantly, for the sake of faithfulness to their calling. That is an essential part of their vulnerability which we have considered. But congregations also are often unfaithful to their calling as they, chameleon-like, take on the coloration of their environments in an uncritical way. In such instances, they are overwhelmed by events in their contexts and captive to the social worlds of their members. This kind of vulnerability is not what is called for to be faithful to the Christ who, in and through his own vulnerability, remained faithful unto death. Rather, the calling of congregations is to ministry and mission in the particularities of their time, place, and culture—always being vulnerable yet faithful to the One whose body they are. Such *faithfulness in vulnerability* requires, at the least, congregational knowledge of *who it is* (a strong and positive identity) and *where it is* (strategic understanding of its context). And it also requires the gift of *leadership,* lay and clergy, who can help the congregation to gain the necessary clarity and to develop modes of responding, in programs and processes, that are faithful to its identity and appropriate to its context.

Why Do People Congregate?

DAVID S. STEWARD
Pacific School of Religion

This chapter is written especially for church leaders who are concerned about the meaning and vitality of congregational life. It seeks to affirm that God is active in the affairs of the world, and to acknowledge the many ways that God's activity occurs both within and outside congregational life. This chapter invites church leaders to examine the meaning of congregational life for themselves and for those they wish to recruit into membership. It asks, specifically, "What IS the church, for Americans?" and "What do people want from a congregation?" It suggests ways church leaders can think about their congregational life and make it vital, both for themselves and for the nonchurched.

The question "Why do people congregate?" has to do with the church as we experience it in our everyday lives. When we talk about the church we experience, we are not talking about a church different from the one theologians talk about.

But we are talking differently about that church. We are talking out of the particular experiences we have had in a local church which is framed, as we ourselves are, by American culture.

This chapter presents two responses to what stands behind a person's affiliation with a congregation. Each response points beyond the congregation itself, to a context which influences our understanding of why people congregate.

The first response has to do with what the church *is* for American Christians. In some countries, persons affiliate with the church pretty much by virtue of their birth. In America, persons *decide* to go to church. If we are to understand why Americans congregate, we must have some understanding of the role the church plays in American society, and how that role has come to be. Specifically, we must understand what it means for church affiliation to be voluntary—for people to be free to decide for or against membership in a congregation.

The second response explores the decision to congregate. Theological libraries are full of volumes which tell us why, as the people of God, we should congregate. Experience in congregations interprets these reasons, revealing the desire of people to belong to a church community to worship and remember together; and to have a means through which to express their religious experience in the larger world.

Some Americans, however, understand themselves to be deeply religious, and even to be Christian, but do not attend our churches. Many of these persons once were participants, but have dropped out. They know the church from the inside out. What is involved in the decision to congregate becomes especially transparent in conversation with persons who once were congregants, but who have decided not to continue their church affiliation. Surprisingly, what they have to say helps us bring into focus how the congregation can be most alive.

What Is the Church, for Americans?

For Americans, the church is a voluntary institution. Frequently, we forget that voluntarism was not characteristic of the European church heritage. Sidney Mead found the church as it has developed in America so distinctive that he called it *The Lively Experiment*.[1] The final results, he believes, are not yet "in." The reflections of his book are important and interesting because it is not clear yet whether the church, as Americans know it, finally will work.

Forty-five years ago, the great church historian, Kenneth Scott Latourette, said: "The Christianity which developed in the United States was unique. It displayed features which marked it as distinct from previous Christianity in any other land."[2] For Americans, there is "a separation between church and state." The denomination, which is the institutional form assumed by the church in America, "unlike the traditional forms of the church, is not primarily confessional, and it is certainly not territorial. Rather it is purposive."[3] What does this mean for an American understanding of the church?

Throughout Christendom, from the fourth century through the eighteenth century, Christians were organized in established churches. To be a citizen meant that a person was a member of the established church. Church membership was not something for a person to choose, or necessarily even to think about.

The rise of nations, followed by the Protestant Reformation, increased the complexity of the role of the church in governance, but did not change its established character. Kings and princes needed the church to undergird and validate their right to rule, and to teach the people those values which would give cohesion to their governance. As regions developed both political and economic independence toward nationhood, regional expressions of the church became important to undergird the new territories. The Protestant Reformation both reflected and encouraged such territoriality. The confessional differences lifted up during the Reformation came to characterize regional churches, with the result that nation-states could claim Divine support through their own established church. Nations could mobilize and fight or support one another, buttressed by the sanctions of a confessional and territorial church.

There could be power struggles between established churches, for example, between Roman Catholic and Anglican authorities in England. But it was the dissenters from any established churches who were most persecuted. Their assertion that, as citizens of one country or another, they could CHOOSE their church struck at the core of authority as expressed in the church/state alliance. That the choice reflected a commitment to Scripture and immediate religious experience did not matter. Dissenters were unwelcome in established churches and in nations which relied on established churches.

But it was the circumstances of dissenters that most influenced America. In part, this was due to the fact that so many dissenters emigrated to America. In part, it was due to the absence of European tradition once they came. Mead quotes George Santayana to make the point: "(The American people) have all been uprooted from their several soils and ancestries and plunged together into one vortex, whirling irresistibly in a space otherwise quite empty."[4] The nation had to develop from this vortex. It had to cultivate and support the diverse religious passions of the "new American" while turning them to serve a national identity. Through the separation of church and state, a new proposal was made for the relation of those institutions, which reflects the twin authorities of citizenship: religion and nation.

The basic idea which stood behind the new proposal for church/state relationship was what Alexis de Tocqueville called "government by the people."[5] No longer could an individual claim a Divine right to rule, nor could an institution assert traditional prerogatives. Authority resided in the experience and good sense of the citizens. The state existed to preserve those rights through which individuals could come to participate in government. No institution, not even the church, could coerce or in any way replace the judicious individual. In American churches, coercion was replaced by persuasion, and tradition by immediate religious experience. Denominationalism was the result: an institutional form which was required to compete for the loyalty of its members in a land where everything was new. Is it any wonder, then, that the efforts of American churches to gain converts replaced the efforts of European churches to support the order of the state?

The American solution has been to reject the church as a power in matters of state. Now, if the church cannot effect its will on the nation, does that make it unimportant? That question raises significant issues for those who would ask: "Why do people congregate?"

Many Americans believe that the church can be independent of any institutional form. The issue is a complicated one. Emile Durkheim said: "Religion is inseparable from the idea of a church."[6] At the same time, he reported his observation of "private religions which the individual established for himself and celebrates himself." He set the problem when he commented: "Not only are these individual religions very frequent in history, but nowadays many are asking if they are not destined to be the pre-eminent form of the religious life, and if the day will not come when there will be no other cult than that which each man will freely perform within himself."[7] Durkheim acknowledged individualism in religion and understood that, for some people, it could take the form of an outlook of common religion without the church.

Ernst Troeltsch[8] analyzed individual religion, which he called "mysticism," along with his more famous categories of "church" and "sect." He spoke of an "invisible church" to cover the mystical relationship between the person and God. This spiritual relationship "invisibly rules all believers, without external signs or other human means."[9] The mystic, residing in the "invisible church," is called to a life of Christian charity. For such a person, neither church nor clergy held authority; authority rested in the Holy Spirit.

"Why do people congregate?" becomes a compelling social and psychological question, as it becomes clear to us not only that church membership is voluntary, but also that persons can understand themselves as members of an "invisible church" with no affiliation whatsoever with an institutional church. Whereas individual religion is the natural outcome of the separation of church and state (and the consequent competition of churches for the loyalty of individual persons), individual religion is the source of a "spiritual church" apart from institutional forms. At the same time, Durkheim and Troeltsch tell us that individual religion requires social expression. It is the church, Durkheim insists, which provides the outlook that makes the individual religious. And Troeltsch defines a religious action in social terms, as a relationship of caring. The context for individual religion, then, is a community.

It is within this community-based individualism that we come to understand better the phenomenon of the "unchurched." The unchurched, says Lauve Steenhuisen, "had once turned to a church, for a number of reasons, yet something had changed, either in the church ... or in their lives ... which had made the church no longer a viable proposition."[10] The unchurched in America are understood, largely, to be the previously churched, rather than to be people with no history of church experience. They are considered to be institutionally apostate—to have abandoned the church.

There is a range of brittleness among churches when it comes to the issue of the unchurched. At the harshest extreme are those churches which define Christianity moralistically, that is, in terms of behavior prescribed by their group. For those people, change in the prescribed behavior is a lapse which requires repentance on the part of the offender. The responsibility assigned to the defector for the move away from the church is caught up in the question: "How can the gospel best be explained to those who have turned away?"[11]

Toward the other extreme are those churches, usually more attuned to the rhythms of nature and culture, which continue to affirm a person as theirs, so long as their basic religious ceremonies (for example, baptism, marriage, and burial) are observed. For those people, there are fewer unchurched; it requires a major wrench to disaffiliate. Thus, there remain plenty of "inactive" members. A mild version of this position is expressed in Greeley's lament: "The first melancholy conclusion for those who embark on evangelism must be that

... most of the problem (is) in the past experience of adults."[12] It is, specifically, their experience in the church.

For the institutionally aggressive church, there is little, if any, room for an "invisible church." Too much is at stake in the marketplace. For the more acculturated church, it is acceptable to entertain "seasons" in a person's life wherein religious experience may continue to be vital without exhibiting itself in institutional form. Neither, however, feels overly comfortable with the autonomy gained through an "invisible church." If not unfaithful, such persons are at least "alienated"[13] or "crypto-believers"[14] or "apathetic."[15] Frequently, churches set as their purpose the reclaiming of these "lost souls." That is by no means an easy task in a pluralistic society. When it ignores the "invisible church," the result is often a further distancing from the church of the person to be evangelized. These days the option to disaffiliate from church life, while continuing to see oneself related to God through an invisible church, colors the question, "Why do people congregate?

For many churches, outreach has come to mean self-support. Even though the European understanding of church (as bounded by territory and confession) has been transformed in America to a church with a purpose, neither territory nor confession has been eliminated. Jack L. Seymour traces the domestication of church purpose during American history. The story, using education as the focus, goes like this. In Europe (and pre-revolutionary America), the church provided training in the basic values and skills of citizenship. Since social life was understood to exist in covenant with God, the church's activity was both central to and pervasive in the public arena. It was this role which was adjusted in the American experiment of the separation of church and state.[16]

The American experiment did not intend to exclude the church from public affairs; it simply could not let the church rest at the center of things. The question was, "How can training in the basic values, on which both the nation and the church depend, be accomplished?" Since the denominations had been defined confessionally, and the nation wholistically, this was not an easy problem to solve.[17]

At the beginning of the nineteenth century, the Sunday school exploded onto the American scene. Both its form and its purpose matched the experimental temper of the new nation. Its purpose was to advance literacy and Christian values which were considered necessary by both the nation and the church. A vital electorate had to read, and had to develop enough value coherence to accomplish an effective political "mind." Organizationally, the Sunday school was a voluntary association. Anyone concerned with its purpose could join. The larger public agenda compelled membership across denominational boundaries. As a special interest group, it got things done which could not be accomplished through rival churches. Such voluntary associations continue with us today, especially in the causes and political action groups which invite participation based on commitment to the special interest represented rather than on creed.

By the middle of the nineteenth century, the common school, as the public school system was initially called, preempted the national political purpose of the Sunday school. For awhile, the two coexisted, but the formalized public school system came to replace the voluntary association. The energy that had served the Sunday school movement as a voluntary association was diverted in two directions. First, church people expanded their vision of literacy and Christian values into the world mission movement. Missionaries from America circled the globe to carry the good news of their Christian nation. American values and methods were linked with Bible translation in an effort to "save the world." Both denominational and independent boards sent missionaries. Sometimes missionaries would work together "in the field," regardless of denominational affiliation. Sometimes the denominational rivalry persisted, and whole countries were divided into denominational spheres of influence.

The second development was a withdrawal, during the first half of the nineteenth century, by the churches from the public arena.[18] The public concerns present in the Sunday school were replaced by concerns of church status and survival. By the middle of the nineteenth century, evangelization of America was complete (it was now a full-fledged Christian nation, with few who failed to identify themselves with one denomination or another). Further evangelizing would require taking members from another church. The power balance among denominations was delicate enough to make this a bad idea for everyone. Therefore, the denomination had to look within itself for survival. Perpetuation of the denomination required rearing one's own to active membership. The church's vital effort shifted from evangelical outreach to the education of the church's own children. This fundamentally defensive posture resulted in doctrinal education, to insure the adult loyalty of the church's children. It set the churches apart from one another, and solidified their marginality when it came to public issues.

What is the church for Americans? It is the most explicit value ground for our nation and culture. But it has been separated from the power of the state and forced to use persuasion rather than coercion to effect its role. Its voluntary nature encourages it to be competitive and combative with its several forms. Since it is not permitted to operate with political power, it must operate at the "grass roots." This may be just the right place for it in an America based in "the power of the people," but the experiment is not finished. Some have argued that a secular religion has replaced church religion already. Others come to church because they believe its pluralistic, persuasive form is indeed the "last, best hope of earth."[19]

What is the church for Americans? It is a spiritual reality which can take a very personal form. It involves the relation a person has, directly, with God. For some, it does not require an institution at all. In fact for many, the institutional church violates loving relationships so dramatically that it is seen to hinder rather than to promote the Christian life. It is not easy for an institution to deal with the individualism that is so central to the American experience. Some Americans come to church to seek help in their own spiritual journeys which are based not in church tradition, but in their own, individual experience.

The church, for many Americans, has become a fragile island in Santayana's whirling vortex. The forces that have made it what it is continue to value it, but at an arm's length. It is acknowledged as a source of value and commitment. These are needed by the nation, but there are limits to how they can be tapped. Some churches acknowledge their marginal role in American society and content themselves to provide support for the social expression of vague, private religious sentiments. Other churches acknowledge the pluralism of America, and sharpen their self-understanding while remaining tolerant of the commitment of other persons and communities. Still other churches seek to reclaim the nation, and to make it in their own image. Despite their different purposes, each of these groups responds to a public beyond itself. In that encounter each must answer the question, "Why do people congregate?"

What Do People Want from a Congregation?

The dominant reality of American experience is the choosing individual. It is this person who, for better and for worse, constitutes the pluralism with which both nation and church must deal. It is through the choosing individual that the value ground of our nation and culture will be expressed. It is through the choosing individual that spiritual reality will be made manifest. It is through the choosing individual that affiliation with an institutional church will occur.

The question, "Why do people congregate?" is, of course, a question about churches. But, dramatically, in the American context, it also is a question about individual persons. Why do people congregate? The personal thrust of the matter is caught up in the question now under discussion: "What do people want from a congregation?"

"People participate in churches—or they stay away—" says Carl Dudley, "based on what they believe the congregation stands for . . ." (see "Using Church Images for Commitment, Conflict, and Renewal"). Dudley presents eight images of the congregation which he finds operative in local churches, and enjoins leaders to become aware of how these images interact in the life of every local church. Pastors and lay persons need to do this, and then fine-tune their leadership so the church can be seen by its members to be clearly responsive to their needs.

But there is a larger audience for congregational ministry which results from the voluntarism of American society. As Dudley notes, people participate—or stay away. The unchurched have many of the same yearnings as the churched— yearnings to which churches seek to respond. Why do some people leave the church and stay away? What do church leaders need to understand about these yearnings of the unchurched, and how they can be met? What do the unchurched want from a congregation?

These are unpleasant questions for church people to face. The unchurched remind us that we don't always do things right or make good impressions. But to face the outsider may reveal to us a range of needs our congregations must meet, and may challenge us to become more sensitive and intentional as congregations.

The great majority of Americans perceive themselves to be religious. Christian institutions understand and accept, at least in their rhetoric, the voluntarism in religion which is part of a pluralistic nation. Evangelism is softened by this realization. Proselytizing is generally frowned upon. The major market for evangelism is the previously churched; those who understand themselves already to be within the tradition, but who are not now active in any of its voluntary institutional expressions. These are the disaffiliates to whom the question is best put: "What do people want from a congregation?"

It has not been easy for church members to ask this question effectively. How do you talk about someone who has declined to participate in the church which means so much to you? It is easy to use disparaging language. One researcher has presented the unchurched as "more likely than the churched to be characterized by misanthropy, normlessness, and despair."[20] How does a church person who feels this way engage in conversation with an unchurched person, let alone listen to that person?

"Disaffiliate," "apathetic," "dropout," "unchurched" are names that have been given to those who have withdrawn from active church life. All convey the presence of an outsider rather than the presence of a member with independent views of what it is to be a Christian. It is easy to "personalize" these names, and to assume that the unchurched is a person who has chosen to be alienated. This lets us off the hook. Since their withdrawal is seen as their decision, it is not necessary, we might argue mistakenly, for us to look at ourselves or our church to understand their alienation.

Dean Hoge finds this view too simple. He refuses to see dropouts as entirely outside the church. He seeks to soften the unfortunate bias of names by describing dropouts according to the way they relate, despite their disaffiliation, within a broadly conceived church. He identifies five types of dropouts.[21] "Young dropouts" reveal tensions their family members have concerning church participation. "Older dropouts" reveal weariness with church participation. Disagreement with church positions on morality or doctrine can result in more liberal "lifestyle dropouts" and more conservative "anti-change dropouts." Some individuals find that the church is no longer an important factor in their spiritual journey. They may be called "spiritual need dropouts." In every case, the dropout is defined by events in which the church has been involved. Hoge concludes that the decision to drop out is seldom rational or logical. Rather, it is a judgment resting on the blend of experiences an individual has in the larger context of living. Each dropout has a story about life in the church, which the church needs to hear.

Joseph H. Fichter also refuses to cut off the dropout. He speaks of the "degree of unchurchedness."[22] His description of "factors of marginality" reveals an often angry story heard by researchers who have listened to the unchurched. For marginal church people, says Fichter, the church holds unrealistic expectations about their lifestyle; proposes an unacceptable moral law; is authoritarian; and can't provide for their particular needs. He finds that both family and church contribute to marginality, with the pastor's personality and style of leadership as the most important factor.

J. Russell Hale interviewed the unchurched about their perception of themselves and their perception of the church.[23] His conclusion is very much the same as that of Hoge and Fichter: people leave the church because of the church's inability to meet their expectations. There are, Hale reminds us, "several worlds of the unchurched."[24] He labels ten: anti-institutionalists, boxed in, burned out, floaters, hedonists, locked out, nomads, pilgrims, publicans, true unbelievers. People have so many different needs. It is not surprising that some disaffiliate.

It is important to know about the different worlds of the unchurched. It is also important to know how the unchurched remain similar to the churched. Researchers tell us: "Comparisons between churched and unchurched have found dissimilarity in demographic characteristics and similarity in matters of belief and theology."[25] What a stunning message this is! The unchurched are like us precisely at the point which makes us Christian. We share a common commitment to the God of Jesus Christ. It is demographic characteristics—matters of age and sex and social circumstances—which set us apart.

Churches contribute to the process through which individual believers come to feel excluded. Nearly thirty years ago, Bruce Reinhart[26] showed how the practices of church life—the scheduling of programs, the conduct of worship, the organization and leadership of committees—served to screen people in and out of local churches. These "hidden persuaders" helped maintain the social uniformity of the local church, and kept people with different backgrounds out. John Westerhoff currently argues that the local church must draw the differences of our pluralistic nation into itself explicitly.[27] The church exists to help us value and interpret our differences within God's world, rather than to divide us according to social prejudices.

What motivates a person to disaffiliate from a church? Researchers agree that the origin of disaffiliation is not usually due to matters of belief. It is due to the career of the person—in the experience an individual has of the church through a family and over time. Again and again, the support of the family is revealed as a base point. Hartman found that church attendance "was highest among families with church school aged children, that parental encouragement was decisive in church attendance in later life, and that the commitment of the spouse to church attendance was crucial to maintained membership."[28] When Hartman interviewed nonattenders under the age of 30, he found that they did not feel themselves loved or wanted by church members. Nonattenders over the age of 30 spoke of "personal" changes in their lives which made church attendance irrelevant. Although researchers have uncovered many factors external to church life, which condition a person's experience of rejection or independence in relation to church, these two general reasons for disaffiliation are mentioned again and again as researchers talk with the unchurched.

John Kotre makes clear just how complicated the issue is of what people want from their congregation. He insists that the confessions and accusations people make about their experiences in the church must be understood in light of the experiences each individual brings. His study highlights the concept of "predisposing factors" (such as age, sex, and family situation) as being crucial to the experiences people will have in the church. These factors will combine to shape the perception a person has of the church. Kotre is clear that a member and a dropout will view the same church differently. "The church that the Ins are in is not the church that the Outs are out of."[29] For those persons who have a past which predisposes them to stay "in," the church will be redefined over time to take account of the changes which growth and the circumstances of living make inevitable. Without such redefinition, the church cannot last over a lifetime as a community of orientation.

John Savage focuses on how intensely the unchurched feel about the events which led to their disaffiliation.[30] He suggests that church dropouts feel driven from the church, psychologically, due to experiences with church leaders or members (and in some cases, with family members in and around church matters) which leave them feeling "depersonalized." The experience of being hurt this way within the community of the church produces bitter memories. The ongoing anxiety present in the interviews reveals how expensive it was and continues to be for some persons to leave the church.

It is in this context that the unchurched want and need to be heard. "Studies on the unchurched," summarizes Steenhuisen, "have found that they are not unreligious; in fact, many studies have shown that the unchurched are more religious than the churched, that is, they pray more, read the Bible more often, and turn more often to their faith for guidance in their daily lives."[31] It is somewhat unexpected to find Steenhuisen's conclusion to be: "(The Disaffiliated) did not leave the church for religious reasons and they left with their faith intact."[32] In fact, what dropouts want from a congregation is to be heard. Fulfill our needs and aspirations, they say; and acknowledge our gifts. This is the Good News they ask from the church. The church can become Good News for the disaffiliate as it becomes a diverse community, listening to Christian believers who differ in their response to God's call and providing resources for living according to different gifts.[33]

Thinking About Our Congregational Life

These are confusing times for church leaders. The whole world is changing, and the church with it. The church should be a quiet place in the storm—a place for renewal and a launching pad. But we find the church itself, and its people, uncertain. Congregational life too frequently alienates rather than supports. It seeks to compete with other institutions in society, and finds itself on the losing end.

Many church leaders see this as a time for our beliefs to be clarified. I agree. I would like to point to beliefs in three areas which church people need to sharpen: beliefs about what the church is for us; beliefs about who our own people are; and beliefs about what makes a congregation a powerful force in persons' lives. I understand these areas to require prayerful, theological response. They are questions with a personal, social, and historical "bite," and they are questions about God's people and the church of Jesus Christ.

Beliefs are, on the bottom line, what individual people hold. Doctrines and creeds may represent beliefs, but a creed without a believer is pretty empty. One does not clarify a belief by simply dusting off an old doctrine and proclaiming it more loudly from the pulpit. Belief becomes clarified as individual believers struggle to understand and accept both the reality and meaning of things for themselves. Clarification of beliefs begins with people. It is they who need to think about their congregational life. The result of their struggle will be more relevant than the wisest answers offered from an outside authority.

I want to end this chapter by presenting three questions which church people need to answer in order to understand why their people congregate. They are questions for which there is no single answer. The result for people who struggle to answer them will be a clarification of what they believe.

What Is the Church for Us?   We have already traced several answers to this question. More importantly, we have set the question within the context of American history and society. We have seen the church in America as a denomination, set apart from politics and made marginal in terms of the power of the state. We also have seen the church in America as an idea which goes beyond institutional form, an idea with which individual persons can still identify when they reject or dismiss a local congregation.

These are circumstances which exist. Our answer to the question, "what is the church for us?" will clarify matters only if it takes these circumstances into account. In addition to the many biblical and doctrinal responses we will make about what we believe the church to be, we need to deal also with the questions: "How is our church related to the public arena?" and "How is our church related to the lives of individual persons?"

The question about the public arena acknowledges the church's location in society. It acknowledges its social limitation, and the fact that it has to compete for public attention. It also makes clear that there is a role for the church in a larger society. It raises the issue of evangelism and outreach.

The question about individual persons acknowledges the composition of the church itself. The church is its people. It is through church people that the activity of the church takes place. It is church people who must be clear about who they are and how their activity contributes to the church's mission. This question opens up the issue of nurture and discipleship.

Who Are Our People? We have discovered that churches "own" people in quite different ways, and, perhaps more startling, people "own" churches in different ways. Some churches find people who differ from their practice in most any area to be unfaithful and "outside the wall." Other churches allow for great variety in church practice, insisting on compliance only in a few life-transitional sacraments. And some people see themselves as religious, and even Christian, practitioners while avoiding the practices of the institutional church altogether.

These, too, are circumstances which exist. The answer we give to the question, "Who are our people?" helps us see who we include and exclude; and who excludes and includes us. How wide is the scope of "our people" in your church? Does it include only those who participate actively in church practice? Does it include others? What about those who see themselves as members of a "hidden church" beyond institutional form? What about people who have left the church, apparently for a season? Are they still "our people," or are they named "backsliders" or "unfaithful"?

We relate to family members and strangers in different ways. When we confuse the two, we frequently breed misunderstanding. How must it look to the people who believe themselves to be "family members" when we try to convert them? How must they feel when we pray for them to return to a place they don't think they've ever left? What about the people who feel a need to follow a different drummer for a season . . . who seek a vacation from what they feel to be the burdens of church practice? And what about those who find the spirituality of church practice too limiting . . . who seek beyond the local church for more satisfying relationships with God? Can we let them go, and still pray and care for them?

Those are not easy questions. Because a church is its people, the questions go to the core of our corporate identity. When we are not clear about who our people are, we become fuzzy about who we are. That is why church practice is such a powerful norm for membership. But a rigid, behavioral norm always leaves people out who believe themselves to belong, and inevitably makes it difficult for us to listen seriously to those whom we define as different from us. When Jesus dealt with tax collectors and Samaritans he pointed us to a broader norm. If we believe that we are all God's children, we must be clear about how that affects membership, not only in the human family, but in our churches. We may know somewhat less than we thought about how to choose those who are to be included. We may need to listen more widely than we thought . . . even to outsiders, if we are to be clear about who and whose we are.

When Is a Congregation Full of Power? It is the Christian's witness that power comes from God. A congregation is filled with power as it acknowledges that its power comes from God. This is not an invitation to turn away from the personal, social, and historical dimensions of life. Every congregation HAS power . . . to draw and sustain members of its communion and to influence people it meets. This power is the resource from which it acts. The congregation which is filled with power is clear in its belief about this, and understands that church practice is framed by God's power.

For the power-filled church, congregational life is understood as celebration. Sometimes we find it hard to know what there is to celebrate. We are like the elder brother of the prodigal son. For Christians, celebration is an acknowledgement of gifts received. Liturgy is much more than the rehearsal of ancient forms. It is giving thanks for what God is doing now among us. We know of God's activity now, as we listen to one another. Effective listening is possible only as we pay attention to the people who form and are influenced by the congregation. Celebration is the acknowledgement of the gifts to which they bear witness. Power comes to a congregation through the gifts its people bring. Congregations need to listen to people in order to acknowledge the gifts God has given through them, and to glorify God for these blessings. What happens to a congregation when it understands God's power as flowing into it through gifts people bring, if only it will listen?

The power-filled church exhibits congregational life as mission. The power of the church is the power of discernment. The church announces what it is time for. This is accomplished as members of a congregation find their needs and aspirations fulfilled. Announcement of the times is not a mere matter of grand ideas and words. The times are announced as the poor are fed, the blind given sight, the oppressed set free. The needs and aspirations to be fulfilled are not the needs and aspirations of the marketplace . . . of TV advertising or personal/national glorification. The needs and aspirations to be fulfilled are those of the outcast . . . the tax-collector and the leper. Power is exhibited as we listen to those in our congregation, and those beyond, at the points where we have trouble hearing. Power is exhibited as we faithfully respond to what is missing in the lives of those we love, and those who cross our paths by accident. The power does not come from us, nor is it our job to diagnose the need and remedy it with our own favorite solution. The power comes *through* us as we hear what we would rather not hear. We cannot listen this way without responding. In our response to what we hear, the announcement is made about what it is time for. And in the same response is a power-filled action to satisfy the needs of those whom God has set before us.

In the final analysis, people congregate to be listened to and to listen. Congregations do these things as they acknowledge the gifts people bring and announce through their actions "the times" as they are experienced by those in need. Clarification of our beliefs about what the church is for us, and about who our people are, can lead to congregational life as celebration and mission, to a living revelation of why people congregate.

Using
Church Images
for Commitment,
Conflict,
and Renewal

CARL S. DUDLEY
McCormick Theological Seminary

People participate in churches—or they stay away—based on what they believe the congregation stands for, or their image of the church. The most compelling education by the church is found in images which it evokes in the community it serves. Every motivation toward church activity, from its public appeals for participation and support to its emotional conflicts and intimate satisfactions, is grounded in images of what the members believe the church both is and ought to be.

In church conflicts, members who have a common language for discussing their church images can at least agree on the nature of their disagreements. When members accept the importance of differing images held by other members, the conflicts do not need to be experienced as contests of power or personalities. Members who understand and agree on the choices of church images gain a strength in their decisions, even when they disagree with a particular choice which the church has made.

Leadership is related to the use of those church images in language and behavior which the membership understands and supports. The relationship of leaders and members is symbiotic: each makes demands upon the other, and each responds to expectations of the other. Therefore, trusted church leaders promote, articulate, and embody the values which the church claims for itself. Members can follow a trusted leader who talks their language, even if they disagree with a particular decision or activity. Shared images make possible both continuity and change.

To the outside observer, the church "teaches" by the images that it projects into the community. In part the church is known by the architectural symbols in which it is housed, the activities which it supports, and the public image that it projects through the pastor and the press. More importantly, a congregation affects the community through self images of "church" that inform and guide the lives of its members.

Since every action of a church is symbolic, each congregation provides an endless source of self-images. This chapter will consider several ways in which these images have been organized and utilized by the church. First, we will survey briefly five common and historic typologies (analytical classifications or models) of church images, and suggest the usefulness and limitations of these images. Second, in a longer discussion we will offer eight specific images which have been drawn from work with congregations. Readers not interested in historic ways of organizing images may wish to proceed immediately to the application of "Eight Images" suggested in the second part.

Types of Church Images

Since this discussion seeks to reflect the images that teach and guide the behavior of the local church, two of the most frequent types of church images need only be acknowledged in passing.

The first image is significant because it is attached to the sign which designates almost every congregation: the denominational label, such as Lutheran, Presbyterian, Method-

ist. The denominational tag designates a particular strand of
Christian witness with a historically shaped range of liturgy,
polity, and membership. Although this image is significant for
some discussions, such as clergy preparation, church financing,
and sociology of religion in America, denominational differences are not the determinative factors for the images that
guide behavior within the congregation and teach the meaning
of the church in the community.

Church size provides the basis for another popular typology of churches, as the congregation records membership or
recognizes attendance in worship and other events. Although
congregational size directly affects the leadership, resources,
and process of congregational life, size alone does not define
the functional images by which the membership participates
in the church, and the church influences the community. In
discovering the way the images of the church educate the community and guide its own members, we must look at three
more basic areas: images drawn from biblical sources, from a
congregation's social setting in its community, and from the
programmatic purpose of the church.

Biblical Images

As a gathered community, the New Testament church
spends much of its energy defining what it means to belong "in
Christ." No paragraph of the New Testament exists without an
underlying image of the relationship to which the believer is
called. When we look for images of the church as the focus for
Bible study, the text is rich with imagination drawn from a
wide variety of experience. New Testament images of the church
include: (1) *objects*—such as salt, rock, road, boat, table, and
cup; (2) *products*—such as building, garden, flock, and house;
(3) *living things*—such as body and blood, and also seed, fruit,
vine, branches, and tree; (4) *significant events*—such as the
happy times of festivals, feasts, and weddings, and the crises
of exile, sacrifice, and poverty; (5) *feelings*—such as love, judgement, rejection, election, forgiveness, redemption, and reconciliation; (6) and, most of all, *human relationships with God
among Christian family and fellowship*—such as daughters,

sons, friends, community, citizens, priests, ambassadors, guests, slaves, servants, disciples, brides of Christ, and "members" of the body. The list of New Testament images is extensive, even without including the Christian appropriation of ecclesiastical images in the Old Testament.

Paul Minear in his classic study of *Images of the Church in the New Testament* [1] discussed ninety-six metaphors to suggest a dynamic theology of tension between the history of the faith in Israel and the constantly renewed creation brought by the intervention of the Holy Spirit. He viewed this combination as producing communal images of continuity within the church and "the body of Christ" images of the church in the world. Hans Küng, in a much more extensive review of church images and their meanings,[2] used the same formulation of continuity, creativity, and community to affirm the necessity of tension among images in the dynamic of God's continuing activity in the church. No single image is sufficient. In most congregations this diversity of images provides the energy of commitment for particular activities in the life of the church.

Twenty centuries of reflection, proclamation, and liturgical use have not exhausted the meanings of these biblical images. In the imagination of the church, they have been researched, amplified, and applied in endlessly different settings and moments of human need. But we have paid for such diverse application by dulling the edge of clarity. For example, "People of God" is a generic term which may distinguish the church from secular groups, but it does not suggest the unique character of a particular local congregation. Such a metaphor could be used as easily by a synagogue or mosque.

"Body of Christ" is another frequently used biblical image. For Christians it has the advantage of identifying the source of our faith in Jesus Christ. But it has been used with different and sometimes conflicting meanings. Thus the diversity implied in the various "members of Christ's body" has been applied to different characteristics within a single group, different groups within a congregation, different congregations within a denomination—anything that is different has been justified by its application. Claiming to be the "body of Christ" has been used, for example, to legitimate such different gatherings as (1) a sacramental moment of quiet personal communion, (2) a sanctified group which was alienated from the world, and (3) a servant community which seeks to continue the ministry of Jesus in the world without regard to their recognition as Christians.

Biblical images remain the inspiration and nourishment from which we are continually renewed. They are a sacred source of symbols used to clarify, reinforce, and sometimes challenge images drawn from other sources. From the biblical record, we see the use of many images gathered into coherent themes. We should expect a similar diversity of images in our congregations, and we must look for those unifying themes. These themes should be grounded in the biblical record but specific to the location, role, and lifestyle which define the character and mission of the congregation.

Images Based on Social Location

Congregations are strongly affected by their social environment. The church in the city must deal with the fragmented character of urban life while the rural church can often make assumptions about social networks in the community. The middle class suburban community draws from a population in which organization and good management are expected from its leadership. Immigrant churches often gather around strong cultural leaders and do not give a high priority to organizational clarity. In significant ways, different images of the church are related to the social location of the congregation.

In *Parish Planning*,[3] Lyle Schaller has listed more than a score of church images based on social context. When we see the names they seem remarkably familiar: from the downtown Old First Church, through a variety of congregations serving neighborhoods, suburbs, and cultural groups; to scattered churches in the "dying crossroads village" and "the open country congregation." Each image has its own architecture and patterned behavior, based on the expectations of the membership served. Douglas Walrath[4] has developed a typology of twelve turf-based congregations and has expanded these images by noting differences in the ways congregations develop leadership and relate to their target populations. Ezra Earl Jones[5] has suggested six basic community-related images (characterized by a unique appeal to a particular theology, ethnic-cultural group, or institutional base): Old Downtown, New Metropolitan, Neighborhood, Rural, Open Country, and Special Purpose. Clergy, especially denominational leaders, find these images of location especially helpful.

However, images based on social location are uninteresting to most local church members. People in congregations tend to assume the local environment as their universe. They recognize that other churches exist differently: most other churches are not competitive, only different. Various images based on different target populations are essential for church planners and program developers, but they are almost irrelevant to the regular participation of most members. Members assume that their style of commitment and behavior is "the church" for their community.

Church leaders and planners also carry other images which, though they may be significant for shaping the program of the congregation, generally are not regarded as important in the conscious definitions of most church members. Thus some consultants[6] have suggested a wide range of church images which reflect other influences of context, history, and organization, such as: stages in congregational development, unique pastoral influence, style of congregational leadership, crises in community change, average age of members, organizational efficiency, and membership commitment. All of those factors are significant for leaders who compare one congregation to another. As with the effects of social context, most typical church members acknowledge the influence of other factors only in offhand comments and frustrated sighs.

Images of Purpose in Ministry

Church members do understand and rally to support images which are grounded in the program and purpose of the church. These images are usually presented in either of two forms: one emphasizes the way the church relates to the larger society, and the other suggests the program which the church offers to the society. We shall consider them in turn.

The uses of pop-theological language for church images (such as fundamentalist and liberal, radical and moderate, charismatic and activist) can be seen as attempts to gather into single concepts a relationship between the faith of the congregation and the world in which it lives. In a more systematic way, H. Richard Niebuhr[7] has developed, from the Weberian concepts of church and sect, a classic typology of images which reflect a particular relationship between "Christ" and "culture," that is, between various Christian traditions and the communities in which they witness. He noted that churches see themselves, in relation to their society, as taking a stance of rejecting, accepting, leading, living in paradox, or transforming.

In more recent research, Roozen, McKinney, and Carroll[8] have reformulated the categories of Niebuhr based on congregational self-images which are guided by two criteria: the priority they place on this world or the next, and their emphasis on inner life of the congregation or health of the larger community. They present congregational case studies based on four images developed from those two indexes: *Civic Church* which seeks to serve the community with caring programs, and *Sanctuary Church* which provides a spiritual haven; *Activist Church* which seeks to change the world, and *Evangelist Church* which places a primary emphasis on saving souls. Their data strongly support the conclusion that church members have made functional commitments to the church based on images of the relationship between church and culture.

Secondly, a different set of congregational images can be developed from the program emphasis which the congregation offers to the community. One popular expression of these images is found in the writing of Avery Dulles, *Models of the Church*.[9] Dulles defines five images around which congregations (and denominations) organize their life and work: *institutional* church with an emphasis on order, *mystical communion* with an emphasis on personal relationships, *sacramental* church which celebrates the intersection of human and divine, *herald* church which puts priority on proclamation, and *servant* church which seeks to touch humanity at the points of greatest need. With a collection of case studies, Dan Baumann[10] describes a similar set of images, calling them: the *teaching* church, the *family-centered* church, the *soul-saving* church, the *servant* church. Baumann's own congregation, like the sacramental model for Dulles, combines all of the others in an emphasis on the (sacramental) Presence of God moving through particular persons and events. This programmatic emphasis on images has the advantage of immediate response among church members. Laity can see the images of the church in its actions: the church is what it does.

But churches, like people, are always more than behavior. There can be depth and texture to images of the congregation, not just program activity. The same program may have different meanings in separate churches, or even among different members in the same congregation. Images that move members are a combination drawn from all of these areas. They are biblical in basis and, like the biblical material itself, they are varied and in tension—pointing toward a mystery. The images are drawn from the populations served and the cultures they carry, even if they find their identity in being "counter-culture." The images of church members are reflected in the congregation's programs and projected into the community. Effective images among church members need to combine all of these elements.

Eight Images Which Teach Faith in Community

Each of the previously mentioned classifications has been developed for particular purposes, especially for church leaders, to provide symbols to focus the life and work of the church. Using these typologies can be intellectually stimulating and experientially satisfying.

However, when working with congregations we find that the members do not limit themselves to the rational typologies recognized by seminary curriculum. Clergy often bring to the church the images which they learned in the subculture of the seminary and from the literature of established authorities. Of course, some tension between clergy and laity is essential to the prophetic leadership of the ordained religious calling. Clergy are expected to see some things differently, "through biblical eyes," for example. But all too often clergy tend to import and impose a set of images that seem more like personal bias than prophetic insight.

In our work with members of mainline congregations of various sizes, denominations, and cultural settings, we have tried to be sensitive to the language and symbols which emerge from laity and reflect the sources of their commitments in faith. We have rediscovered a New Testament-like tension of images that exist together without necessarily being resolved into patterns of rational coherence or theological consistency. We have tried to bring these images together into a tapestry of congregational commitment without losing the diversity or forcing an alien pattern. We have clustered the countless images into fewer centers of meaning and a more manageable number of choices. Based on these data, we suggest eight images as basic to the commitments, conflicts, and energies for renewal in most congregational settings.[11]

These eight images assume that members are committed to the Lordship of Jesus Christ, but that people understand and express their commitments differently. All eight images imply priorities of faithful Christian behavior and belief, which are not better or holier in themselves but may be more or less relevant in a particular situation. Each of these images can be legitimate, and each can be corrupted or carried to the extreme (which is heresy). Individuals and congregations may hold two or more of these images, and usually do, even though they might appear to be in theological contradiction. In some settings there is a kind of balance among the images, each needing the others to generate a larger and more holistic expression of the Christian faith.

We have grouped the eight images in pairs around four issues of faith to which the members may be responding, consciously or not: (1) What relationships hold us together? (2) How do we carry the faith? (3) How do we serve the community?

(4) How do we seek change in others? Thus we see the eight images as affirmations of faith and belonging.

   1. "What relationships hold us together?" Personal relationships provide the most frequent image, and for many people the most compelling. This image is expressed in two ways: (1) *The Christian Family Church,* which assumes a common language and cultural heritage, and sustains a sense of family even if the members are not kin. (2) *The Christian Nurture Church,* which must develop a common language and establish a network of relationships to care for individuals and to sustain family life in a highly mobile world.

   2. "How do we carry the faith?" For many members the dominant images relate to a sense of the sacred in and through the life of the church: (3) *Old First (Denominational) Church,* which carries the faith with patterned presentation of historic denominational traditions (language, liturgy, leadership, etc.) as they are remembered and practiced in the region. (4) *The Christian Sanctuary Church,* which carries the faith through specific, local attachments to symbolic objects, persons, and spaces which are associated with God's presence in transitional crises and seasonal rhythms in the lives of the members.

   3. "How do we serve the community?" For a fewer but significant number of people, the means of service seems the most salient image: (5) *The Christian Citizen Church,* which sees itself as actively participating in the community primarily through the use of the building, by seeking to bring into its space varied social groups and political dialogue as an affirmation of its centrality in the community. (6) *The Christian Servant Church,* which provides a way for its members to act out their compassion, both in the church and through church connections, for people who need help.

   4. "How do we seek change in others?" The final two images are found least frequently, though they are expressed with great intensity. Both seek to challenge and change the world, but their priorities are different. (7) *The Social Prophet Church,* which begins by seeking to change the destructive horizontal relationships of oppression and injustice wherever they are found, in the world, the community, and the church. (8) *The Faith Evangelist Church,* which begins by seeking to change the disrupted vertical relationships between God and humanity, seeking to bring individuals into the life of the church.

Interpersonal Relationships.[12] Interpersonal relationships provide the base for the most typical and significant image of the church. Although some of these images are drawn from other sources (e.g., a team or an army), most interpersonal ideals are grounded in the caring intimacy of a family. For people in a highly mobile and fragmented society, this finds particular expression in the continuity of family from the past, and in the reunion of families.

Christian Family Church

The Christian Family Church assumes a common cultural base, and builds upon this Christian heritage. The continuity of the congregation is often provided by several extended families, whose well-known names are associated with particular pews in the sanctuary and jobs in the church.

Worship for the Christian Family Church is rooted in tradition and carried on with determination. Often the choir is the backbone of the congregation, from the music they render in worship to the information they share in rehearsal—they are the switchboard that makes things happen. The style may be friendly and casual, but not informal or easily changed. The family church has a strong commitment and a deep satisfaction in "the way we do things around here."

Since the "family" is held together by a cultural or ethnic base, the congregation embraces by name a rich mix of different ages, educations, and incomes. All the family members are accepted, even—or especially—those who are seen to be a little odd. Typically, the old families have a history of relationships, both intimate and stormy. Stories of events may be almost forgotten, but emotions linger on. For the family, "home church" is a place of memories, with all the strength and limitations which it implies. It is often haunted by the Golden Era which glows a little with increased distance and immediate difficulties.

If the extended family image dominates the congregation, then growth and change may be a problem for the Christian Family Church. Evangelism tends to be more biological than programmatic: they like "to grow their own" new members from birth. Anyone can join who learns to "talk our language," especially if they participate in the annual events—the birthday parties of the church. In the annual Christmas pageant, for example, you can recognize the surnames and family ties even if you do not know all the children by name. Typically the pastor is an "outsider" for a long time, but sometimes pastors remain for a generation since the family makes staying feel so good.

Ministry may be more important than mission in most Christian Family Churches—that is, the care of our own. But they will be naturally generous if the distant mission is defined as "one of the family." Stewardship tends to be "as needed," with no problems in the crises, while the regular bills are hard to meet. In the family, funds are given more in celebration than in sacrifice. Care becomes associated with particular saints, with Martha who runs the kitchen and Fred who repairs the boiler.

Caring in the family is the universal character of the Christian Family Church—both its remarkable strength and its frustrating limitation.

Christian Nurture Church

The Christian Nurture Church is a "new" and more open family composed of people with different backgrounds who are bonded by their common faith and a covenant of mutual acceptance in the Lord. The congregation sees its ministry in responding to personal concerns and family problems. Lifecycle issues are the focus for most groups which the church sponsors and houses in its building, such as singles groups, young mothers clubs, sports teams, couples clubs, and a parish shepherding plan. Members participate for personal nourishment and growth. They are united in worship, in a variety of special interest groups, and in the person (or figure) of the pastor.

The social issues which concern the congregation have emerged from personal and family needs, such as alcoholism, abortion, child rearing, divorce, family discipline, single parent support, health services, public schools, and care for the elderly. Church members may hold very divergent views in political and economic issues, but these are off limits for discussion in the Christian Nurture Congregation. Conflict on these issues, or for any reason, is seen as disruptive and distracting to the primary mission of the church—to help people. When church conversations turn to controversial public issues, members avoid stating private views and may even withdraw from the conversation. Extended controversy is considered in poor taste.

A relationship with the pastor is important to most members. The minister is expected to be sensitive to personal need and effective in pastoral counselling. Former pastors are recalled as "really present with us" in times of crisis and transition, a person who visited regularly and was warmly received. Non-members may not be impressed with the pastor's skill in the pulpit or organizational strength as a leader, but many members consider the pastor to be "a rock in times of need" and "a close friend to me personally." In the intimacy of these relationships, the prophetic ministry may be limited to public statements and personal guidance for individual and family issues.

In the Christian Nurture Church, leaders are chosen from those who listen carefully and respond effectively to the needs that members experience in the world. Although the church may have a denominational label, it is far more invested in meeting the needs of individuals and families in the area it serves.

Sense of the Sacred.[13] For many believers the church building represents a kind of sacramental presence in the community, both for themselves and for others who live in the shadow of the steeple but never become official members. This sense of the sacred can be expressed in the high church traditions of a cathedral-like congregation or in the low church traditions of a neighborhood church.

Old First (Denominational) Church

Centuries of faith come to focus in the solid architecture, the flow of liturgy, and the articulation of the Word in the Old First Denominational Church. The tall steeple breaks the flatness of existence and, even in a cluttered skyline, it points upward with human aspirations. Physically, the building looks like a church, a monument of faith built to a scale larger than life. The Grand Christian Tradition makes its appearance as a solid base surrounded by a world of constant change.

Old First Church is a way of thinking, even if there is no Second. Whatever they do, it is done in the style of their tradition: they do it right. In Old First, the ushers may still dress alike and walk in stride, and a woman with a hat and gloves is never out of style. Its members may repair the organ even before they fix the roof, or print the order of worship when mimeograph copies would do as well. They will give sacrificially to sustain their witness "as it should be done."

Old First Church serves a cross section of the community, but in different ways. Sunday worship is a combination of the old community leadership who drive past other congregations to support this center of denominational witness, and of younger families and single people who reside near the church building. They may make formal decisions for the church, while informally they are preparing the next wave of community leaders.

On weekdays the church might house an array of programs to meet a wide spectrum of community needs. The building looks large enough to embrace the city, with a sanctuary that could shelter great gatherings of civic or religious celebration. Yet even with its size, the church retains those festival seasons and intimate places where the anonymous believer can quietly return and rekindle the faith.

The pastor is expected to be a little larger than life. As a well-prepared professional (preferably with a touch of accent from the old country), the pastor must move with ease from the drawing room and the parlor to the pulpit and the board room, and very likely will be more respected than loved, more poised than personal. First Church pastors are known for good sermons, delegated management, sensitive funerals, and leadership in significant places of community life.

Old First Church cares about community morality more in conscience than in personal contact. As guardians of historic Christian concern, the church seeks relief for the dispossessed and justice for the oppressed. But the members of Old First are unlikely to deliver pronouncements or engage in public protests. Rather, they legitimate an issue when they provide an arena for its discussion. And they respond to personal crises by telephone, through professionals with agency connections.

Cultural arts provide a living link with past culture, and an instrument of challenge toward appropriate change. For both reasons Old First Church is often a curator of the best in the arts: music, drama, poetry, fabrics, fine arts. And it is a place where all these elements come together, especially in liturgical worship. Old First is the visual and visceral affirmation of faith in the grand denominational tradition, evangelizing, appropriately, with a medieval passion play, a jazz mass, or a Bach cantata.

Christian Sanctuary Church

The Christian Sanctuary Church is a place where the transitions of life are celebrated and the crises are interpreted. Here Holy Communion is celebrated as nourishment for the community in the journey. Here the Word is read, preached, and enacted in the lives of believers. Here the young are introduced in baptism, joined in marriage, and separated in the solemn joy of funeral services. Faith is the experience of God's presence in our time of need, but it is remembered and renewed in the place and traditions of the local church.

Symbols, shapes, and even spaces can become carriers of our sense of the sacred: the pulpit and the altar, the pew, the cross, and the stained glass window may, over time, take on a unique power to evoke a sacred consciousness in the believer. These objects were present when God seemed especially real, when help seemed available. The people who shared that experience may be gathered in those memories, especially the pastors who have been the stewards of the mysteries of God. Even the exterior shell of the building may become a sacramental presence for people who attend infrequently, but who know the church "is always there." Many congregations receive substantial gifts from non-members who want the church as a part of their community even if they never attend.

The Christian Sanctuary is the most short-lived image among Protestant believers. Some will claim it constantly, but for most people it recedes in the routines of daily life, briefly returning to consciousness during the annual seasons or the seasonal changes of life. It often is associated with significant transitional moments, and with the people who shared in those adjustments. Recent use of the Sanctuary symbol for the sheltering of Central American refugees has helped to unmask the ambivalence with which we have treated this powerful, earthy image in the experiences of many believers.

The Christian Sanctuary Church has been accorded ambivalent treatment because it affords believers a haven from the world, a place of rest and renewal in one's journeys of faith. For some it can be a closet of permanent withdrawal, but for most it is a shelter for prayer and preparation for what lies ahead. For most Protestants, the image of Christian Sanctuary has provided a temporary "anchor" in transitional times. This anchor of faith is portable most of the journey, and seems most helpful when it is out of sight but stabilizing in a stormy time.

Service to the Community.[14] Service to others is embedded in the values and images of Christian commitment. For many people, whether church members or not, the church exists for service. Service requires a volunteer ethic, where members are willing to share their time and resources to help the lives of others. For some people this means service to the community in which they live, as a means of helping the community realize its potential and become a healthier environment. For some people, Christian service implies reaching out to others who need help, especially to those living in less fortunate circumstances. These two different understandings of service produce separate images of the church.

Christian Citizen Church

The Christian Citizen Church is a place where the diverse people of the community can gather to affirm their differences and share their common goals. Its architecture is more broad than tall, with an openness to all the issues that concern the community. The congregation takes pride in two areas: the pluralism of its membership and the variety of its programs (from pre-school to senior citizens, from Boy Scouts to peace groups, from Alcoholics Anonymous to the Daughters of the British Empire, from quiet discussion groups to controversial town meetings). The church provides common ground for people who need a place to affirm their identity.

Most Christian Citizen Churches have a history of caring with the community for the common good. Some churches have been the point of entry for waves of immigrants and newcomers, and some churches have provided the arena for historic debates and community decisions. Groups using the building may have radically different viewpoints from the Right to Life and National Rifle Association to advocates of hand-gun control and nuclear freeze (with meetings on different evenings). Providing space for groups to use the church facility is both its ministry to the community and its source of recruitment from the community. Surprisingly, new members join the church primarily not because they belong to the groups using the church, but because they want to be part of a church that cares for its community.

The pastor of the Christian Citizen Church is expected to be an informed citizen who shares a concern about community issues without making "irresponsible" (unauthorized) pronouncements which alienate the members of the congregation. By providing meeting space, most Citizen Churches feel they have fulfilled their obligation for social concerns, and avoid taking sides or making controversial statements. The pastor also is expected to orchestrate the variety of church and community groups into a harmony of ministry, more to negotiate than advocate. Typically the tensions of this church revolve around the use and limits of their resources, the appropriate spiritual awareness of non-church groups who use the building, and the amount of financial responsibility which should be shared with these community groups.

Church programs are intentionally diverse to demonstrate their theology of concern for the whole person: prayer groups and tutoring, church music and social ethics, young mothers and Gray Panthers. Their Christmas celebration might include a tree in which every group contributed an ornament to symbolize the wealth of their diversity. They might use the season to bring church and community groups together to learn from one another, break down stereotypes, and help to build a better world.

Christian Servant Church

Members of the Christian Servant Church worship with their hands and feet: they enact the gospel in deeds of care and service. They are not particularly concerned if the choir cannot sing or the organ is out of tune. Their ministry is one of Christian presence in places of pain, need, and alienation. They simply want to be helpful.

Success for the Christian Servant Church is marked by the sustained activity of caring for those who need it most— the homeless and hungry, prostitutes and prisoners, bag ladies and derelicts, refugees from every source and kind of human condition. Recognizing the gospel bias for the poor, they find their deepest satisfaction in serving people in marginal, deprived, and impossible situations. Theologically they believe that healing only comes with suffering love. In the paradox of faith, they see that the worst can be redeemed and, unfortunately, the best can be corrupted. There are no permanent successes, only perseverance in love. In the larger church they provide an awkward presence, since some of them delight in twitting the church about its bias toward wealth, and its distance from the places where they believe the ministry of Jesus took place—among the poorest people with the greatest need.

Typically, the Christian Servant Church develops volunteers to staff a variety of programs of direct service such as meals on wheels, soup kitchens, food pantries, clothing resale shops, para-legal clinics, and neighborhood medical centers. If these programs are not sufficient, these congregations may push the church boards to open their building as overnight shelters for the homeless and food centers for the hungry. In their desire to be helpful, Servant Churches often bypass existing organizational structures. They do not seem overly concerned with the clarity of church membership or the rules for institutional care. They want to work with anyone who will join with them in response to their perception of human need. They love being generous and hope to be helpful, but without the burden of expecting to correct the causes of the evil they find in the world.

The Christian Servant Church prefers pastors who are model servants, often with a compassion which leads them to reach out to everyone in need, exhausting institutional and personal resources in times of peak demand. Too many responses and too few resources often lead to burnout for pastors and members, and sometimes for their families as well. Sometimes the Servant Church develops a condescension of the wealthy toward the poor; and sometimes it protects enclaves of special interest long after the service is no longer needed. Often called paternalistic and naive, still Servant Churches dare to maintain human contact and potential channels for love and care across the barriers of class, race, and cultural differences.

Commitment to Change.[15] For some people the church is the instrument for change, the vehicle through which God is at work making a difference in peoples' lives. Since they see themselves especially called to do the will of God, they develop programs with a sense of urgency which may be experienced by others as confrontational and divisive. For some who are committed to change, the emotions of division and conflict may be seen as affirmation of their calling. A "good fight" with the proper opposition affirms their faithfulness.

However, their priorities and agenda often are different. Some people experience God as most concerned about oppression and injustice, about the broken relationships and inequitable distribution of resources among people in the world. Some people experience God as most concerned about the barriers and broken relationships between God and humanity, the inability of people to recognize the saving power of God in Jesus Christ. These perspectives are not necessarily exclusive, but people are strongly committed to them and, as noted earlier, they are affirmed by conflict with those who have another view. Characteristically they are a committed minority with an influence far greater than their numbers.

Social Prophet Church

The Social Prophet Church understands God to be calling them to bring good news to the poor, "to proclaim release to the captives and recovering of sight to the blind, to set at liberty those who are oppressed" (Luke 4:18). Sympathy for the oppressed or empathy with the outcast is not enough. The Prophetic image suggests that only through solidarity with the poor can the gospel be understood at all. It seeks to understand and transform the systems of injustice from the bottom up.

Members of the Social Prophet Church feel no need for permanent structures of building or organization. They could gather in a home, a store front, or church basement—the cause is important, not the place of meeting. Often they are a cell of believers within a larger congregation, or individuals drawn to a cause from several congregations, even attracting Christians who have "given up on the church."

They are incensed by oppression and injustice—a righteous indignation which they identify with the prophetic figures of the Old Testament and the ministry of Jesus. In the prophetic tradition, they share feelings of hostility and dismay with the evil of the world, and a remnant-like rebellion which takes risks to challenge the existing power structures. They want others to see the evil "as it is" and join in the transformation of structures to the world "as it should be." More than the commission to make disciples (Matt. 28:19–20) or the commandments to love God and neighbor (Matt. 22:37–40), they feel God's judgement of the nations' wealth and poverty (Matt. 25:31–46), and imagine an alternative.

They choose no small issues: nuclear armaments and world peace, the family farm and industrial unemployment, abortion and the right to life, multi-national corporations and hunger throughout the world. But they will engage in specific actions, such as declaring the church a sanctuary for politically unacceptable refugees. Locally they will take on major institutions, even among their own: one church group tried to change the name of a familiar and friendly organization to the League of "Person" Voters. They wish to sensitize individuals, mobilize groups, and transform structures. More than resolving the problems of individuals, they want to make the systems functionally acceptable in the kingdom of God.

The Prophetic Church image attempts to mobilize the congregation as an agent of change in the mission of social transformation. They are understandably weak on counselling, institutional continuity, and historical patterns of worship—unless we see public demonstrations as their form of liturgical worship, the vigils as their prayer, and boycotts as their sacrament. They tend to be uncritical of persons who share their common cause, but they measure institutions by the standards of biblical justice. They find unity in clarity of mission for which they will make unusual sacrifice.

The leaders of the Christian Prophet Church are expected to speak out on issues and live with conflict. Since they are more united in their issues than in their institution, the leaders often become the focus of the group coherence and continuity. In their prophetic causes they find common voice and can have an influence far greater than their size. However, over time, they are institutionally unstable.

Since their style is confirmed in confrontation, they are sometimes experienced as abrasive. Social Prophet Churches have been characterized even by some of their own members as "often wrong, but never in doubt."

Faith Evangelist Church

Equally self-assured is the Faith Evangelist Church's image, with its emphasis on God's call to personal salvation. These people are united in the clarity of their message which defines who should belong and what programs the church should offer. The language of personal salvation can be heard throughout the church, from the small children in Sunday school to the heights of the pulpit, from the echo of the choir to prayers of the youth group on a skiing weekend. Special events of the church year, such as a world mission conference in mid-winter and the great preaching and joint choirs of a revival in late summer, reinforce the same message on a larger scale.

Worship in the Faith Evangelist Church is a central event, a flow of presentations that weave common themes of everyday life with the intervention of divine salvation. Music is drawn as frequently from folk and popular styles as from the historic melodies of the Christian church. The liturgy and prayers are a mixture of contemporary phrases, personal experiences, and biblical commentary. Typical worship themes concentrate on personal crises; and the pastor has a dramatic, sometimes flamboyant, style of talking the language of the people. The place of worship is often defined as an auditorium rather than a sanctuary; and the worshiper is made to feel socially welcome and physically comfortable, even as the soul is convicted of sin and then saved from judgment by the grace of God. Sometimes the contemporary language becomes expressed in clever names for church groups, for example, the dieters who call themselves Gracious Losers and the martial arts group which is dubbed Karate for Christ.

The Faith Evangelist Church image is manifest in the disciplined faith, moral lives, and evangelical zeal of its members. Since God is merciful and just, some believers are rewarded with worldly success and the responsibilities of wealth and leadership. These church leaders are seen as models of God's intervention and are expected to live exemplary lives for the guidance and uplifting of others. The social issues about which they are concerned revolve around individual decisions, such as fidelity in marriage, strength in family life, and resistance to any legitimation of abortion, homosexuality, drugs, or alcohol. They are concerned with such issues as hunger, poverty, and world peace, but feel that the church should "not get involved in politics."

All who claim the image of Faith Evangelist Church, clergy and laity alike, are expected to share in the propagation of the gospel. Their commitment is expressed in a worship that is grounded in personal experience which is a liturgical "sacrament" that unites the membership. The faith must be offered to all who do not belong to the church, to people who are already active in other congregations, and even to members of the same congregation who have not shown the signs of experiencing the transforming power of God in their lives. This sense of immediacy is reflected in the numerous offerings and the large size of financial contributions which are typical of the Faith Evangelist style of commitment.

Just as the church is understood as having a special responsibility to carry the truth of God throughout the world, so too the nation often comes to be seen as a unique instrument in the providence of God. The Evangelist Church image places high value on the church and the nation in the hands of God, and views with alarm any internal criticism or external threat against either the church or the nation.

Implications

Each of these images exists, in some degree, in every congregation; for these images are not mutually exclusive, though they are competitive. Moreover, every congregation has one or two primary images which they put forward as their face to the world. In these images churches would like to be seen as modeling their faith and teaching their community what it means to them to be Christian.

On closer examination we discover that many church

members, who accept and even champion the public image of the church, personally cherish a different image (or combination of images) for themselves. This diversity of images is usually not a problem. In fact, there seems to be a kind of symbiosis among combinations of images: the strong advocacy of some seems to assume the strength of others, as if they have become mutually dependent for a sense of the whole congregation.

Most church events, for example, are based on motivations which combine several church images, such as a covered dish supper (Family) followed by a program in the chapel (Sanctuary) on church missions in Haiti (Evangelist), drilling wells in east Africa (Servant), human rights in Central America (Prophetic), or the choir's rendition of St. Matthew's Passion (Old First Church). The typical Sunday worship in most churches includes some symbols from each image, although some are more prominent than others. Most images are included "naturally," since they all can be legitimate expressions of our Christian faith.

We have not found that congregations conform to preestablished patterns of theological consistency. They make curious combinations, such as Old First and Christian Nurture, Christian Family and Evangelist, Sanctuary and Prophetic. For every congregation, at any given time some images dominate the thinking of the church, some are subordinate but present, and some images frequently are "unthinkable" for that church at that time.

Congregations can trace their history through the primacy of various church images: they talk about "our First Church era," "the Servant days," and so on. There is no discernible pattern to the image with which they begin and the order of the journey which they follow over the years. Additionally, it is evident that church leaders are more intuitive than intentional in their use of congregational images. Even in the planning process their stated goals may be explicit, but their images often remain unexamined. Yet long after their objectives have been achieved or forgotten, their images still direct the behavior of the board and the decisions of committees.

In another dimension, when congregational controversy occurs, the issues are usually larger than the particular problem. Some controversies involve power issues and personality conflicts. These conflicts can be traced to different church images which people hold, each with its distinctive priorities for program, leadership, and resource allocation. When the church experiences controversy, we ask: "who can make the decision?" (authority); and "what do they believe ought to happen?" (functional images of the church). As we listen to the different perspectives, we seek to hear not only the details of their differences, but also the images of their commitments which are directing their decisions.

Surprisingly, different images are evident when the church plans, and when it fights. In the planning process, church leaders put the "best face" on the church and use those images that reflect the church in the most favorable light. In conflicts, members often reveal the "shadow side" of their commitments to images that are more sharply controversial. While planning, the church can agree that we should "help the needy"; but when in conflict, the Prophetic Church may feel constrained by the Sanctuary Church's image of sacredness, or the Nurture Church may feel invaded by "those people" whom the Servant Church attracts. Images provide a method for (1) understanding differences among members, (2) depersonalizing conflicts, and (3) allocating resources in a manner which is understandable if not acceptable to most members.

These eight church images exist cheek by jowl in every community, and are represented within most congregations. Each image can claim to be part of the authentic Christian tradition, and each can be corrupted if isolated or carried to extreme. The energizing task of church leadership is to maintain the mix that is appropriate for each changing situation and is consistent with an unchanging gospel. In the providence of God, all of these church images reflect the divine ecology and remind us how much we need each other.

Centers
of Vision
and
Energy

DONALD EUGENE MILLER

Bethany Theological Seminary

Previous chapters have focused the reader's attention on the congregation as an organized community, especially as it is shaped by motivational, historical, and social factors. Now we turn our attention to the congregation as a center of vision and energy. We shall be concerned about how the congregation teaches and how leaders can direct and enhance education processes, both formal and informal.

People attend churches for a variety of reasons that represent a mixture of theological, social, and personal concerns. Congregations are strongly influenced by biblical, theological, and confessional traditions, as well as by social class, race, ethnic origin, size, location, age and gender makeup, regional and national ethos. In this kaleidoscope of influences how can ministers and lay leaders foster the growth of vision and energy in a congregation?

The Living Story

To begin, we must know what we mean when we speak about vision and energy in a congregation. Vision refers to a commonly held perspective, and energy refers to commonly experienced power. How then can leadership, ministerial and lay, foster a congregation that is powerfully and discerningly alive?

The distinction between vision and energy is similar to the biblical references to Word and Spirit. Biblically, the Word of God becomes embodied and active in human life through the power of the Spirit. In human relationships Word and Spirit come together in covenant, God's gracious love that undergirds human love and justice. The congregation is a community that seeks its vision in God's Word, its energy in God's Spirit, and its covenant in God's love. In doing so the congregation lives out a story; indeed the congregation is a living story.

Energy does not come automatically with vision, nor does vision always accompany energy. To understand better why this is so I find it helpful to consider three additional factors through which vision and energy interplay. These three additional factors are ethos, commitment, and context.[1] One might diagram these factors in the following way:

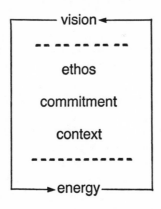

By ethos I mean the living and shared practices, customs, procedures, and feelings that are present in every congregation. Not only are these customs and practices present, in a very real way they are the interactions that define the congregation. I sometimes refer to the ethos as the living covenant of the congregation. The covenant is the body and blood of the congregation.

Ethos can be present only where there are committed individuals. Commitment is the foundation of a congregation. The energy of a congregation comes through the commitment of its members. Their loyalty, devotion, and continuing support allow a pattern of life to develop. So there is ethos only where there is commitment.

The life of the congregation also is affected significantly by the context in which it finds itself. The context includes persons, meeting place, the surrounding community, economic circumstances, social attitudes, and historical events. Whether a congregation is in the inner city or a rural area makes a dramatic difference for its life. Whether the nation is at war or peace strongly affects the congregation. Economic circumstances, income, employment, and occupations of the members radically affect the congregation.

Perhaps a way of stating these relations is to say that vision *guides* ethos, which in turn guides commitment and influences the context. Conversely, the context *conditions* commitment, which in turn conditions ethos and vision. At every level the congregation lives in the dynamic interaction of guiding factors and conditioning factors, the interplay of vision and energy.[2]

Let us look more carefully at the factors in the preceding diagram. Every congregation shares a vision, a common perspective on the world. The perspective includes beliefs, theology, and doctrines. Beliefs will vary from one tradition to another. The fundamental reality of the congregation may be seen as enacted sacrament, preached Word, forgiving grace, or outgoing love. Though the belief and sense of reality may vary, the congregation is nevertheless a shared perspective. The congregation provides a common language for expression and a mode of thinking. The congregation creates a functioning credo of shared beliefs and purposes.[3] The story of the functioning credo is the story of the congregation.

Not every participant shares the functioning credo of a congregation. In fact, the many participants and members may have many different beliefs, and they may view the purpose of the congregation in many different ways. However, the act of participating in a congregation entails some degree of acceptance of shared faith, perspective, and language.[4] To resist the shared perspective is to be cut off from any basic communication. Of course persons may give some preliminary consent to the shared beliefs without adopting them in more profound ways.

Power comes in a congregation as participants genuinely share the functioning credo. Pastors and leaders can discern the functioning credo by studying the accounts that various individuals give of the congregation's beliefs, and by studying how these beliefs actually function in the lives of people. Which beliefs actually guide church government and program? How are beliefs and behavior actually related to various individuals? Compare what various individuals want the congregation's purpose to be with what the same individuals perceive the congregation's actual purpose to be. Such a study can help get at the functioning credo and common beliefs.

Consensus about vision, belief, and purpose may come by discussion and agreement, or it may come by an energizing sense of being of the same mind. Otherwise stated, consensus can come by deliberation, or as a gift of power. In fact, consensus always involves elements of both. The dynamic interaction of guidance and conditions is always present. Consensus often combines deliberative, political, and celebrative dimensions. Leaders therefore work for a common vision by conversation, persuasion, education, and worship. When a strong consensus of vision, belief, and purpose occurs, with it comes a community sense of power and energy.

Every congregation shares not only a vision but also embodies an ethos. An ethos is a way of life, a shared set of values and practices. It includes the authority, norms, customs, government, rules, organization, roles, and informal relationships which bind a people together. A congregation gives people a common way of relating to one another. Only by looking at the embodied ethos can one tell how beliefs actually function in the life of a congregation.

Authority in a congregation may be given to an ordained minister, a group of elders, the church board, or the assembly of the people. Traditions have different modes of authority. In the episcopal tradition (Catholic, Anglican, Methodist) authority resides with the bishop. In the presbyterian tradition authority is vested in the elders. The congregational tradition places authority with the assembly of the people. Many congregations have constitutions that prescribe authoritative procedures.

Informal authority may vary from formal or prescribed authority. A bishop may consider it wise to allow decisions to be made by the assembled people. A congregational church may be dominated by one influential person who has the functional power of a bishop. The constitution of a congregation may suggest certain procedures, but the functional procedures may be quite different. The officials of a congregation may have certain designated responsibilities, but customary practice may be quite different.

Congregations gain vision and energy when formal and informal authority mutually support one another.[5] Pastors and leaders of a congregation can study the embodied ethos of a congregation by comparing what is actually done by officials with the expected responsibilities of that position.[6] A study that compares normal procedure (common expectations) with what actually happens can show the degree to which the two support one another. Who are the most influential persons in the congregation? How are they related to persons who have official responsibility? What are the official lines of communication and what are the informal lines of communication (e.g., gossip)? In which conversational groups are decisions actually made? How do such groups relate to the groups officially responsible for those decisions? Unless formal and informal authority support one another, vision will be divided and energy dissipated.

We have said that every congregation shares a vision and embodies an ethos. It also is true that every congregation incorporates a constellation of commitments and loyalties.[7] To be loyal is to be committed to the common beliefs and the common way of life in a congregation. Participants may have a variety of motives and a variety of understandings of the congregation's beliefs and ethos. In spite of variety, participation in a congregation implies some degree of shared commitment, however minimal.

From the commitment of individuals the congregation gains its energy. The vision lives and the ethos becomes powerful as individuals give their commitment. Members grow by participating, by receiving the ministry, by accepting responsibility, and by becoming more faithful to God and more loving to one another. Whatever their degree of participation, they are somewhat guided by the common vision as they give devotion to it. The devotion of individual participants is the congregation's energy.

Every person has mixed motives for participating in congregational life. Each person wants something from the congregation and each expects certain things of the congregation. Furthermore, these wants and expectations are nearly always disappointed at one time or another. A young man in his twenties may spend five years as a dynamic youth leader with seemingly boundless energy. Suddenly he announces that he is withdrawing from the church and does not want to be approached again. Such an incident is all too common in congregations. Like the disciples who expected Jesus to become Israel's ruler, he may be keenly disappointed in what the congregation has given him for all his effort. After Jesus' death many of his followers returned to their previous life but some were driven by the Spirit to continue in a new way of life. In the typical congregation some people move beyond disappointment to a new vision of life in Christ, and through them the congregation gains increased vitality.

The congregation is not simply a collection of individuals worshiping together. It is rather a living vision and powerful ethos which is energized by the commitment and loyalty of the participants. If the vision of the congregation mobilizes the energy of individuals, the commitment of individuals energizes the vision. Pastors and lay leaders can study the energy level of a congregation by studying the motives of participants. Why do people attend? What satisfaction do they get? How does attendance make their lives different? In what ways are they disappointed by the congregation? What more do they wish from the congregation? When the congregation is more fulfilling to individuals, then they contribute more energy. Loyalty is commitment to the love of God through Christ as that is mediated in a congregation, however provisionally.

Every congregation not only incorporates a common vision, ethos, and commitment but also entails a set of interactions within a given context. The congregation is located in an urban, suburban, or rural area. It has a certain size and is growing or declining. It represents a certain social class and ethnic background. It has certain financial resources and a certain level of stewardship. Regional and national differences as well as wider cultural and political realities affect the church. These kinds of factors have been mentioned in previous chapters, and so we shall not dwell upon them here. Simply stated, contextual factors are decisive in the life of the congregation. They set the conditions that affect commitment, ethos, and vision.

Pastors and lay leaders can study the contextual factors of a congregation.[8] How many people of different ages and gender attend? What are the members' talents? What are the economic resources of members? What are the characteristics of the larger community? Who are the people to whom the church's mission is directed? The congregation can hardly have vision and energy unless it is aware of such conditioning factors. An educational program for children is useless when no children are present. Aiming for a growing membership may be senseless in a declining community.

A congregation may be viewed in terms of the interaction of vision and energy in its ethos, commitment, and context, as we have been suggesting. However, in all of its dimensions a congregation is constantly changing. The account of the ongoing life of the congregation is the congregation's story. Each congregation is a living story.[9] That story includes the continuing vision, ethos, commitment, and context of the congregation.

A story is a narrative account of continuity and change. Stories are told in narrative form, and narrative is a way of describing ongoing continuity and change without losing the uniqueness of individual events. The Bible is predominantly a story, a narrative account of a people. Each congregation's story seeks to intersect and extend the biblical story.

One way to rehearse the story of a congregation is to gather people together to share their memories. Place a timeline on newsprint paper on the wall and mark off the timeline in ten-year periods. Begin with the founding of the congregation and extend the timeline a decade or two into the future. Then recall significant events decade by decade, noting them on the timeline. Recall pastors, leaders, and other significant persons. Recall issues, programs, and customs. Recall changing emphases in doctrine and teaching. Note building programs and changes of location. Also recall events in the community, nation, or world which have affected the congregation. Is the "golden period" of the congregation in the past, present, or future? Is the story a comedy in which difficulties are always certain to be overcome? Is it a tragedy in which circumstances are overwhelming to the congregation? Is it a romance with certain persons or programs? Is the story an ironic, hard-nosed, realistic assessment of changing conditions?[10] What is the special vocation of this congregation? When has the vision and energy of this congregation been most focused?

Finding the Way

We have been discussing the elements that constitute the congregation as a living, ongoing story. We have suggested

questions and exercises to help people become more aware of
these elements in their own congregations. Now I want to suggest a procedure to encourage the enlargement of vision and
the focus of energy in a congregation.[11]

No procedure or method can provide what is not in some
way already present. A method cannot provide what God's grace
is not already giving. However, a method can seek to be faithful
to what God is bringing about in a congregation. A method
may serve to open new possibilities, give birth to new visions,
and release new energies. Therefore I want to propose a method
with six identifiable steps. Each step is closely related to the
congregation's story, and each is in touch with the ethos and
commitment of the congregation.

The six steps are as follows:

1. Rehearse a present practice about which there is interest
    or concern.

2. Locate the present practice within the ongoing narrative
    of the congregation's story.

3. Identify causes and cultural wisdom which help to explain
    the present practice.

4. Bring the present practice into dialog with some part of
    the Christian story and arrive at an evaluative vision for
    the congregation.

5. Review the vision in terms of justice, emotional wholeness,
    and faithfulness.

6. Identify a procedure to embody the vision, by enacting it
    and telling the congregation's story.

The method begins and ends with actual practices within
the congregation. These practices are not to be seen in isolation,
but as part of the congregation's ongoing story. The storied
practice is then to be explored in terms of its causes and meanings. The new understanding is to be brought into dialog with
Christian belief, especially the biblical story, and perhaps denominational teaching.

Discussion and prayer can open new possibilities, a revised vision. However, we should test the vision in terms of who is to gain, who will bear the emotional weight, and where we understand God to be leading us. The congregation should then be at a point of acknowledging weaknesses, repenting the inadequate ways, reaffirming its faith, and identifying revised procedures or programs. As the congregation acts on this new vision, it again sets the action within its ongoing story.

Let us illustrate the method with one actual experience. In a midwestern suburban congregation many members were concerned that people who left the church were promptly forgotten. This practice was set within the congregation's story of moderate growth in numbers, considerable change in membership each year, and steady outreach ministry. An evangelism group identified such causes as the large number of people who move, the difficulty of keeping in touch with everyone, and the reluctance of church members to visit. A study of the New Testament story brought up the basic motives of love of others, hospitality to them, the joy and blessing of the gospel.

The desire to visit was examined in terms of justice and wholeness. People acknowledged their primary desire to enlarge the church, their resentment of some who had left, and their lesser concern for those they were to visit. They decided that they would begin by confessing their own need, that they genuinely wanted to hear from those who had left, and that the gospel was impelling them to reach out. A visiting team made the visits simply to hear the stories of those who had left rather than to compel them to return. People were responsive to the visits, and the congregation began to plan how it might minister so as to lose fewer people.

This method of six steps can be used with a small or a large church, with a very formal or a very informal ministry. For example the analysis of causes can be done with expert opinion or by informal conversation. The dialog with the Christian story can be done in extended Bible study and prayer, or by informal conversation. Identifying a procedure and enacting it can be done in the form of management by objectives, or it can be done as informal agreement about what to do. The contribution of the method is to keep a balance between what is currently believed and practiced, the larger congregational story, and reasonable assessment of cause and meaning. There also is an interplay between the biblical story and the congregation's story. Throughout this method, vision, ethos, commitment, and context are balanced. The method moves toward a continuing repentance, renewal, formation, and reformation within God's ongoing story.

Models and Types

Any procedure, such as the six-step method just described, must be very flexible to meet the many situations of congregations. Energizing a congregation's vision will depend a great deal upon the predominant ongoing story of ministry in that congregation. Even radical changes in congregational life are accommodated to the ongoing story.

Ministry within a congregation usually is organized around certain typical activities. Such activities include preaching and worship, counseling and care, teaching and nurture, social relationships and service, mission and evangelism, stewardship and benevolence, prophetic witness and action, planning and administration. Care includes visiting those who are ill, as well as other visitation and spiritual guidance. Worship includes all the celebrations of the church year. Teaching includes confirmation and other training of new members. These ministry activities can be very informal and not well differentiated, or they can be distinct and administered by separate committees.

While most congregations carry out all of these typical activities to some degree, they cannot put equal emphasis upon all of them. Inevitably some are featured more than others. The particular program that evolves is guided by vision and ethos, conditioned by commitment and circumstances.

The ministry of different congregations falls into several types. These types, to which we now turn, offer clues about where the church may be energized and the vision enlarged.

No congregation fits into any one type exactly. In fact, most congregations may have something of every type. Yet these typologies (analytical classifications or models) may be helpful, for they help to clarify real possibilities and illuminate relationships. In the final analysis the source of vision and energy remains a mystery, a gift of God, something to be received with thanksgiving. The types we shall consider are as follows: liturgy, management, primary group, growth and development, prophet, and interpretation. The reader will notice a rough parallel between those six types and the six steps identified earlier.

The Liturgy Type

Liturgy, celebration, and worship have been at the center of the church for millennia. Powerful worship energizes people. Pastors and lay leaders can nurture a vision of the Christian life by strengthening and enlivening worship and celebration. Worship gains power as Scripture and tradition are dramatized and proclaimed in a lively manner. Worship gains power as it touches the beliefs, ethos, policies, loyalties, and circumstances of a congregation.

Some Christian educators are calling for a recovery of the teaching function of worship.[12] People learn the meaning of the gospel as much by the dramas and celebrations of the church as by formal instruction. Church celebrations offer excellent opportunities for reflecting upon not only the meaning of the celebrations but also of the gospel and Christian life. Church celebrations can be planned and explained meaningfully for children and youth as well as adults.

Many congregations present a Bible to each of their younger elementary-age children who are just becoming proficient readers. Often these presentations simply involve having the children come to the front of the sanctuary during worship, reading their names, and handing a Bible to each of them. When no more or less happens in such an event, the congregation misses significant opportunities not only to add a special note of celebration to its worship service but also to dramatize the importance of receiving and giving the gift of God's Word.

However, careful planning of these Bible presentations can help both to model a vital unity of worship and education and to create truly celebrative and dramatic events in the life of the congregation. The following are illustrations of the planning and activities which might be involved in effective Bible presentations:

- Include especially the pastor, members of the worship and education committees, and the younger children themselves in the planning of this special event.

- Design the event so that the children are central participants in the whole worship drama, by

  * Helping each child to choose and to read a favorite Bible passage, and

  * Working with the group to select and prepare for other kinds of worship leadership, such as reading the call to worship, leading in prayer, collecting the offering, and others.

- Ask some of the older children or youths to give a brief account of how the Bible was transmitted before the invention of printing, and of the effects of having printed Bibles available. As additional or alternative activities, have these young people read selected passages from different versions of the Bible, perhaps including dramatizations of the stories being read or a presentation about the origins of different versions of the Bible.

- Plan the sermon of the day to focus on how we receive the Word of God and to involve testimonies from adults about what the Bible has meant in their lives.

- Prepare a special sharing time with preschool-age children, perhaps using a scroll to portray the ancient history of Scripture or by giving a Bible storybook to the children.

- Use a litany (perhaps one that the younger elementary-age children have helped to create) to lead the congregation in both a dedication of the children and a rededication of adults to the study and guidance of Scripture in their own lives, which may entail urging individuals and families to commit themselves to a discipline of daily Bible reading.

• Encourage intergenerational planning and leadership of the Bible presentation service, so that all ages of people are energized by this shared experience and thus are helped to nurture a common vision of the congregation's reception and proclamation of God's Word.

These suggestions illustrate some ways to aid the recovery of the teaching function of worship. Of course there are numerous ways to do so. Many other special events and seasons of the church year are opportunities for the joining of worship and education. We can learn from the traditions of Advent and Christmas, because this celebrative season is a time of the year when the whole congregation, by accident or design, often is dramatically engaged in a unity of worship and educational events. Baptism, the Lord's Supper, weddings, and other special rituals or activities of the church present opportunities for an intentional joining of education and worship. Moreover, receiving new members, welcoming visitors, praying for the sick, celebrating graduations, experiencing the trials of daily life—all offer a unique context and content to a recovery of the teaching function of worship. Unfortunately, many congregations merely mention such events in announcements, prayers, or newsletters, and then move right along to something else. But again, any and all of these events can be invaluable opportunities to join worship and education and thereby to nurture the congregation's shared vision of God's sustaining presence and direction.

The danger of such an approach is that it can become stylized, frozen, magical, or trite. What is potentially interesting can become humdrum. However, for example, around the giving of Bibles to children a congregation can develop traditions which are anticipated with great expectation each year. Patterns from previous years may grow. Often there will be a remarkable coincidence between a lectionary text and the event being planned. One of the great advantages of such an approach is the way in which the pastor is able to work with a variety of people in planning worship. Not only the worship and education committees but also children, teachers, families, and others are drawn in. All of the contacts allow the pastor to nourish the congregation's vision.

The Management Type

The management type is characterized by leaders who identify needs, specify objectives, assign responsibilities, supervise activities, provide resources, evaluate the results, and revise the objectives.[13] This model is the dominant one in most organizations in the United States. It goes under the popular name of "management by objectives." There is no doubt that management by objectives can energize almost any organization.

However, many congregations resist a management model. One complaint is that spiritual realities are not readily objectified. Furthermore, some people believe that the church does well not to take too many of its methods from the self-serving business world. Consider the second objection first. Where did the modern business world learn such methods? Economic historians point out that the mission focus of the Reformation church, especially the Reformed and Believers' Church traditions, emphasized mission as prevailing over all else in life. That conception became the foundation of the modern corporation. When a congregation sets clearly defined mission objectives, it simply claims what belongs to it historically.

With regard to the first objection, one need only recall that Jesus spoke of putting first things first, of seeking first the kingdom of God, of the signs of his messianic work. Paul spoke of the Christian life as running a race, achieving the goal. There is nothing unspiritual about having clear goals, so long as they are not simply self-serving.

Education may be closely related to a management style. Studying the situation, diagnosing need, establishing objectives, devising procedures, training leaders, selecting resources, and assessing consequences—all require study, deliberation, and decision. They are the essence of education in the pragmatic tradition. The great advantage of study in the management model is that study is for the sake of mission goals. The study at each point belongs to the mission.

Leadership tends to be hierarchical in the management type. However, final decisions about policy are in the hands of the whole congregation, a church's board, (depending upon the tradition) and the informal procedures. The pastor usually is related to a board, many of whose members very likely chair a committee. The hierarchical model can be made more democratic by letting the responsible groups actually make decisions and by letting the persons affected be a part of the decision-making process. For example, the youth group should be represented when decisions about a youth counselor are made. The management model works best when the whole congregation knows and accepts the mission objectives, when responsibilities are clearly defined and performed, and when there is careful assessment and revision of objectives. The following is an illustration.

An Appalachian pastor was concerned about the amount of unemployment in his community and about the way unemployment was sapping the energy of both the community and his congregation. More and more people were leaving the community to move elsewhere. A group of concerned persons, under the pastor's direction, began to question what could be done. They set an objective to discover how the church could be more helpful to those who were facing unemployment. Their first procedure was to visit those who had moved from the community in the past year because of loss of a job.

The study group accepted the responsibility of carrying out the interviews. Together the study group and the pastor devised the questions that would be asked. The visits and the interviews were conducted and the group came together to discuss the results. They concluded that the church's most important task is to stand by people, helping them find meaning in times of great stress. The study group's assessment of the interviewing project was that it was very helpful to the congregation. Next they set the objective to stand by people and help them to discover God's purpose in times of trial. They then established a mutual aid committee. The pastor developed a sermon and a Bible study series about God's presence in the time of trial. The group turned apathy in that congregation to a vision with growing energy.

Some congregations have a variety of mission groups and require every member to participate in one such group. Each mission group worships together, but also works at a missional task. These groups have considerable latitude to establish their own objectives. In my view the mission groups fit within the management model.

One limitation of a management model is that clear objectives are very difficult to achieve. Seldom does everyone in a congregation agree about an objective. The diagnosis of the situation may be wrong, and the situation itself is constantly changing. To set specific goals runs the risk of triviality or irrelevancy. Too much attention to achieving objectives leads to overworking some persons and therefore to their loss of interest. There must be a strong balance of maintaining good relationships as well as achieving goals.

Most congregations feel the need to achieve some goals. Even very informal congregations need some achievement. To that extent they cannot completely bypass the management model. In my opinion goals and objectives should always be considered within the context of the congregation's story and the biblical story. Things are better chosen because "they belong to our story" and "they belong to the Christian story" than simply because "we feel a need for them." Following the management model, according to the steps given in the previous section, will balance story and objective. The management model can sharpen vision and focus energy, when it is skillfully, sensitively, and prayerfully carried out.

The Primary Group Type

A primary group is a face-to-face group whose basic emotional needs are satisfied by the close relationships between its members. Examples of primary groups are families and close friends. A congregation that is a primary group usually consists not only of families but also of close friends, whose friendships often have been lifelong.[14] In this type of congregation worship often is informal and conveys a strong sense of the warmth of being included.

The primary group lives by the stories it tells. There are many stories about past events and about persons who belong or who for some reason are no longer present. When people come together they share what is happening in their lives. They feel the pain and the hopes of one another. When one suffers, all suffer; and when one rejoices, all rejoice. The telling of the stories, events, and feelings serves to weave a net which binds people together. Storytelling also is a process of repairing and reweaving the net.

Not all persons get along well. Often church members are in conflict with one another, even to the point of shunning one another. Occasionally people have not spoken for years. Sometimes all efforts to reconcile the personal differences fail. Nevertheless, hostile parties often are included in the fellowship, and other persons make allowance for the animosity. Likes and dislikes may run high, and they may serve as an unending source of conversation. However, even such conversations generate some of the stories that are the lifeblood of the congregation, the net holding them together. Of course hostilities must be overcome, and one of the functions of a church community is to encourage repentance and reconciliation. Failing this, persons may leave and the congregation will suffer, or even die.

The leadership strategy in this type of congregation is to love people and to enter into the storytelling. People in a primary group want leaders who love and accept them. They want leaders whom they enjoy being with and who help them weave the net of stories that constitutes the church community. The ministerial image is that of shepherd or pastor. The leader's primary responsibility is to care for people, to visit them when they are sick, to talk to them when problems arise, to help extend the net that holds them together. Often the congregation has many traditions, such as who sits where and who may serve as a trustee. The pastor respects such traditions because tradition, much more than bureaucracy, is the binding force in the congregation. The pastor who can encourage and embody the values of friendship, of care for one another, of hospitality to the stranger, and of the sense of God's presence can generate great energy and devotion.

The educational style in a primary group is informal, consisting largely of developing friendships and learning the network of stories. Many church school classes consist of primary groups in which the students and teachers simply enjoy each other's friendship and presence. The objectives of the lesson are not nearly so important as learning the latest news and feeling one another's appreciation. For such classes the revelation of God's Word comes first of all as a friendship-creating reality. Teachers are aware of this and are more interested in friendship than in getting a task completed. For that very reason the learnings in all the gatherings of the church group outside the classroom are equally as important as the classroom learnings. Participating in informal relationships is the primary way learning occurs. Such informal participation may be as powerful as more formal instruction in communicating biblical values.

An example of the primary group type is that of a new pastor who came into a small declining congregation. He quickly visited all the people who attended, and he soon became acquainted with the traditions and stories of the congregation's life. He visited the sick and the shut-ins immediately and regularly. Before and after the worship services he circulated among the people, exchanging greetings and stories with them. He began to visit persons who were in the network of friendships of those who attended the church and he found ways of including neighborhood children who had not been coming before. The mood of the congregation changed to one of optimism. The new pastor became a center of storytelling.

The examples we have given have been of primary groups in smaller congregations. However, larger congregations can be made up of a series of overlapping primary groups. Church school classes or various informal groupings can very well be primary groups that last for decades. With multiple primary groups, as well as with a single group, the leadership nourishes the informal sense of community, mutual care, assistance when needed, welcome to the visitor, and the network of stories.

The strength of primary groups is the love, care, and strong sense of community that can be provided to everyone. They indicate the reality and great power of informal relationships. The weakness is that such groups can become cliquish and ingrown. New persons may never quite feel included. Members of the primary group may lose their sense of mission and outreach by only providing for their own needs. Layers of resentment and gossip can build, sometimes splitting the group. Primary groups sometimes are dominated by one family, and usually by the matriarch or patriarch of that family.

Nevertheless, the primary group is a predominant and recurrent expression of Christian congregational life. It seems closely related to profoundly needed family values. The primary group congregation often dreams of becoming one of the other types listed here, but other styles of leadership frequently fail when they are actually attempted. Leaders should believe that vision and energy can be nourished within the primary group fellowship and should remember that the primary group is a most enduring model of congregational life.

The Growth and Development Type

The growth and development type of congregation encourages persons to mature, calls out leadership, and generally works and prays for the maturation of the congregation.[15] Attention is given to the life stage and special situation of each person. People are given challenging tasks according to their growing abilities. Prayer, worship, and spiritual direction are central to growth and maturation. Social and emotional development usually are considered to be a part of spiritual growth. Moments of transformation are very important, although as much emphasis is given to continuing transformation as to the moment of conversion.

A growth oriented congregation often gives careful attention to teaching and learning. Church school classes typically are as closely graded as is possible for the size of the congregation. Teachers of children confer with one another and with parents, giving continuing attention to how children are developing. Appropriate and flexible learning goals for each child are established. Adult classes are established to meet adult life tasks (e.g., parenting, business ethics, problems of aging, and spiritual growth, to mention only several possibilities).

Learning, however, does not occur only in the classroom. The growth oriented congregation is aware of how all of the church's activities contribute to the maturation of participants. Youth are encouraged to go to summer camps, political responsibility seminars, and international work camps. Adults are encouraged to participate in denominational, ecumenical, and wider community responsibilities according to their abilities. Special awareness and celebrative events are planned to meet the needs of various persons at their particular life stages.

The pastoral leadership understands ministry primarily in terms of spiritual growth. Much attention is given to assessing the abilities of persons and to providing opportune and challenging responsibilities. Groups are created to meet the special needs of persons. Tasks and responsibilities are judged as much by the growth of the persons involved as by whether objectives are achieved. The pastor and other leaders give much attention to counseling and to giving spiritual direction. People are encouraged to accept spiritual discipline, and spiritual discipline groups are established. Much attention is given to prayer for individuals and groups within the congregation.

People participate in congregations for a variety of reasons. Some do so for status, respect, friendship, or to resist loneliness. Others do so because they get caught up in the congregational pattern, accept responsibilities, and feel included. Still others catch a vision of the church as Christ's body and desire to conform their lives to Christ. Others find all of their efforts to be spiritually impoverished and so they deeply desire the grace and love of God in their lives. We see that some people's reasons for attendance are external, while others' reasons are integral to the purposes of the church. A growth oriented leadership attempts to provide activities, groups, and experiences for each level of participation.

An example of a growth oriented congregation is one in which the pastor and the pastoral committee created a series of small groups in which the participants were to study and discuss faith development. The committee discovered that only the most committed leaders in the church could gain satisfaction from guiding such groups. Because of the promotional effort, a large proportion of the congregation began to participate in these groups. However, as many as half dropped out after several weeks. Those who remained became devoted to the groups. The pastor came to realize that people were at different places in their spiritual life, and that different experiences must be provided for different people. Some people were concerned to see results from their activities. They were like Jesus' disciples, expecting things to happen. Others desired to get beyond activism, and they were more open to groups for spiritual guidance.

The development type has certain limitations. There are no commonly accepted stages of spiritual development. The vision of the leadership will therefore be somewhat arbitrary. The development model requires much sophistication from the leadership. Not all congregations have teachers and leaders who can serve as mature spiritual guides. Like the primary group model, the growth model can turn in upon itself, losing its sense of evangelism, justice, and mission. To expect maturation can itself become a barrier that hinders growth.

Nearly every congregation, however, has spiritual giants and leaders, though their leadership may be quiet and hidden. Every teacher has a sense of the next step of growth for a child. Such a sense of guidance may not be well schooled, but is nearly always present. Nearly every congregation anticipates greater maturity. The growth model is a way of giving articulation and energy to a present reality. The growth model as presented here moves beyond the classroom and becomes a vision for the whole congregation.

The Prophetic Type

The prophetic type of congregation recognizes that conflict is inevitable in life and seeks to witness to the creative possibilities of conflict.[16] The prophet senses the degree to which God's covenant has been broken by the community. The prophetic community lives in the pain of that brokenness, expressing it, acknowledging the conflict, and calling for a return to the ways of God.

Some sociologists suggest that groups cannot live simply by authoritative procedures nor by informal authority.[17] Rather every group is caught in a continuing process of conflict. Groups are better off to accept conflict and to learn to struggle creatively. In terms of our typology, most congregations cannot live only by the management model or by the primary group model. Both of those models tend to cover conflict. Rather, genuine conflict must be encouraged between the appropriate parties. At times the issues are better aired in public.

The prophetic congregation recognizes the importance of expressing conflict in order that devotion to the covenant will not be lost. The strategy is not to arrive at a total consensus, but to arrive at a workable balance of conflict. Acceptance of conflict is a virtue rather than a vice, although conflict is best settled at the lowest possible level. The prophet values conflict not for its own sake, but for the sake of justice. A congregation that is open to conflict within itself is much more likely to be able to witness to injustice beyond itself.

Striving for justice and resolving conflict requires study to understand the conditions and opinions of others. It requires discussion of strategy and public expression of opinion. Concern for justice often requires being present in places of injustice. The prophetic community participates in public discussion and works to make its view known in the public forum. Effective expression of prophetic opinion necessitates a great deal of research and study. A prophetic congregation has many persons and groups studying and discussing issues for which there is concern. Classes in a prophetic congregation work at serious problems with genuine disagreement. Often the congregation is drawn together in mutual support and prayer as they address a threatening issue.

The pastor may be a prophetic leader, a person whose vision on congregational and public issues is much respected. Or the pastor may work more unobtrusively, encouraging a group of leaders to address questions of justice, finding resources that are needed, and generally supporting other persons. The latter pastoral style fits together better with a more pastoral model. Even when a congregation does not address dramatic issues, its style may be prophetic to the extent that it encourages the expression of genuine differences. Prophetic leaders sometimes call in experts in conflict resolution to move beyond an impasse.

An example of a prophetic congregation is one that has decided to provide sanctuary for political refugees from Central America. Finding such refugees in their midst and learning more of the circumstances of their flight from their homeland, some members of the congregation become convinced that the Christlike response is to provide sanctuary. This requires much study and debate at both the committee and church council levels. A number of persons is strongly opposed to doing what may be illegal. The pastor preaches a series of sermons on the issue. After six months of considerable struggle the congregation decides to vote for sanctuary. The vote of course leads to further debate.

The weakness of the prophetic model is that it may emphasize witness at the expense of nurture, although that is not always the case. A prophetic congregation can become cause oriented, losing persons who do not share those concerns. To accept conflict brings with it a risk. The risk is that conflict can be harmful to some persons or groups, though not to express conflict can be seriously harmful too.

The concern for righteousness is everywhere present, even when covered by unrighteousness. Furthermore, the call to righteousness is central in the gospel. God's grace and love are the source of righteousness. So it is not surprising that the prophetic type of congregation readily may be found in such places as the base communities of South America, the congregations dedicated to civil rights in the United States, or the churches witnessing to peace in Western Europe. In less dramatic ways, many congregations encourage people to speak the truth to one another as they see it, to feel the pain of injustice, and to find ways to attack the oppressions of our time. In these ways they follow the prophetic model of nourishing a center of vision and energy.

The Interpretation Type

The interpretation type of congregation seeks to find meaning and significance in the events of life.[18] The strategy of the interpretation model is to let the biblical tradition interpret the present situation. An analogy is to be found between the biblical text in its situation and the congregation in the contemporary situation. The biblical text is the result of conversation and debate about the way God was present in past events. An understanding of contemporary events requires an understanding of how God is present in these events. Biblical interpretation is not complete until contemporary events are considered. The interpretation may be related to an individual's joy or crisis, or it may point to national or international events.

Learning in an interpretive congregation involves a continuing conversation about the relationship between biblical stories and life events. Preaching is not so much a matter of providing the answers as it is a part of a larger conversation, a way of making the congregation's interpretive conversation public. Formal classes also work at the interrelationship of biblical meaning and present meaning. From the youngest to the oldest members an appropriate level of conversation takes place to uncover meaning. The interpretive congregation searches out God's meaning in all dimensions of life and in all functions of the congregation, not just the pulpit and the classroom. Family prayers, the welcome to church pot luck meals, and various celebrations all become the occasion for interpretation. Learning in an interpretive congregation is respectful of what others believe. Teaching is not telling so much as conversing.

Leadership in an interpretive congregation requires considerable study. Teachers, speakers, and chairpersons must study to be well informed. But all private study is generally balanced by conversations with others in the congregation. Interpretation is ongoing conversation rather than a private vision. The goal is that the whole people be engaged in the process of interpreting their lives in relationship to the Scriptures. The entire congregation becomes a community of moral and theological discourse.

As an example, consider a university chapel whose attendance began to swell when the preacher began a series of messages addressing issues of university life. Visiting preachers were invited to the pulpit because they were known to be well informed about current issues. A series of afternoon teas was set up to discuss issues raised by the sermons. The church school classes were taught by persons who had the same skills. The prayers and litanies constantly broadened the vision of the persons present. Many conversations began to revolve around the interpretation going on in the chapel.

The interpretation model also has its weaknesses. It may substitute conversation for actual engagement in issues. The delight of the conversation can be an escape from facing life's realities. The preacher may become the centerpiece rather than an interpreter of the congregation's ongoing conversation. Interpretation can become arbitrary, bigoted, or trite in the name of wisdom. There may be an idolatry of understanding with the loss of genuine pastoral care for one another.

Nevertheless, the interpretation model seems close to what the Scripture means by the Word of God. Interpretation does not preclude what is emphasized in the other models cited earlier. It seeks rather to give proper perspective to all that the congregation does. It seeks to keep the Scripture and God's

will central in a life that is threatened to be overcome by sec-
ularity and triviality. It takes seriously the reality of the congregation as a living story.

The Growing Center

How then do ministers and lay leaders of a congregation
foster the growth of a center of vision and energy? A congregation is already a center of vision (no matter how unconscious)
and energy (no matter how suppressed). Leadership seeks to
recover and enrich the vision, release and concentrate the energy. A congregation is a living story, constantly being formed
and transformed, seeking to discover and embody God's purposes. A congregation is a functioning credo, an embodied ethos,
a constellation of loyalties.

To discover the vision and receive the energy, leadership
should articulate present practice and set it within the congregation's ongoing story. They should identify causes and
meanings of the stories and practice and bring them into dialog
with the Christian story. Finally leaders should be willing to
identify weaknesses and points of unfaithfulness, select a plan
for the future, act it out, and tell the congregation's story.

Congregational types of vision and power include the
following: liturgy, management, primary group, growth and
development, prophet, and interpretation. Most congregations
likely have elements of several of those types. Nevertheless,
congregations cannot feature the characteristics of all of the
types at once. Congregations will find themselves drawn toward one type or another, or perhaps toward one or another
combination of types.

A congregation's vision and power comes from its story,
its ongoing beliefs, purpose, organization, leadership, communication, commitment, and resources. A change in any of
these may lead to a disruption or renewal of vision and energy.
The direction forward requires careful attention to the congregation's living story, for therein does the ever-present power
of God to form and transform become most evident.

Meeting in the Silence: Meditation as the Center of Congregational Life

MARY ELIZABETH MOORE
Claremont School of Theology

LORD, teach us the silence of humility
   the silence of wisdom
   the silence of love
   the silence that speaks without words
   the silence of faith
LORD, teach us to silence our own hearts and minds
   that we may listen to the movement of the Holy Spirit
     within us
   and feel your presence in the depth of our being.
   Amen.[1]

    I sat in the large ballroom for session one of my second conference in two weeks. This was more sitting in conference than usual for me. "What am I doing here?" I asked. Getting here was a challenge of completing correspondence, classes, and meetings with students. Getting here required time and support with my children, grocery shopping, preparing meals, and washing clothes. Getting here required catching up with some responsibilities and postponing others.

But I sat and listened to the lectures, and I *knew* why I was there. I had come to find sacred space for silence. In that room no one would call me to wash their clothes, arrange an appointment, or sign a petition. The lectures, of course, would be interesting, but the dialogue within myself was the more significant work of silence.

As I sat in that first session, I began to write, taking notes at first but soon writing my own thoughts. I wrote intensely, only occasionally making contact with the speakers. Later in the day I saw someone who had been present in that first session with me. She said, "Wasn't that a dull meeting?" I answered, "Not for me; I was in my own world." I realized that I had sought silence and I had found it.

This is not a story of the purpose of conferences, but of the purpose of silence. The particular conference in which this story took place was actually a very enlightening one, and I did participate more attentively in other sessions. What is important to me in this story, however, is that silence is an opportunity to enter into oneself and speak with God and other people there. The silence is like a clearing in the woods where the sky can be seen in its expanse and where grasses and wildflowers grow. The trees of the woods surround you there, and you know you will reenter the forest when you depart from the silent space.

The forest in which I wandered as I approached that conference was a very active one, and I was very conscious of its activity and noise. The conference itself was busy and loud, but I sought silence there and I found it. Perhaps my story is not unusual. Perhaps many of us in our individual and congregational lives experience a flutter of activity and only catch moments of silence as we stop for a moment in the clearing between one forest path and another. This may be a particularly apt metaphor for many North American Protestant churches that conceive of their mission as *actively* carrying out the work of Christ in the church and the world.

Meeting in the Silence: The Possibilities

The purpose of this chapter is to explore the possibilities in silence as an organizing center for congregational life. Silence is an opportunity to listen and wait for God, and other activities grow from that. Imagine educational ministry that is centered on meeting in silence—meeting God, others, and ourselves.

The educational options discussed in earlier chapters of this book largely are attempts to direct the life and work of the congregation in an active mode. These have value in themselves and have certainly borne fruit in the work of the churches. But the purpose of this chapter is to make a case for meditation to be at the center of congregational life. Meditation represents that broad range of activities through which we commune with God. The problem in our congregations is not really the absence of prayer and meditation. The problem seems to be that these efforts to apprehend God's will for our lives and our situations are not put in the center of congregational life; and we do not seem to know how to wait until we know what God would have us do. We are more prone to move ahead with decisions and actions than to pray and wait in silence.

If silence is the organizing center of educational ministry, then, listening for God becomes the central activity. This does not refer to a quick prayer at the beginning of a meeting, or even to an occasional classroom session on prayer and meditation. What is called for is a pervasive listening for God in the midst of everything.

Listening for God is an art to be cultivated. We can listen for God in the people near us, in the life of the congregation, in the world, and in the written texts of the Christian tradition (the Bible and the Church's traditions in hymns, prayers, creeds, and so forth). In short, we can learn to be attentive to God's Word not only in the Bible, but also in the midst of visiting a family in the hospital. The question before us now is "What are some of the possibilities for cultivating this art of listening for God?"

Meditation, Prayer, and Contemplation. Certain disciplines need to be cultivated. The most obvious disciplines are *meditation, prayer, and contemplation.* These three are considered together here because they are intertwined, and because the mystics and others who write of spirituality often move from one to the other without imposing rigid boundaries. Meditation is a deep reflection on the mysteries or truths of faith. It is often seen as a penetration into one's inner life and as a preparation for prayer. Because it is so fundamental to all of the life of silence, it is used in this chapter as the general practice that is foundational to all of the others. Prayer is basically communion with God, and it usually is associated with giving thanks or making supplication to God. In much of Christian tradition, the acts of thanksgiving, petition, or intercession actually grow from the sense of God and the union with God that are the heart of prayer. Contemplation is a concentrated focus on God. Traditionally, it does not depend on rational faculties, but simply on being opened to God.[2]

These disciplines are extraordinarily important to meeting in silence. Through them the barriers we place between ourselves and God are broken down. Thomas Merton says that meditation can be summarized in one idea: "the idea of *awakening* our interior self and attuning ourselves inwardly to the Holy Spirit, so that we will be able to respond to His [God's] grace."[3] And of contemplation he says:

> The fact remains that contemplation will not be given to those who willfully remain at a distance from God, who confine their interior life to a few routine exercises of piety and a few external acts of worship and service performed as a matter of duty. . . . In actual practice, their minds and hearts are taken up with their own ambitions and troubles and comforts and pleasures and all of their worldly interests and anxieties and fears. God is only invited to enter this charmed circle to smooth out difficulties and to dispense rewards.[4]

The distance from God and the barriers we put in the way are the problem. The hope is that we may be attuned to the mysteries and united with God.

This unity with God does not ignore the world. In fact, Merton recommends that persons actually meditate on their everyday duties and difficulties.[5] Sometimes the very frustrations and frenzied activities which seem to block our silence can be the best starting points for our meditation. The danger, of course, is that we will have a heightened awareness of our loneliness and pain. The hope is that God will address us at those very points. Merton pushes even beyond that to urge people to be aware of the whole world. He says:

> I would be inclined to say that a nun who has meditated on the passion of Christ but has not meditated on the extermination camps of Dachau and Auschwitz has not yet fully entered into the experience of Christianity in our time.[6]

What is needed is not a blindness to the world but a centering, or what Merton and the historical mystics call recollection. It is a form of withdrawal from those things that bombard one's senses and from the modern pressures to buy more and seek passing satisfactions. Recollection is a kind of self-denial that makes it possible to give attention to God. Recollection is obviously needed at the time of prayer and meditation; but it also is needed to some extent throughout the day in order to create an atmosphere of faith.[7] The challenge in all of this is to live in a spirit of prayer and carry out educational ministry in that spirit.

These disciplines of prayer, meditation, and contemplation might be understood not only as ways to be united with God, but also as ways to know and live in harmony with the creation. Among some Native American tribes the primary education in past generations was to sit on a mound or rock or natural formation for hours contemplating one's surroundings. Such an education aroused sensitivities to the world that are not cultivated in classrooms with walls. We need not wonder

why Native Americans were so often sensitive to the movements of the sun and moon and seasons.

Study and Reflection. Other disciplines may be less
obvious, but they are equally important to the art of listening
for God. One of these is *study and reflection.* Actually, study
and reflection often are activities in silence. Jewish men traditionally have gone to the Synagogue or House of Study to
read and reflect on the Scriptures. Likewise, when I was a
young mother I sometimes arose in the middle of the night to
study in silence for a class I taught on Sundays. When my
family awoke I felt fresher and ready to enjoy the day with
them.

Study and reflection in silence are themselves meditative. As one studies and reflects on the people, the earth, the
social and political situations in the world, and the written
texts of the Christian faith, one encounters God. Both critical
reflection and depth reflection are involved.[8] In critical reflection one probes the texts and reflects on what they do and do
not communicate. In depth reflection, one reflects into the texts,
attempting to experience them from their own points of view.

Both critical and depth reflection are important in listening for God. The former enables us to analyze the texts from
new perspectives, such as the perspectives of the poor or women
or children or ethnic minorities. These perspectives can liberate
us from oppressive readings of the texts that foster classism,
sexism, ageism, or racism. Depth reflection serves another
function, that is, to help us hear more fully what another is
trying to communicate. Both the critical capacity and the capacity to enter deeply into the life of another can help us to
cross over into the depths of the other and listen to the Word
of God.

Receptivity. Another discipline is *receptivity.* Just to
call this a discipline is strange to the ear because receptivity
usually is seen as a passivity that reveals the absence of effort
and intention. Receptivity is itself a discipline, however, and
it can be cultivated. It is an attitude of appreciation for what

can be offered to us through other people and through the earth.

Receptivity is similar to what Charles Foster calls child-likeness. Among other things, it includes an ability to receive with open hands and an expectation that we are growing.[9] This is very different from assuming that we have all of the gifts to give, or that we know answers to every question (even those not asked!). It is different too from using our own preconceptions to analyze every new situation. Actually, people do typically function out of their preconceptions, as when they cite a proof text from the Bible to prove a point or explain everyone's behavior with the same psychological interpretations.

The challenge is to move beyond simply giving gifts and giving answers, and move into a discipline of receiving the gifts and answers that others have to give. Sometimes we need to be silent in a conversation in order to listen to others. Such a practice can move us away from classifying people and creation. It moves us in the direction of being a community with one another and with the earth—a community that listens and receives and appreciates the gifts of one another. In such a community persons can receive the gifts of God more fully as they listen to voices other than their own.

Awe and Reverence. Another discipline that can be encouraged is *awe and reverence*. These, like receptivity, are attitudes, and they are the way by which we recognize the presence of God in everything. They are the way we become sensitized to the mystery of God's movements.

The significance of these attitudes is called to attention by Philip Phenix, who refers to wonder, awe, and reverence as some of the dispositions that are associated with transcendence and are important to the educational enterprise.[10] For Phenix, awe and wonder have to do with one's awareness of transcendence, and reverence has to do with a sense of participation in it.[11] Each contributes to the other.

Awe and reverence are named here as disciplines of silence because they are habits that can be practiced. We can draw on symbols that quiet our souls, such as taking off our shoes for an event focused on listening for God. We can offer retreats into the natural surroundings, which themselves stir awe and reverence. The practice of awe inspires the feeling of awe, and the practice of reverence engenders more reverence. Awe is a sense of wonder before the greatness of God and grandeur of creation. Reverence is respect and love for God and the creation. These are clearly intertwined. As we practice both of these attitudes, we become more open to the mysteries of God and to meeting God in the silence.

All of the disciplines named here offer ways to enter silence and to listen in the silence of God. What happens in the silence is a meeting, not only with God, but also with ourselves and with others.

Meeting in the Uproar: The Problems

The practical problems in the previous proposal are obvious to anyone who is deeply involved in a parish or congregation. The very nature of congregational life (in most parts of North America anyway) is active and busy. People are born and they die; they marry and divorce. Political, economic, and personal issues emerge, and decisions have to be made. All of these can be ignored, of course, but only at the expense of the people in the congregation who need the rituals and personal care of the church community, and only at the risk of making congregational decisions by default. In fact, to ignore the events and issues emerging in and around the congregation is to abandon the mission of the church.

But the problem we face is uproar, an uproar that distorts and distracts from the world and the church's mission in it. Richard Foster has described the problem well in the introductory pages of *Celebration of Discipline:*

> In contemporary society our Adversary majors in three things: noise, hurry, and crowds. If he can keep us engaged in 'muchness' and 'manyness,' he will rest satisfied.[12]

The question is how we can live in this uproar without either being overcome by it or ignoring the uproar and avoiding the need of the church to respond to the world.

The proposal of meeting in silence really is not intended to encourage persons to ignore the community's life and all of the happenings that take place within and outside the congregation. Rather, it is intended to challenge the common approaches to education in a whirlwind of activity. Much of the educational ministry now taking place could be characterized as "meeting in the uproar." The problems in this approach will be analyzed briefly here.

In the uproar, a community is likely to *forget that community itself is a gift to be received, not made*. The belief that the community is a gift of God is deeply woven into the fabric of the Jewish and Christian traditions. Bruce Birch highlights the biblical accent on God's initiative toward the community in his essay in this volume. This accent is easily forgotten, however.

In an effort to build community, church leaders often exert great effort and use all of the latest techniques to get people formed into small groups, to encourage people to share their lives, to create grand celebrations of anniversaries or high holy days, and to sponsor attractive events that will get people's attention. All the while, the roots of community life may remain very shallow. The grand efforts to build community can sometimes even distract the church, and thus can work against the openness to receive the gift of community.

Another problem with efforts to build community in the uproar is that we *tend to build the community in our own image*. We feature those gifts that we value the most, whether they are the ability to speak smoothly, to share about one's personal life, or to make music. Thus, the communities we build often center around these valued gifts. These communities, of course, have value, but they are limited. The limits are especially large when we have failed to seek out God and one another.

The failure to listen for God and the other is evidenced in the frantic or partial attempts churches sometimes make to build community. Sometimes they try to reproduce ideas from other churches, or the pastors and lay leaders try to repeat ideas they themselves have led successfully in other churches. Sometimes churches create partial communities which include some people and exclude others, e.g., including only the athletes, musicians, actors, or intellectuals. Of course, learning from the experience of other churches and creating communities of people with shared interest are not problems in themselves. The problem is a lack of listening to God in the present situation. The problem is that the church can too easily be satisfied with partial communities and have no sense of a larger call.

This attempt to build community in our own image also can take the form of structuring communities according to our own self-interests. Paulo Freire has highlighted the impossibility of oppressors' liberating the oppressed.[13] Only the oppressed can liberate themselves (*and* their oppressors) from unjust social structures. In other words, those in control of communal structures are likely to perpetuate their own control. As long as clergy- , male- , Anglo- , wealthy- , professional- , intellectual- , or any other elite are shaping the community, the community will very likely reflect their values and power interests.

The problem with meeting in the uproar is that some voices are not heard in the midst of all the confusion. The quieter voices especially will be missed, such as the voices of the poor or the elderly, or the handicapped. Also, in the uproar, the easiest path may seem to be "the way we have always done it." The voices of God and others may be dimmed by our efforts just to keep moving, and we build the community in our own image.

Still another problem of meeting in the uproar is that *the congregation's teaching will be limited by its own discernment, or lack of it.* As noted in the discussion earlier, some voices cannot even be heard in the uproar, and these are usually the voices of the least powerful in the community. We cannot learn from them if we do not hear them. Furthermore, the church can easily close out the still small voice of God by avoiding silence. The danger, of course, is that the tradition is limited to those voices we do hear, and the fresh breath of the Spirit is closed out.

This problem is of particular concern to women and ethnic minorities whose contributions and histories largely have been ignored and who only now are being introduced into general and religious history books in this country. The movement to revise history has come from the willingness of some of these women and ethnic minorities to enter into their own silence and ask, "What is missing in this account, what is distorted, and where can I go to find the missing pieces?" One of the most notable examples of this historical reconstruction is seen in Elisabeth Schüssler Fiorenza's work.[14] Fiorenza is trying to do a feminist critique of biblical texts and interpretations, and to reconstruct the missing pieces in regard to women, using textual fragments and critical interpretation to put together a fuller picture of women during biblical times.

If the church is to teach, it must teach with an understanding of its own tradition which is as full as possible. Furthermore, the church needs to hear God's voice in the quiet and in the quiet voices of the others all around. Meeting in the uproar can limit the degree to which we actually meet God and the other, and even ourselves. Meeting in the uproar can be very brief and casual, so that it is hardly a meeting at all.

Because the active approaches to Christian religious education have so dominated churches in the United States, the question must be raised as to the adequacy of these approaches. Some limitations have been highlighted here, and others are possible. Certainly the meditative approaches need to be considered as complements to the more active approaches which are normally offered as the base for educational theory and practice.

Consider, for example, the approaches described in Jack Seymour and Donald Miller's *Contemporary Approaches to Christian Education*. These approaches are centered around: religious instruction, faith community, development, liberation, and interpretation.[15] Meeting in silence could be part of any of those approaches, but the idea is usually not developed in theory or practice. Much less does meeting in silence become an organizing center in any of those approaches. The meditative approaches can offer both critique and complement to the approaches described in the Seymour and Miller book.

They also can offer critique to common practices in the churches. Certainly, meeting in silence is different from the programmatic thrust in Christian education that leads even to subsuming education under the category of program in some congregations. Certainly, meeting in silence is different from the kind of order and control that does not allow for unfilled gaps of time or unanswered questions or unexplained stories. When we fill all of the time gaps and analyze the stories until they make sense, we sometimes allow mastery to undercut mystery. But mastery is not important for its own sake. The challenge is to seek after God and to respect mystery, a challenge that requires both active and meditative approaches to Christian religious education. The focus here is on the latter.

Meditation as a Context for Action

The title of this section suggests an interesting connection between action and meditation. Perhaps the active and meditative approaches are more than complementary; perhaps they are so integrally related that each actually enhances the other. Meditation, then, is a source for action, and action, a source for meditation. But the relationship cannot be described in terms of simple cause and effect. One does not automatically cause the other, but each creates the context in which the other can be deepened. Therefore, if one is neglected by the Christian community, the other will be slighted as well.

Meditation and Action. No one has understood this connection between action and meditation better than Thomas Merton. His passion for recovering silence comes out of his own passion for the world:

> We are living through the greatest crisis in the history of man [sic]; and this crisis is centered precisely in the country that has made a fetish out of action and has lost (or perhaps never had) the sense of contemplation.[16]

Merton is not concerned simply with inspiring prayer, meditation, and contemplation as a complement for action. He is concerned too with reforming the way these meditative acts are viewed. They often are defended as a way to get action from God. Merton notes that people often justify the life of the contemplatives by explaining that their work is effective in a spiritual, invisible way; they call upon God to act. The greatest limit of this view is that it assumes a cause-and-effect universe in which the purpose of everything is to affect something else.[17] In fact, for Merton, the value of prayer and contemplation should not be judged by the emotions aroused, answers given, or practical results achieved.[18] Those measures of value evade the heart of the matter.

The relationship with God that is made possible in prayer is more important to Merton than the effectiveness of prayer in getting things done. For him:

> The real point of the contemplative life has always been a deepening of faith and of the personal dimensions of liberty and apprehension to the point where our direct union with God is realized and 'experienced.'[19]

This sense of union (sometimes called a vision of love) often will lead people to pray for the world.[20] But in this case, the prayers of petition come out of the sense of union with God. These prayers have actually played a role in opening the eyes of people to the needs of the world which cry out for their prayers of petition and intercession.

Meditation is not a source of action in a simple sense. Meditation is a source of life-giving relationship with God, and this relationship helps us to see the world and its needs and to respond. Our action, then, can be fuller and wiser if nurtured by a life of meditation. Furthermore, those persons whose life vocations are to be contemplatives enrich the Christian community by their presence, and those contemplatives who are themselves called to speak need to be heeded. This includes those living in solitude in monastic communities and also those contemplative spirits who are part of any congregation.

Meditation and the Life of One Community. Much has been written on this subject, but the focus of this particular chapter is on learning in congregations. We will look at one particular community that did, in fact, take meditation as an organizing center during one period of its history. This was not a single congregation but a diocese of the Anglican Church in Coventry, England. The story is told by Stephen Verney in his book *Fire in Coventry*. Some highlights of the story will be offered here to give a sense of how one church community acted on some of the ideas shared in this chapter.

The city of Coventry had been levelled by war bombing in 1940, and the old cathedral had been destroyed by fire. Only the walls remained as an empty shell to remind visitors of the cathedral's former glory and of the horrors of war. A new, modern cathedral was built by the side of the shell, and today both structures witness to God and the hope for peace. The old cathedral has a simple altar with a cross made of charred timbers that fell from the cathedral roof during the Blitz. Behind the cross are engraved the words "Father forgive." The mission of the parish is defined today as a ministry of reconciliation, and it reaches out into the world.

Stephen Verney begins his story of the Coventry Diocese in 1959 at the time he began his work as Diocesan Missioner there. He began that work by visiting the Chapters, small groups of clergy who met on a regular basis. His purpose in these meetings was "to talk as little as possible, and to *listen* carefully, and to try to hear the answer to this question, 'What is the Spirit saying to the Churches?' "[21]

During one of these early Chapter meetings, someone marveled at the opportunity for the diocese that would be offered by the consecration of the new cathedral which was to take place three years later. The opportunity for spiritual renewal was discussed in that gathering, and the clergy expressed the desire to be a consecrated people surrounding the consecrated cathedral. They decided to begin with themselves by meeting together for a quiet day. They did so, and at the end of their day of silence, they discussed their mission and decided to meet for one hour every week.[22] Those early events already gave some sense of the kind of challenge that can arise from meeting in silence. The clergy in this Chapter were *not* looking for ways to spend their time. They already were very busy people and laughed at the thought of finding an hour a week to meet together. But they were trying to respond to the movements of the Spirit.

The fruits of those early meetings were bountiful. Verney reports:

> As the weekly meetings continued, Monday after Monday, these men grew less and less suspicious of each other. As they studied the Bible together, and each spoke of the truth as he saw it, they began first to know that the other man was genuine, and then to discover that he had something to teach them which they hadn't quite grasped before. As they knelt together in prayer, perhaps above all as they were silent, they began to know that they belonged to one another, and cared about each other's work, and that the mighty task to which they were committed, and which was overwhelming them individually, was something which they could tackle together in a strength greater than their own.[23]

This story is already revealing something of the depth of meeting that was taking place in silence. The clergy were listening to one another and spending time together in prayer and "above all" in silence. The silence was joining them together rather than separating them off into their individual worlds.

The Chapter that met together those first weeks wanted to spread the idea, so they wrote the Bishop to recommend the idea to the other Chapters in the Diocese. The Bishop chose not to operate in that way. Instead, he invited the originating Chapter to write the others and share its story, inviting the other Chapters to move in similar directions. Most did, though considerable variation was found from Chapter to Chapter. The variations gave proof to the words of the Archdeacon of Warwick that the Holy Spirit "will not be stereotyped."[24] An awareness was beginning to develop in the Bishop and clergy that this wind of the Spirit needed to be allowed free movement and not to be controlled by large structures and organization. Note that more organization would have saved time and energy, but the early communication was kept personal and unrestrained by requirements imposed from the hierarchy.

The next movement was a plan to spread the experiences from the Chapters of clergy (first ripple), to small groups of clergy and laity (second ripple), to the congregatiòns of each parish (third ripple), to the final dramatic acts of the diocese (fourth ripple), to a new, but unknown, starting point (fifth ripple). This plan was adopted, especially after an impassioned plea from a lay woman for the clergy to listen to the laity and for the laity to listen to one another.[25]

The plan did proceed from ripple to ripple, and the result was a growing sense of unity in the diocese. In fact, Verney describes the culmination in the fourth ripple of the diocesan mission services: "[T]he diocese became a person, a body alive with a spirit."[26] Conflicts and important decisions were faced along the way, but the culmination of meeting in silence was a sense of unity and celebration.

Verney himself reflects on the experiences described here and draws out several meanings. Some of his observations are particularly apt for our discussion here. He highlights the importance of people organizing their time so they can love as Jesus loved, which means making time for prayer and rest as well as work.[27] He also emphasizes the importance of people praying together and for one another, putting themselves at God's disposal.[28] In another vein, he calls attention to the shift in evangelism from a one-way instructional task to a sharing of one person with another in a search for the truth that already abides within each.[29] All of this represents a radical shift in consciousness—from an accent on human activity to seeking after God, and from an accent on instructive Christian witness to a shared search with other persons, Christian and non-Christian.

This kind of respect for God's Spirit alive in persons all around, and for the possibilities of meeting God and one another in prayer, is one fruit of Stephen Verney's experiences in the Diocese of Coventry. Those experiences and reflections form one picture of a community meeting in silence. The Diocese of Coventry continues, even today, to be a lively body. It has been a leading force in the religious arts, in a worldwide ministry of reconciliation, and in ecumenical work.

The Coventry story is told here not as the ideal model for meeting in silence, but as one model. It is a model that calls attention to some of the ways silence and prayer can be integral to the busy life of a large community. It also calls attention to the unforeseen turns in the life of a praying community. The Diocese of Coventry was engaged in waiting for God. Plans and organization were allowed to emerge in response to God's voice, but the action grew out of meditation rather than vice versa.

We can look similarly to the base communities in Latin America where people meet regularly to study and pray together. The experiences of those communities have been equally transformative of their members, and the cause of liberation has been advanced by people willing to listen to the voice of God and one another.

Educational Ministry in the Silence

If meditation is at the center of congregational life, then educational ministry will grow out of that center. Education will be planned to respect and nurture mystery. It will be planned to anticipate and nurture the relationship with God in all of its dimensions.

Three dimensions of the relationship with God will be examined here in particular: the personal/interpersonal relationship, the congregational relationship, and the relationship with God in the world. The first focuses on meeting God through personal and interpersonal relationships; the second, on the congregation's relationship with God *as* a congregation. The last gives attention to meeting God in the world, that is, in voices from different parts of the world, from the poor, from the children, and so forth. These are three dimensions of the same all-encompassing relationship with God.

Dimensions of Relating with God.   The central purpose of educational ministry, when meditation is at the congregation's center, is to foster the relationship with God in all of its dimensions. The three dimensions discussed here can become a way to evaluate what is happening in the congregation's life and to plan for the educational ministry. For example, to what extent does corporate worship or Bible study in your congregation foster the personal/interpersonal relationship with God, the congregation's relationship with God, or the relationship with God in the world?

I have worked now with two classes of seminary students who have used these questions to study four different congregations and make proposals for their educational ministry. Pastors and lay leaders of those congregations responded to the final reports and were amazed at what they learned about themselves. They, of course, had participated in the study, and at the end they contributed insights that amplified the students' reports. More will be said of this in the descriptions that follow.

Personal and Interpersonal Meeting with God.   One role of educational ministry is to foster the personal and interpersonal relationship with God. This is perhaps the most obvious dimension, due in part to the North American valuing of individual persons and of their close relationships (especially family and close friends).

In this dimension, the church recognizes that each person communes with God in a unique way, and that the forms of meditation that enable persons to move into the depths of their own beings are vital to the relationship with God. Important to educational ministry, then, are such practices as: silent times for listening after a story or musical offering; silent times for meditation on Scriptural texts or on a dilemma in society or in one's own life; and question-posing, in which questions of faith are raised not so much for answers as for facing mystery.

Also, the church recognizes that God is mediated to persons through their close relationships. God is incarnate in the parent with child, the sister with brother, the friend with friend, the wife with husband. These relationships can be enriched if people participate together in the various disciplines that have been discussed earlier. It also is important to recognize that these relationships are holy. Not only is the church called to foster healthy relationships but also to foster a sense of the sacred in those relationships. The hope is that people will meet in silence so that they really can listen to one another and appreciate the revelation of God in the other.

In the congregations studied by my class, considerable attention was indeed being given to the personal and interpersonal dimension of relating to God. Pastoral prayers and sermons in worship, pastoral counseling, and prayer and Bible study groups were among the contexts where the personal and interpersonal dimension of spirituality was getting particular attention. The focus, however, tended to be directed more to psychological adjustment and to reaching out to God with prayers of petition. What is being suggested here puts less emphasis on getting immediate results and more emphasis on sensing and relating to God's presence. In this proposal the relationship with God would be allowed to grow in silence, and then that relationship can guide the people in knowing what results to seek.

Congregational Meeting with God. Meeting in silence also requires a sense that the congregation as a whole body relates with God. If educational ministry is to foster that relationship, the congregation needs to begin to see itself as a people, relating to God in the way of the Hebrews who were delivered out of bondage in Egypt as a people.

We are reminded then that worship is not simply a time when the church provides quietness for individuals to talk with God, but a time when the community prays together for God's will. This idea challenges the basic assumption that church life exists for nurturing individuals in their relations with God. If the congregation knows itself to be in relationship with God as a congregation, then it recognizes its call to be silent as a congregation and to engage in the spiritual disciplines as a body.

This, of course, does not mean that every member has to be gathered for every event, but certainly corporate worship and congregational meetings are critical centers for gathering. Worship is especially important, not only because the one congregation is gathered, but also because the connections with the historical and worldwide Christian body are named and symbolized in the liturgy and, especially, in the sacraments.

Worship is the center for the congregation's relating with God as a corporate body connected with the body of Christ.

The congregation's relationship with God can be underlined too in a prayerful approach to the business meetings of the church and in certain churchwide emphases and disciplines that take place in classes, small groups, persons' homes, and so forth. One church launched a study of its mission by beginning several small groups to read and discuss books that raised missional questions for the Christian church. The members of these small groups were then invited to meet in a churchwide conference to discuss their congregation's mission.

Congregations will seek and follow God in various ways. In this book considerable discussion has been offered by David Steward, Donald Miller, and Carl Dudley concerning multiple types or images of the church. The proposals here cut across those various types and images, urging each congregation to take itself seriously as a body relating with God.

My seminary class studied congregations that were faced with major decisions about what directions to take in their ministries. These decisions were being much discussed, and prayer was a regular part of church decision meetings and of worship and prayer meetings. The sense of seeking God's call to the congregation was less evident. Decision-making was taking place in more of an active mode with little silence. God was being called upon, but listening in silence was not a major feature of congregational life.

Meeting God in the World. The third dimension of relating with God is relating with God in the world. This is perhaps the most difficult to hear because the social focus of North American churches often is described in terms such as "social action" or "mission." These activities usually are seen as the *consequences* of relating with God, rather than as the *context* for meeting God.

In this dimension the church recognizes that God is not revealed simply in our own homes and congregations, but also in the people of the world and in the earth itself. Wisdom was offered to Jesus by the Syro-Phoenician woman who reminded him that even the dogs under the table could eat the scraps

(Mark 7:24–30). Likewise, wisdom is offered to us by many people whom we may not expect to do so.

Especially important is listening to the voices of those who have little power, such as the poor and the children. These are the ones who often can help us see our own blindness and see God in a new light. These meetings are not easy, especially since we who have more power usually are talking, and even controlling the meetings. That is why silence is so important—so we can listen for those quiet voices.

Also important is meeting God and others in the social structures themselves. These structures typically are seen as impersonal entities; but the work of feminist, Black, and Latin American liberation theologians has demonstrated repeatedly the way in which social structures are formed by human societies and then shape those societies. They often become the tools of the oppressors to limit the power of the oppressed. If we are to meet God in the world, we need to meet those social structures that are humanizing and speak of God, and we need to meet those that are dehumanizing and speak against God. We need to be careful and critical listeners and not to assume blindly that all communism or all capitalism is automatically of God.

In some of the congregations studied by my seminary class, social action was prominent. In fact, some of those congregations had a long and proud history of action in their communities and in global mission. As one might expect, the sense of serving the world was stronger than the sense of meeting God in the world. Likewise, the active approach to naming and addressing the needs of the world was more prominent than silently meeting God in the world.

Foundational Assumptions for Education

If meditation is at the center of congregational life, then educational ministry will grow out of that center. With this statement I introduced this final section of the chapter on educational ministry in the silence. Now we will turn to some of the foundational assumptions that are inherent in that statement.

First is the assumption that *the most profound meetings with God and others and ourselves take place in silence.* The church, then, needs to provide opportunities for silence and to teach us to make those opportunities for ourselves. Examples of these opportunities were mentioned earlier, and many others can be cited. Members of the Diocese of Coventry began by holding weekly meetings for listening to one another and to God. The base communities in Latin America meet regularly to pray and reflect on their social structures in light of the Gospel. One congregation in this country sponsors a monthly retreat of silence in its church buildings, offering space, a light meal, and resources for prayer and meditation. People come and go through the day as they can.

A *second* assumption is that *God is present in all things, and therefore, we can meet God as we relate with all of creation.* This is not pantheism (God *is* all things) but pan*en*theism (God is *in* all things). Educational ministry needs to help people listen. The problem, of course, is to discern the voice of God amid voices that may not be God's. This problem itself is a reminder that God's presence and call always will be a mystery, never fully heard or understood. But the problem also suggests why we need silence—silence in which the voice of God *can* be heard.

That is why we need to listen for voices other than our own and those of people close to us. That is why we need to listen to the Christian tradition, meeting the corporate memory in silence. Furthermore, that is why study and reflection are included in the disciplines we have discussed. Persons need not only to listen but also to test their hearing in relation to the Christian tradition and the people around the world who need their concern.

This assumption may seem mild and non-threatening, but actually it is a very large challenge. If God is present in all things, then virtually no elements of creation can be ignored. All things, living and not living, are sacred and in need of our care. We cannot, for example, ignore the land; rather, we need to care for it and allow it to teach us as did the Native Americans who went out onto the land to sit and meditate.

Just as challenging is the repeated idea that we should not listen only to those people who are like us. If God is in all things, we need especially to listen for the voice of God in persons different from ourselves. We sometimes can approach this effectively through literature and film, which enable people to cross cultural boundaries. Such books as Alice Walker's *The Color Purple,* Maya Angelou's *Why the Caged Bird Sings,* Thomas Merton's *Seven Story Mountain,* John Neihardt's *Black Elk Speaks,* and Maxine Hong Kingston's *The Woman Warrior* become important to persons who want to cross into another's world and listen for God there.

A *third* and obvious assumption here is that *education takes place in all of the contexts of Christian life.* Those who lead the congregation in educational ministry are challenged to understand, plan for, and work with all parts of the church community. The churches will need to seek some very different leadership structures and styles of planning for educational ministry than those found in most North American congregations today.

Persons concerned with education will need to enter into dialogue with persons planning for worship, mission, general administration, and so forth. The educational leaders will need to seek ways to provide more silent time in the services of worship, in the planning meetings, and in the midst of action. They will need to encourage the congregation to engage more intentionally in listening to one another and to those they serve. For example, a congregation might take time in decision meetings for unprogrammed silence and prayer. They can plan a time for persons to share the issues that are of greatest concern to them, and they can invite people who will be served by a new project to come in and share what they really expect from the church.

A *fourth* assumption is that *spirituality is inherently both personal and social.* Personal and social concerns are not put over against one another, nor does one aspect come first and the other follow. We really cannot speak of spirituality that is not affected by the dynamics in one's personal life and close relationships and, also, by one's social location (such as one's gender, ethnic group, national and regional identity, and so forth).

This assumption is, perhaps, the most startling to the common-sense assumptions of our day. A more common assumption today is that spirituality, or the relationship with God, is a personal matter and that social concerns grow from our personal experiences with God. This idea is being questioned, however. Several contemporary writers on spirituality are recovering a muted strand of the Jewish and Christian traditions that recognizes the social nature of spirituality. Increasing recognition is being given to the fact that our relationship with God is inseparable from our relationship with our culture and the social structures.

This idea is highlighted by Dorothee Soelle and J. B. Libanio who believe one's social position affects one's spirituality and that one's spirituality affects one's participation in the social order.[30] For both of these authors, spirituality requires a critique of one's own social position, as well as a social response to the world. Persons need to be alert to possible distortions in their spiritual intuitions which arise from their own social positions. They also need to seek the spiritual insights of persons in other social positions (such as other social classes and other parts of the world). In other words, the society is recognized as both shaper and recipient of our spirituality. This idea is discussed by Francis Meehan, who calls the phenomenon "social spirituality."[31]

In addition to what these authors are highlighting, the possibility of enhancing the spirituality of an entire community is also being encouraged here. If spirituality is both personal and social, God addresses not only individual persons, but also whole congregations and denominations. The congregation as a whole can spend time in silence (including prayer, study, and reflection) as it seeks to reshape its mission for the future.

A *fifth* assumption about educational ministry in silence is that *the teacher will be part of the meditating community*. Teachers themselves will need to spend time in silence, listening and discerning the movements of God's Spirit. In addition, they will have important roles in naming the presence of God both in the historical tradition and in the midst of the world today. They will have roles in inspiring devotion, teaching people how to meditate and pray, and leading persons in the practice of the disciplines discussed earlier in this chapter. The teacher becomes a spiritual guide, or what I have called elsewhere "a wise companion."[32] The critical importance of receptivity and spiritual formation to leadership in teaching are highlighted also in the essays by Janet Fishburn and Maria Harris elsewhere in this volume.

And finally, a *sixth* assumption about educational ministry is that *educational ministry will move with the Spirit.* This is not a repudiation of careful planning and administration, both of which are very important. But the experience of the Diocese of Coventry may become our experience, especially if we allow the Spirit to bubble up and lead us in some new directions, rather than deciding in advance what the Spirit will do and planning for that to happen. Planning and preparations were very much a part of the life of Coventry, but time was spent first in silence, and some unexpected turns took place. Perhaps if we put meditation at the center of congregational life, we too will come to expect the unexpected.

Several ideas have been briefly offered in this essay to cultivate the art of listening in silence. These can be amplified by other resources that guide persons and communities in their meditative lives.[33]

What is most important, however, is to know the *power* of silence. Many ideas and images are offered throughout this book to guide the congregation in knowing itself and its social context and in knowing what directions it might move in. The challenge of this chapter is to urge the reflective study of these ideas and the seeking after God amid the voices of this book and those in your own situation. The promise is not that you will have perfect hearing or vision but that you will have a deepened sense of reality and of God's presence in it.

Belonging:
A Sacramental
Approach to
Inclusion and Depth
of Commitment

ROBERT L. BROWNING
The Methodist Theological School in Ohio

One of the most troubling issues before the church today
is the matter of what it means to belong to the body of Christ
and the accompanying questions concerning the level of commitment, involvement, and preparation expected of members.
Churches that are inclusive and open sometimes have large
numbers of members on the rolls but only one third of their
members actively participating. Churches that have high standards for membership (in terms of Christian education, giving,
and personal commitment to concrete forms of ministry) often
have much tighter memberships in terms of numbers but a
more intense pattern of participation and engagement in ministry. Denominational leaders, responding to shrinking memberships, are calling for aggressive evangelism programs and
strong Christian education efforts in order to increase mark-
edly the numbers of persons who belong to the church and who
serve with abandon and significance. Internal conflicts are ev-

ident when church leaders seek to agree on the standards for membership and levels of expectation regarding education, liturgical life, and concrete expressions of ministry within and beyond the faith community.

These conflicts can be seen quickly in the current discussions about the sacraments of baptism and communion, and about such rites or rituals as confirmation and ordination. Issues of inclusion and exclusion of infants and children, women and men, formally and informally educated, active and inactive, and believers of particular doctrines and persons whose beliefs are more "in process" are evident in our views and practices. Issues of belonging are resolved in our decisions concerning infant or adult baptism; open or closed communion; the nature of and age for confirmation; and the preparation of persons for various forms of ministry in respect to the ordained, the lay professionals in religious education, music, and other specializations, and consecrated lay ministers (i.e., universal priesthood of all believers).

In this study, I propose to: (1) explore the issue of belonging to the body of Christ in our post-Christendom age; (2) examine the dynamics associated with the rites and sacraments of belonging; (3) present an ecumenical model of sacramentality which has potential for unifying Protestant, Roman Catholic, and Orthodox understandings and practices concerning the sacraments of inclusion and depth of commitment; (4) highlight the educational and liturgical life which uniquely can accompany the sacraments of belonging (baptism, communion, and confirmation) and the sacraments of vocation (consecration of laity for ministry and ordination of clergy).

Belonging to the Body of Christ in a Post-Christendom Society

The issue of who really belongs to the body of Christ has been with us from the beginning. Paul encountered the problem in the early church—some Christians thinking of themselves as belonging to Apollos, or Cephas, or Paul rather than to Christ (1 Cor. 1:12).

One of the most penetrating critiques of what it means to belong to Christ came from the pen of Søren Kierkegaard in his *Attack Upon "Christendom."* Published in 1854 and 1855 at the end of his life, the book identifies the key problems of being a faithful firsthand disciple of Christ in his day. At a time when Christianity was the official religion of the state and when ministers and theologians had rationalized Christian teachings with the values and norms of society, Kierkegaard maintained that it was very difficult to find a genuine Christian who actually knew or radically followed the contemporaneous Christ. This criticism was symbolized for him by the issue of infant baptism which he perceived to be more of a function of the state than of the church. The assumption was that every child should be baptized in order to be an acceptable member of society. Even more scandalous was the practice of confirmation. Here again, this was more a civil ceremony, which every fourteen- or fifteen-year-old went through in order to have proper credentials, than a commitment to be a follower of a Christ who was crucified because he was upsetting the established beliefs about religion. Kierkegaard said that confirmation was a comedy in which the priests of the established church led people in a deception. "Confirmation is in itself far deeper nonsense than infant baptism. . . . The significance of confirmation really is the certificate issued by the priest, without which the boy or girl in question cannot get along at all in this life."[1]

Here we see the crucial issue of belonging to Christ and following Christ truly out of an inward commitment based on self-understanding rather than belonging to Christ because it is acceptable in society. To Kierkegaard, such acceptability and such harmonization of the Christian faith with secular values of success, power, and position can actually distort the Gospel to the point that it is inauthentic and unrecognizable in relation to the picture of Christ given in the New Testament. Kierkegaard questioned infant baptism and confirmation not because they were inauthentic from a biblical or theological perspective, but because they had been distorted.

In the twentieth century, Karl Barth observed the empty forms of infant baptism and confirmation in the state church in Germany and saw how persons could become so deceived as to believe that they belonged both to Christ and to Hitler. The distinctive message of the Christian faith could not be communicated or taught profoundly to persons who had the perception of themselves as members of the body of Christ through infant baptism and confirmation but who did not attend church except for ceremonies such as weddings, funerals, and festivals of the church year. Barth lived in a time when Christendom was assumed to be in place when, in fact, it was clearly crumbling. Barth opted for a strong, committed minority rather than a large, uncommitted majority. Therefore, he searched the Scriptures and reflected theologically upon the essential nature of baptism and confirmation in an attempt to recapture what Kierkegaard sought to distill: the dimensions of an authentic, firsthand Christian discipleship. Barth could not find a defense of infant baptism in the Scriptures or in doctrine. From the standpoint of a doctrine of baptism, infant baptism can hardly be preserved without exegetical and practical artifices and sophisms, the proof to the contrary has yet to be supplied! One wants to preserve it only if one is resolved to do so on grounds which live outside the biblical passages on baptism and outside the thing itself.[2]

Barth started a movement which coincided with the recognition that we are in a post-Christendom age. What he was after was a movement toward a healthy church that can celebrate Christ-centered values and commitments in a society given to dehumanizing and materialistic values. From biblical, theological, and sociological perspectives, Barth saw the need for a preaching and teaching that brought persons to a radical decision to die to the values of the society and to rise again with Christ. The most powerful symbol for this phenomenon to him was adult baptism. He concluded that what is needed is simple:

> Instead of the present infant baptism, a baptism which on the part of the baptized is a responsible act. If it is to be natural,

the candidate, instead of being a passive object of baptism, must become once more the free partner of Jesus Christ, that is, freely deciding, freely confessing, declaring on his (sic) part his willingness and readiness.[3]

While others, such as Oscar Cullmann,[4] provided biblical and theological evidence for authentic infant baptism, there was a ground swell for a restoration of the power of adult initiation, particularly and strangely by the Roman Catholic community. I say strangely, because we normally associate infant baptism with the Roman Catholic Church and we associate the concept of belonging to the body of Christ *because* of infant baptism with the Roman Catholic Church. In Protestantism, infant baptism often made the child a "preparatory member" whose full membership would be achieved through Christian education and confirmation. Barth correctly criticized this practice as promoting two "half sacraments." Recent studies of the catechumenate (the process of instruction in the Christian faith) of the second to fifth centuries, together with the realities existing in a post-Christendom environment, have prompted the Roman Catholic Church to inaugurate the Rite of Christian Initiation of Adults. The candidate is brought into an agreement, through sensitive evangelistic ministry, to become a catechumen, a hearer and learner of the way, for a period of from one to three years of Christian education, liturgical participation, and ethical reflection. The catechumenate culminates in the unified initiation of adult baptism, often by immersion, confirmation through the laying on of hands, and the eucharist.[5] Some Catholic theologians are so convinced that adult initiation is superior that they are recommending the enrollment of children as catechumens, with the climax of their preparation for authentic Christian ministries to take place in adult baptism.[6] Here we see infants and children *belonging* in terms of acceptance, love, and nurture but *not belonging* in the full sense of being engrafted into the body of Christ through infant baptism.

Another dynamic in a post-Christendom environment has to do with standards for belonging to the church. For instance, various churches have written norms for membership.

Should such statements indicate to parents that their children can be baptized as infants only if the parents themselves are active members who will welcome counseling and education concerning the meaning of baptism and agree to accept responsibility for nurturing their children in the Christian faith? Moreover, should these parents be expected to express their faith in concrete forms of ministry through their family, work, and community relationships? Or, should the concept of the universal priesthood of all believers be taken so seriously that only persons can belong to the faith community who: (1) prepare themselves intellectually and spiritually for Christian ministry through their occupations or volunteer structures, (2) publicly affirm their decision, and (3) are ordained or consecrated as non-professional ministers? The Church of the Saviour in Washington, D.C. is the primary model for a church with such high standards. All members study the nature of ministry; explore their faith seriously over several years in terms of biblical, theological, and ethical foundations; and involve themselves in concrete forms of giving of their talents and resources.Finally, they are ordained as "lay" ministers. The ordaining minister says:

> "Your work and your worship are intimately interwoven. In fact, they are not separate at all. Your work grows out of your worship and your worship grows out of your work. (Name), do you come today to acknowledge that the place where you work is as holy as the place where you worship?"
> "I do." (Kneels)
> "Enabled by Christ's love for me, I shall endeavor to make each day's work a sacrament."[7]

When such standards are put in operation, the number of people who prepare themselves for ordination as non-professional ministers is predictably more manageable. The number of people who participate in various forms of ministry and who attend worship, retreats, the coffee house, and study and action groups, however, is much larger than the membership.

Another trend which reflects an unwritten but powerful set of standards or expectations was to be seen in the patterns of several churches, especially during the "counter-culture" period, which sought to have an effect on the social problems of our time. An ethos (that is, a context of unique characteristics and tone) developed in such churches, so that to belong meant that you would be involved in bringing righteousness and love to earth around the issues of racial, sexual, and social justice.

Such churches again developed standards of participation in study, celebration, and service which were rather demanding. Much mutual ministry and support was needed. Smaller task groups and ministering units were essential to planning and organizing corporate forms of ministry and witness. One such congregation was Casa View United Methodist Church in Dallas, Texas. The life of Casa View was depicted in a film, "Four Cozy Walls," and in a book (by Wilfred Bailey, and his co-author and neighbor, William McElvaney) about Casa View and several similar churches. The book, *Christ's Suburban Body* (Nashville: Abingdon Press, 1970), described the rising expectations along with the excitement and frustration which tended to accompany such commendable efforts. Again, the membership becomes trimmer and more aware of the levels of commitment and involvement expected. More recently, this trend has been found among leftist evangelical churches—both predominantly white and Black. Richard Quebedeaux describes this movement well in his book, *The Worldly Evangelicals* (San Francisco: Harper and Row, 1979).

A Sacramental Model of Belonging

My colleague, Roy Reed, and I have been working for several years on an ecumenical sacramental model which has universal dimensions of acceptance and affirmation of the total human family while, at the same time, makes possible a clearer vision of what it means to *be* the body of Christ in the world. This work continues, and came to fruition in a recent book, *The Sacraments in Religious Education and Liturgy: An Ecumenical Model* (Birmingham, AL: The Religious Education Press, 1985). In this work we develop a picture of the quiet revolution in sacramental understanding and practice which has taken place over the past several years, especially since

Vatican II. In a very abbreviated form, I will delineate the
major points in this revolution—a promising movement in relation to which Reed and I developed our own model of sacramentality and its meaning for human and faith development
throughout the life cycle from birth to death. After presenting
this encouraging picture of theological consensus between Roman Catholic, Protestant, and Orthodox thinkers, I shall outline the positions Reed and I have taken in respect to the
particular sacraments; and then, I shall draw out the meaning
of these views for the issue of belonging, along with the educational and liturgical life implied. The major points of this
ecumenical model are:

1. All of life is sacred. Life itself is holy because of God's
creative presence in the past, present, and future. Alexander
Schmemann, the brilliant Orthodox theologian, said it well
when he celebrated the fact that God created and continues to
create out of love and goodness. The whole cosmos is visible
evidence of God's goodness. We are those who receive God's
ongoing gifts as priests, standing in the center of the world.
We both receive and bless God's sacred gifts and offer them to
others in God's name. In doing so we transform ordinary life
into eucharist, into communion with God. We all belong to God
as a primary gift. Particular sacraments, such as infant baptism, do not give the child God's love which he or she would
not have without baptism. The sacrament of baptism points to
and participates in that divine love which is given. The sacrament participates in God's extension and focusing of love by
bringing the child into the body of Christ, a community committed to the extension of God's love and goodness in the world.
Fundamentally, all persons and nature belong to God and are
recipients of God's cosmic sacrament.[8] No human being or institution has the power to cut off any one of God's family from
this primary and sacred gift of acceptance and love.

*2. All persons (of every race, religion, sex, and condition)
are sacred and potential channels of grace and truth.* The ecumenical consensus is emphasizing the essential truth captured
by Paul Tillich in one of his final lectures when he said:

> The universal religious basis is the experience of the Holy within
> the finite. Universally in everything finite and particular, or in
> this and that finite, the Holy appears in a special way. I could
> call this the sacramental basis of all religions—the Holy here
> and now which can be seen, heard, dealt with, in spite of its
> mysterious character. We still have remnants of this in the
> highest religions, in their sacraments, and I believe that without
> it, a religious group would become an association of moral clubs,
> as much of Protestantism is because it has lost the sacramental
> basis.[9]

Again, we see God's presence in life with no sacred-
secular split. Essentially all of us and all of creation belong to
God and are avenues of grace and love—of holiness—to one
another.

3. *God's grace, therefore, is built into the very fabric of
life itself.* A commonly held view of the sacraments is inadequate. It goes this way: the sacraments are rites which the
church uses to bring God's grace to persons who otherwise are
without ongoing communion with the divine. The quiet revolution in sacramental thinking is in tune with Karl Rahner's
view when he says that the sacraments point not just to *things*
through which the holy is revealed. Rather, he discerns that
all of nature and history reveal the cosmic grace of God to
which the particular sacraments are witnesses and expressions.
Rahner believes that God's grace is active at all times, bringing
wholeness and salvation at the roots of human life. God's grace
permeates the world.

> The world is constantly and ceaselessly possessed by grace from
> its innermost roots, from the innermost center of the spiritual
> subject. It is constantly and ceaselessly sustained and moved
> by God's self-bestowal even prior to the question (admittedly
> always crucial) of how creaturely freedom reacts to this
> "engracing."[10]

Translated, this means that all of us belong to God and are in
touch with God's grace at the very core of our lives, but we
often do not perceive that God's love is present nor do we open
ourselves to receive and give.

4. The particular sacraments are important. They point to and help us participate in God's grace, already profoundly present. The quiet revolution in sacramental understanding and practice involves a movement *away from* seeing the sacraments as acts by which the church gives or withholds grace in some substantialistic way (that is, as if sacraments involve real substance rather than relationships of love and trust) *toward* seeing the sacraments as action parables which help us recognize, celebrate, and extend the grace of God already present. The grace and love of God are discovered rationally in terms of our deepest human need for belonging to the universe, to God, to one another, to the past, present, and the future.[11]

5. God's grace and love are especially revealed—made visible—in Christ, the primordial sacrament. God's cosmic grace is made visible in many ways (in this sense, there are many sacraments) but supremely in Jesus Christ. The word "sacrament" is not to be found in the New Testament. The word *sacramentum* is a translation of the word *mysterion,* which is found in the New Testament. The word *mysterion* refers to the ineffable, secret purposes God revealed and worked out in the world through the mission of Jesus, the Christ. "To you has been given the secrets (*mysterion*) of the kingdom of God," Jesus told the disciples (Mark 4:10–12; Matt. 13:10–13; Luke 8:9–10). In Christ the grace and love of God burst forth and were incarnate as a presence. The primordial sacrament of God's grace is not an abstraction but an embodied and enacted word given to *you.* "To you has been given the mysterion." God's grace is revealed in Christ in community, through relationships of trust and love. God's nature is profoundly hidden in mystery, but in Christ that mystery was revealed, identified, responded to in faith, enjoyed, and celebrated.

6. The church is the sacrament of Christ in the world. The church is the sacrament of Christ, making visible Christ's ministries of love and justice in all of the arenas of life. Edward Schillebeeckx helpfully maintains that what God's grace has already begun to do in the lives of all persons "becomes an

epiphany in the Church, in other words, completely visible."
The church, like Christ, is a primordial sacrament of salvation
for all humankind, a salvation "which is, moreover, not a mo-
nopoly of the Church, but which, on the basis of redemption
by the Lord, who died and rose again ... is already in fact
actively present in the whole world."[12] The church, through
each member of the body of Christ and also corporately, incarnates God's grace and love, helping all people recognize that
all of life is holy and God's spirit is present to create, sustain,
heal, and renew—if we are open, responsive, and responsible.

7. *The historic sacraments make visible concretely the
sacredness of all of life.* This is revealed by Christ, celebrated
and extended by the church, and related existentially to the
major events and stages of life from birth to death. God communicates with us in many ways. Yet, the historic sacraments
especially point to and participate in the mystery which is God,
and come out of a common history of meaning. They are symbolic, action parables to demonstrate and visualize in graphic
form the story of God's profound love for each of us. They say
"You belong to the holy family—no matter what happens to
you!" The sacraments, while anchored in *mysterion,* are *sacramentum* (i.e., the church's strategy for communicating this story
in the action parables of baptizing with water, breaking bread
and drinking wine, kneeling in prayer, touching and anointing,
confirming and commissioning, along with a host of other signs
and words which reinforce and illustrate the faith stories). The
sacraments, therefore, are grounded biblically in relation to
Christ's ministry, but they also are grounded in the church's
historic expressions of the extension of that ministry. Moreover,
hopefully, the ecumenical church is at a place where it can be
open to a model of sacramentality which employs, at least, the
seven sacraments plus the largely ignored sacrament clearly
initiated by Christ, footwashing, the sacrament of servanthood.
While a discussion of the biblical and theological rationale for
this wider view is crucial, especially for Protestants, it cannot
be undertaken in this chapter. The issues are important and
are analyzed much more fully in our recent publication.[13] The

discussion of belonging, following a sacramental model, will assume the theological and biblical integrity of this wider, and hopefully, deeper view of the nature of sacrament.

The Human Need for Belonging

The human situation is one in which the individual is continually seeking to be genuinely free and self-motivated, as well as to be in relationships of trust, love, and creative exchange with others and with *the other,* either the true center and source of life or some substitute reality such as possessions or power. This profound need both for independence and belonging can be seen in every anthropological study and in all psychological analyses in one form or another. Social anthropologists have recognized the power of rituals, in varying cultures, to communicate these needs—rituals of greeting, naming, feeding, including, excluding, freeing, controlling, kneeling, praying, touching, and not-touching (taboos). These rituals are profoundly religious in that they participate in the natural flow of God's communication, communion, and community with one another and with the source of all of life. As humans we use not only ritual acts but stories, myths, legends, and laws to convey the visions we have concerning the ultimate meaning of life.

Louis Bouyer's research in the history of religion and in anthropology caused him to conclude that such natural rites are the primary stuff of religions and that these rites are the essential *sacraments* on which all later *sacramentalia* (such as the two of the Protestants or the seven of the Roman Catholics and the Orthodox) are based. He saw prayer as the primary human response to the mysteries of life; then, he believed the natural rituals of eating, washing, and others developed. Myths and stories grew up in relation to the rituals not to explain them so much as to expand them imaginatively. The myths or stories were symbolic of the transcendence already present in the rite.[14] These rituals and stories are the primordial creations of people in their desire to transcend their separateness and aloneness and to find community (or belonging) and communion with others and with the divine.

Socio-psychological studies such as Erik Erikson's analysis of the stages of ritualization in the human life cycle, and James Fowler's faith development studies, reveal a similar conclusion. From birth on people have profound needs for trust relationships in which inclusion and mutuality are experienced at deep psychological and spiritual levels. Erikson sees the first year of life as one in which the child not only experiences trust (and thereby develops a sense of hope) but also a sense of the *numinous,* "an indwelling force or quality which animates or guides—evoking awe or reverence." This sense of the numinous is communicated by the parent(s) through such rituals as feeding, greeting, elimination, dressing, and undressing. The loving and affirming eyes and smile of the parent are akin to the warm presence later to be seen in the "face" of God and become the ground not only for a separateness transcended and a distinctiveness confirmed, in human terms, but also the seedbed for the higher forms of religious ritual such as the sacraments.[15]

Fowler's faith development studies also affirm the individual's profound need for separateness transcended but distinctiveness affirmed. At each of the stages of faith development he sees the power of rituals of inclusion and freedom so that the person can grow toward a universal and wide-ranging faith (which focuses on the fact that every creature belongs to the family of God) while always growing honestly at the cognitive, affective, moral, and spiritual levels at each of the stages along the way.[16]

While the seven classic sacraments (plus footwashing) can be related with integrity to the stages of ritualization and to the stages of faith in terms of the church's religious education and liturgical life,[17] I shall limit myself to discussing the primary sacraments of belonging: baptism, communion (the eucharist), confirmation, and ordination of clergy and consecration of laity for ministry. I shall highlight the power of these sacramental experiences to educate us at a deep level concerning the vision we communicate; that is, our images of what it means to belong to Christ's body and to extend that acceptance and sense of belonging to others in concrete expressions of sacramental ministry.

The Sacraments of Belonging and Their Educational and Liturgical Power

It is a somewhat pragmatic rationale for specifying baptism, eucharist, confirmation, and ordination or consecration, as sacraments of belonging and excluding the sacraments of reconciliation (penance), healing and wholeness (unction), and marriage. Certainly, reconciliation has to do significantly with getting back into a relationship with others and God through honest confession, forgiveness, and restoration. Certainly, the sacraments of healing and wholeness in life and death (healing, final liturgical rites for the dying, and the funeral itself) have to do with our relationships with ourselves, others, and God. Finally, marriage is basically a matter of to whom we belong in love and trust. Yet, not everyone marries, and the issue of belonging is as fundamental for those who do not as it is for those who do.[18] All of the sacraments obviously are concerned with belonging, but the four I have chosen to explore in more depth have to do with what it means to belong to the body of Christ and what our expectations and standards are for being educated and prepared spiritually to be in sacramental ministries in the world.

Briefly, let us highlight a more expansive set of expectations for religious education, liturgical, and service life which can develop in relation to the sacramental model already described and in relation to the particular sacraments of belonging which we have chosen to explore. Moreover, the following approach has the potential of avoiding, in most respects, the problem of elitism associated with more demanding standards of membership while, at the same time, affirming patterns of non-manipulative evangelism and growth.

The Unified Sacraments of Initiation
(Baptism, Confirmation, and Eucharist)

Perhaps the most stimulating development in the theology of initiation is the movement toward a unified initiation on the part of Protestants and Roman Catholics. The Orthodox already have such a unified sacramental pattern in their baptism of infants by immersion, followed by confirmation, and first eucharist. The baptized Orthodox infant fully *belongs* to the body of Christ. Geoffrey Wainwright's study of the history of the sacraments of initiation noted that the classic conflicts concerning baptism (infant or adult), confirmation (when it should take place and its essential meaning) and communion (open or closed, before or after confirmation or baptism) could be resolved only by affirming the unification of initiation, but not necessarily by following the Orthodox pattern. The choice would be between: (1) bringing the other events (confirmation and communion) into infancy to join baptism; and (2) postponing baptism until it could once more hold the other events together as a whole.[19] For theological reasons, but especially because of the problems the church has of getting high personal commitment in a post-Christendom age, Wainwright opted for a modified, open baptist approach which recognized the validity of infant baptism but affirmed the unified initiation of persons who had reached the age of discretion and had been prepared educationally and liturgically for the decision to become full members of the body of Christ in ministry. Wainwright saw the need for rites of belonging, such as enrollment of children as catechumens, or dedication, or laying-on-of-hands ceremonies. He also had an open stance concerning children and others coming to the communion table before baptism.

The position my colleague and I take is the following: (1) the initiation of the infants of people *within* the faith community through infant baptism, confirmation (the laying on of hands symbolizing the presence of the Holy Spirit), and communion (symbolizing full engrafting of the child into the body of Christ); and (2) the initiation of those *beyond* the faith community who respond to the good news of the Gospel as adults through a similar unified initiation which focuses on non-manipulative evangelism, strong Christian education, ethical reflection, and richness of liturgical life and spiritual disciplines, culminating in adult baptism, confirmation, and eucharist.

Religious Education and Liturgical Life Related to Infant Baptism. Infant baptism within a unified initiation makes possible a raising of expectations for what it means to belong to the body of Christ not only for the total faith community but especially for parents and sponsors, and for the child as well. The image which is most authentic for the child is that he or she is brought into the ministering body of Christ, into the experience of full acceptance, love, and trust. Of course, the child belongs to the family of God, is in touch with God's grace and love without baptism. However, to be engrafted into the body of Christ is to be in relation to those who see themselves as sacraments of Christ, as those who are *aware* of God's grace and love in the very fabric of life, made known in Christ and extended in the church. Moreover, through baptism, confirmation, and communion the child experiences the primordial or original "ordination" into the ministering community, into the universal priesthood. The child soon ministers unto the whole body in refreshing and unique ways, quite different from ministries of adults, in their spontaneity and playfulness.

The entire congregation should be involved in the unified sacramental celebration at the points of preaching and liturgy which relates the whole congregation to the meaning of baptism into the ministering community. Parents can be counseled and educated concerning the meaning of the unified initiation, into the meaning of sacramental life, into the nature and stages of ritualization and the nature and stages of faith. This education can bring parents to higher commitment to the universal priesthood, especially to the concept of the priesthood of parenthood in which they join other parents in providing depth of Christian nurture and liturgical life in the family, and commit themselves to being agents of change and growth throughout the stages of development for themselves and for their children. The beginning of patterns of spiritual growth, training in the power of personal meditation and prayer, innovations in the use of liturgical resources, following the Christian year and the great Christian festivals—all can be focused on family life which is deep but turned out toward the wider world in inclusive rather than exclusive ways.[20]

Religious Education and Liturgy Related to Adult Baptism. Perhaps the most surprising development is the movement toward adult baptism, using the unified approach, to be found within Roman Catholicism and within several Protestant groups previously committed to infant baptism. Baptists, Disciples of Christ, and others have preferred adult baptism for many years, of course. Even in such churches, the meaning of the sacrament is being reviewed in relation to the standards and expectations deemed essential in our present environment (post-Christendom in the sense that Christianity is now of shrinking influence on the world scene and with the presence of aggressive advocates of other world religions becoming social and political factors with which to contend; or post-Christendom in the sense that smaller, highly committed Christian communities are valued as refuges from society or stimuli to creative forms of witness and ministry in a hurting world).

As was stated earlier, the most imaginative view of adult baptism has come from Roman Catholic studies concerning the unified initiation for adults.[21] These studies and the decision of the Second Vatican Council have resulted in a new rite of adult initiation, built upon the historical catechumenate model.[22] Many Roman Catholic churches are seeking to penetrate the secular community in fresh patterns of evangelism which involve "learners of the way" in one-to-three-year programs with four phases of religious education, liturgical and spiritual development, and ethical decision-making. This program calls candidates to die to secular values and rise with Christ in the new life of faith, climaxing in an Easter Vigil, baptism, confirmation, and communion—often employing immersion as the symbol of dying and rising with Christ.

The four phases include: (1) The *precatechumenate*—where members and clergy form parish teams for outreach to inquirers, through visitation, announcements, radio and television pieces, and dialogue in a non-manipulative way with those who respond. It is hoped that the inquirers will decide to become catechumens and to celebrate this decision in the congregation through the Rite of Becoming Catechumens. (2) The *catechumenate*—where the learners become members of catechetical classes, participate in the congregation's life, receive love, counsel, and acceptance from sponsors, and explore the beliefs of the church in relation to their own honest questions and concerns. Finally, after a decision to prepare for full initiation, they are included in the Rite of Election and are enrolled as catechumens preparing for baptism, confirmation, and communion. (3) The *Lenten period of illumination*—during these weeks the candidate is assigned a spiritual director with whom he or she prepares carefully for initiation on Easter. Religious education continues as the candidate is prepared to understand the sacraments, especially the nature of baptism, laying on of hands in confirmation, and the eucharist. This period also involves clear renunciation of evil patterns of life, personally and corporately expressed, and a decision to surrender to Christ's life of love and justice. This period is fulfilled in baptism, confirmation, and eucharist on Easter. While the candidate has felt included and loved all along, the final initiation brings both a sense of profound belonging to the body of Christ and clear commitment to become a member of the people of God in ministry. (4) The *period of mystogogia*—this period, ending with Pentecost, is a joyous time of parties and enjoyment of the new relationships in Christ, coupled with reflections on the deeper meaning of the Gospel through eucharistic celebrations and preaching. The primary result is a series of decisions about specific forms of ministry to be embraced by the new member of the Body.

Variations on the above outline are described in several fine books concerning specific approaches of particular congregations.[23] Increasingly, Protestant communities are seeking to raise expectations concerning the meaning of membership in the body of Christ and tying these higher standards to baptism. Such communities are learning from their Roman Catholic neighbors.

It should be noted that Reed and I have affirmed the potential of the catechumenate approach but that we see it as a pattern for those primarily beyond the faith community; and, we believe that adult baptism is in itself a form of evangelism. Moreover, we believe that the eucharist should be open at all times and is itself a way of responding to persons' need to belong to God and to others, by responding to Christ's invitation to participate in the breaking of the bread and drinking the cup, symbolizing His real presence among us.

Confirmation—a Repeatable Sacrament Related to the Need for Recommitment at the Points of New Self-Understanding

One of the major difficulties about belonging has to do with the integrity of our beliefs and actions as the experiences of life cause us to question previous formulations of belief or previous behaviors. The studies concerning the stages of faith development, while still "in process," imply that normal growth in faith will, in fact, cause us to question previous expressions and forms of faith. Moreover, faith itself is being seen to be our most basic and fundamental stance in life, involving our deepest values, attitudes, and actions. What we *do* reveals our actual faith. Our behavior reveals our commitments and values more than what we say we believe. Faith and beliefs are different, although related to one another.

If, in fact, there are seven stages of potential growth in faith, as Fowler maintains, confirmation should be repeatable in order for us to reassess our beliefs and celebrate new decisions as we grow from stage to stage. The most common time for confirmation (in churches which employ this form of individual response and affirmation of the Christian faith) is early adolescence. Confirmation education programs often include one to three years of religious education focused on the nature of the church and authentic commitment to the beliefs and practices of the church universal and the particular congregation the adolescent is "joining." Fowler's study indicates that adolescents need this period of reflection and decision-making, but that what they do is to affirm a Synthetic-Conventional faith appropriate for and important to a seventh, eighth, or ninth grader. Soon thereafter, the youth grows to the point of needing to question this helpful, but somewhat conventional, faith and to move to an Individuative-Reflective faith in which he or she is able to question the Christian faith as a system in relation to all of the values piling into the consciousness of the young adult. The church's ministry should affirm this growth and provide clear ways for it to happen, rather than appear to be perplexed and disappointed when older youth and young adults start the process. Moreover, we should affirm ways for the individual to internalize new commitments and celebrate publicly new affirmations. In short, confirmation should be a repeatable experience. Some have called this sacramental celebration baptismal renewal.[24] What is needed is religious education and liturgical life which are related with integrity to the faith pilgrimages of individuals from one stage of life to another, from one life situation to another, so that the individual can feel that he or she belongs to the body of Christ honestly in relation to new challenges to belief and new opportunities for ministry. This should include attention to new dynamics in one's life associated with identity changes in middle or older adulthood. For instance, there is great potential in educational and liturgical life related to retirement. Confirmation as a repeatable sacrament can help older persons prepare for creative ministries, drawing upon their unique talents and focusing their time and energies in ways which meet genuine needs in society and also fulfill real need for self-affirmation on the part of those who serve.

The theological rationale for confirmation to be included in the unified initiation, and also to be a repeatable sacrament, is well discussed in several studies, especially by Max Thurian in his classic, *Consecration of the Layman* (Baltimore: Helicon,

1963). The history of how confirmation became a separate sacrament from baptism and eucharist is well documented by
J. D. C. Fisher in *Confirmation, Then and Now* (London: Alciun
Club, SPCK, 1978). Confirmation resources for youth and adults,
published by various denominations, are sometimes helpfully
written and can be employed when they are integrated into a
unified approach and extended to apply to persons at various
stages of faith development instead of only to one assumed
period of the life cycle. New resources also are needed urgently.
Those who embrace adult baptism are becoming interested in
finding ways for adults to reaffirm their faith as they question
and grow after baptism.

The Eucharist—Christ's Open Table: All Who Respond to God's Love in Christ Belong at the Table

Jesus projects an image of a messianic banquet which
combines the depth of his self-giving with the joy of being
included, with food and drink enough for all. In Luke 14:7–24,
Jesus tells two parables about banquets. One has to do with
who will sit where and who will have the place of honor. The
point is clear: those who exalt themselves will be humbled and
those who humble themselves will be exalted. The second par-
able is about whom to invite to the table. Jesus turns things
upside down by saying that we should not invite neighbors,
friends, or those who will repay us, but the poor, maimed, lame,
and blind who cannot repay us. In Luke 12:35–37, Jesus projects an image of the table which is even more up-setting. The
master will return home from the marriage feast and will reward those who are awake, expecting their master, by serving
them at table. Those who will be at the table will surprise us,
and we will be even more surprised by the fact that Jesus will
be both the host and the one who serves. The image in Revelation 3:20 captures the central truth about who belongs at the
table: "Behold, I stand at the door and knock; if any hear my
voice and open the door, I will come in to [them] and eat with
[them] and [they] with me."

The emphasis on eschatology (that is, on visions of last
or final things) has resulted in an understanding of the eucha-

rist as the table of Christ's reign and that this holy meal is available to all persons without a single condition, not even baptism. Geoffrey Wainwright agrees with J. C. Hoekendijk that it is impossible to lock up Christ's coming kingdom in the church. Wainwright sees the eucharist as Christ's sacrament and as a vehicle of His presence in the world. "In the light of this eschatological purpose, no obstacle of ecclesiastical discipline dependent on a sinful state of Christian disunity must be allowed to block the Lord's invitation."[25]

This position does not mean "cheap grace." It does mean that the table is open to all within the faith community whether baptized or not, and to all beyond the community. It is a table through which the gospel of God's grace to all people is communicated and celebrated. The faith community, of course, has a great responsibility to nurture and care for those who respond. This means careful counseling and education concerning the meaning of such response and the enabling of persons to move toward an act of informed commitment, symbolized by baptism.

Religious educators and liturgical leaders, such as John Westerhoff and William Willimon, see the eucharist as the center of Christian nurture. The service of Word and table is a central communicator of the nature of the life of faith. The liturgy is crucial for education. The central faith story is repeated and related to the themes of the Christian year and to the important issues of life. All learning can be integrated in lectionary readings which ground biblically systematic study in groups, family education, spiritual life, preaching, and sacramental celebrations.[26]

Communion is an ongoing sacrament of renewal and commitment. Its very openness, however, points to the need for continuing exploration of what the gospel really is, who should be seen as members of the family of God, and what the realities are behind the various symbols and codes we use in different traditions and faith communities. These latter concerns are central matters for religious education. There must be an integration of religious education and liturgy without destroying the creative tension needed between these two aspects of ministry.

This means religious education, centered in a sacramental understanding, should help children, youth, and adults become progressively aware of the deeper theological questions implied in open communion, and of the questions of truth and justice which are implied in the way we celebrate the sacred meal. For instance, who is included in celebrating and serving the meal as well as who is invited? Who belongs as celebrants— the ordained only, the ordained with prepared lay ministers, lay ministers alone, men only, women only, men and women? Should children be involved in serving other members of the church family and beyond? Those questions are answered differently in varying denominations and faith groups. No adequate religious education can afford to avoid those questions and still find answers which respect the inclusiveness of the gospel while also facing important issues concerning Word, sacrament, and especially, order. In other words, our conception of the ordination of clergy and the nature and roles of lay ministry may be the most fundamental matter in respect to who really belongs.

The Sacraments of Vocation: The Ordination of Clergy and the Consecration of Laity for Concrete Ministries

The universal priesthood of all believers is quietly but powerfully awakening from its sleep in Roman Catholic and Orthodox as well as Protestant views of ministry. For some time, leaders have been calling for a more inclusive understanding of the sacramental nature of ministry. James White has suggested that a new sacrament of vocation is required in order to raise our expectations concerning the preparation and commitment needed by both lay persons in ministry and the ordained.[27] Thanks to the creative work of Max Thurian of the Taizé Community in France, the concept of the consecration of laity for concrete forms of ministry has emerged as a sacramental rite which complements the ordination of clergy, so that all members of the body of Christ have high expectations for belonging to the ministering community. Thurian sees baptism as the ordination of all Christians for ministry, with consecration of the laity as a strengthening and focusing of ministry in concrete ways and the ordination of clergy as a focusing of ministry in relation to the needs of the congregation for Word, sacrament, and order (or unity, as he prefers to describe it). Thurian believes that consecration to the priesthood is the basic meaning of baptism, but that the laying on of hands can be repeated any time one's self-understanding of ministry becomes more specific or is modified.

> There is no theological objection to keeping the imposition of hands, consecrating to a service, from being repeatedly given with different intentions on the part of the church . . . to confer the diverse gifts of the Holy Spirit; at baptism in the spirit, at confirmation, at the ordination of a deacon, a pastor, a bishop . . . each time with a different intention on the part of the church, in view of a different situation or different service in the church.[28]

The Reformation is unfinished. The universal priesthood is a concept which can be realized in a fresh way in our time. We have not had a liturgical, or sacramental, public celebration to symbolize the commitment of lay persons to be in concrete forms of ministry; nor have we had specific religious education aimed at preparing persons for ministry through their occupations or particular forms of volunteer service. Consequently, our low expectations have been realized. It has been a self-fulfilling prophecy for lay Christians. Likewise, because of an inadequate understanding of the relation of ordained ministry to general ministry (or of clergy to laity), clergy sometimes have cut themselves off from the ministry of the whole people. By embracing the sacraments of vocation (the ordination of clergy and the consecration of laity for ministry), we can genuinely include all members of the body of Christ.

The differences between clergy and lay ministers will relate to the various offices they fill within the faith community. Each needs a high sense of calling to particular forms of ministry. The church needs strong, imaginative, highly committed clergy to proclaim and interpret the Word, to be central figures in leading the whole church in sacramental life, in taking agreed upon responsibility for the organization and administration of the ministering community. Consecrated lay ministers likewise are concerned to participate and grow in their understanding of the gospel and in their ability to be interpreters and witnesses in their contexts of church, family, work, community, and leisure. They also can be deeply involved in sacramental life and in liturgical and educational experiences which correlate with their personal and corporate needs. They should be, and are, crucial to the matters of organization and administration. Beyond that, lay persons are consecrated to ministries of love, justice, and service. Some consecrated lay ministers are full-time members of the ministering team (such as religious educators, church musicians, church and community ministers, and other specialists). All members of the body of Christ can and should have the opportunity to be consecrated for particular expressions of ministry, after education and counseling, related clearly to their self-understanding and perceived talents and to the discerned needs in the world.

The issue is to avoid the phenomenon of first and second class members of the body of Christ. In churches which have raised their standards of commitment and preparation for the ministry of all members, the tendency has been to develop a tightly knit, highly involved group which is prepared and publicly ordained or consecrated along with many others who volunteer, to work with this committed group but who do not belong to the church as such. As noted above, this pattern has been seen in the Church of the Saviour in Washington, D.C. and in other communities of faith with similar goals.

The key issue is for the individual to be able to come to a "conflict-free" decision concerning how his or her sense of Christian vocation can find expression in a particular occupation or voluntary service. The latter should, of course, affirm the commitment of mothers and fathers to the ministries of parenthood in interaction with varying occupational and community involvements. Erik Erikson says that each person needs to find a great fidelity, someone or something to which he or she can be faithful. This fidelity is related to the development of a world view or ideology which has the power to tie the loose ends of ego formation together and to propel the self into the future with some consistency. By making public this world view, the individual is given needed affirmation and support in his or her identity. In finding this "conflict-free, habitual use of a dominant faculty to be elaborated in an occupation" the person can be strengthened not only by the companionship it provides but also by the feedback received and by the symbols and traditions associated with the occupation.[29] I am proposing that both ordained clergy and consecrated lay ministers need this same "conflict-free" self-understanding and need to be supported by the faith community which can confirm and commission them to perform the particular ministries implied. This process allows individuals to find ego resolutions through corporate agreements concerning who each person is and who we are together and what each believes in integrity. It makes possible educational preparation which is much stronger biblically, theologically, and historically, in terms of human and faith development, and in relation to the personal and corporate needs—for both clergy and lay ministers. Lay theological education should not be a mini-seminary course but should have contextual elements which bring depth and focus. The public celebration of these ministries can provide richness of imagery and specificity concerning expressions of ministry in government, business, labor, education, science and technology, law, or in various volunteer ministries within and beyond the church family.

To move in the direction of expecting all members to belong to the ministering community and to have several options for channeling these ministries through the sacraments of ordination or consecration is to embrace a vision of the church that is both demanding and freeing. If hopes are realized, we can know that we belong to God and one another in our successes and in our failures, in our joyous sharing of the fruits of the spirit, and in our desire to fulfill our unique destinies and to celebrate our life together.

In conclusion, what is being proposed is an understanding of sacramentality that includes all persons as active participants in God's grace in the very nature of things, and that includes all persons (not just the clergy or formally ordained) in ministry in terms of their self-understanding. A sacramental approach to belonging helps raise expectations for what it means to be a part of the universal priesthood without indirectly developing first and second class citizens in the body of Christ. The unified sacrament of initiation (baptism, confirmation, and communion) "ordains" all Christians into the universal priesthood; the eucharist sustains and strengthens persons of every status and condition for ministry; confirmation, as a repeatable sacrament, makes possible education and renewed commitment at various stages of personal self-understanding and growth; and, the sacraments of vocation, ordination of clergy and consecration of laity, encourage persons to focus their ministries through their sense of Christian vocation and, more particularly, through their decisions concerning occupation and voluntary expressions of ministry. Each person is supported and loved within the ministering community while, at the same time, challenged to grow in understanding and commitment to the faith in relation to the concrete personal and social issues of life.

While the church as a community will be quite active in nurturing and challenging people to raise their expectations for involvement, the initiative for seeking consecration or refocusing of ministry through confirmation should rest with the individual. The self-understandings of each person should be respected, so that all can feel they are full members of the body of Christ even though only some people seek to embrace new forms of ministry or seek public support for fresh expressions of their commitment.

Leading:
Paideia
in a
New Key

JANET F. FISHBURN
Drew University

The Pastor as Leader

There is considerable confusion in the church these days about clergy roles and identity. Many pastors experience conflicts because of the numerous roles associated with their ministries. The pastoral skills taught at most seminaries include such diverse areas as preaching, teaching, pastoral care and counseling, worship, evangelism, mission, administration, and stewardship. The laity tend to expect their pastors to excel in all of these roles—and more. Some pastors resolve their conflicts by specializing in one of the skills of ministry. Other pastors "burn out," contributing to the modern phenomenon of high rates at which men and women leave the parish ministry. And behind all of this is a basic question: "What distinguishes the leadership roles of the clergy from those of other Christians?"

At best, it is said that the pastor is the last "generalist." The late Urban Holmes, commenting on the tendency of clergy to resolve the conflict by organizing their ministry around management, pastoral care, or social activism, suggested that this was an identification with non-church vocations that was doomed to failure. His point was that the leadership role of the clergy is unique because of the spiritual nature of pastoral ministry.

At worst, when the distinctive nature of pastoral ministry is obscured, it is not obvious, even to church members, how the work of the clergy differs from similar services available from a therapist, a counseling center, or a social service agency. That may be why some pastors experience the demands made upon them by some laity as a form of consumerism. While some laity expect too many services from their pastor, others are resentful that pastors seem to perform so many of the roles associated with ministry. They have been taught that ministry belongs to "the whole people of God." But that has not been their experience.

The members of one pastoral nomination committee refused to use traditional language of the pastor as a "good shepherd" in their job description. They said that it implied that laity are like dumb, passive sheep. They hoped to find a pastor who would lead them into claiming their own potential for leadership in the church and community as Christians. It is tragic that such misconceptions of ministry contribute to clergy "burnout" from overwork and role conflict while laity feel deprived of their rightful role in the church.

The image of the pastor as a "good shepherd" is an allusion to Jesus' way of leading his followers. He taught the people who gathered around him because they were like sheep without a shepherd—straying spiritually. Laity dislike of that image is an indication of two trends in the church today. First, many laity are unfamiliar with this concept as a biblical allusion. Second, if they do know what it means, they do not associate the work of a modern pastor with Jesus' style of giving spiritual direction to his followers through teaching.

It is my thesis that the "good shepherd" is still valid as an image for ministry: Jesus' way of leading his followers is still a good model for ministry. The teaching role of the pastoral leader refers as much to a quality of leadership that infuses all tasks of ministry as it does to formal teaching responsibility. The distinctive role of the clergy is the provision of spiritual direction for the persons entrusted to their care. This is done through preaching *and* teaching, leadership in worship, and by giving consistent and explicit leadership to the task of enabling laity to claim and enjoy their own potential for ministry.

The pastoral leader of a congregation does not have to be personally responsible for providing the many different kinds of service associated with ministry today. Instead, some pastors invest their time and energy in recruiting and training members of their congregations to offer "ministry" to others. This includes service in the congregation as well as the mission of the church in the world.

Of the tasks usually associated with the work of the pastor, teaching, pastoral care, evangelism, and mission/social concern are all valid ministries of the laity. There is a marked imbalance in the respective leadership roles of pastors and laity in the areas of teaching and pastoral care. Most pastors provide far too much of the pastoral care in the congregation, and far too little of the teaching, especially as leaders in Bible study. The pastoral care movement is a very recent trend in the church. It seems to have had the unfortunate effect of usurping the way in which members of a congregation normally express God's love in caring for each other in times of trouble, illness, and death.

Pastoral care, teaching, evangelism, and social concern are all valid ministries through which all Christians can express their conviction that "God is love," in the church and in the world. Laity need their ordained leaders to teach them how to experience and express God's love as they are led in worship, instructed and led in Bible study, hear the gospel proclaimed, and participate in the sacraments. Equally important, they need their pastors to teach them how to give God's love away through their participation in the pastoral care and teaching of the congregation, and in the missional activities of evangelism and social concern.

Pastors and laity alike may object to this description of ordained leadership as a role model for ministry and as the spiritual direction of a congregation through preaching, teaching, and worship leadership. This sounds as if there is no organization or structure to the life of the congregation. However, the official board or elected officers in every congregation exist to collaborate with the pastor in organizing the congregation. Although this takes different forms in different denominations, the organization necessary to leading a congregation is twofold. It includes coordination of all activities and groups that make up the life of the congregation and attention to the corporate business of the church's property and finances.

Church officers are elected to collaborate with the pastor in "managing" the congregation. While they hold office, this is their proper ministry. Put another way, church administration is service given by the pastor and elected officers so that members of the congregation can be the people of God in ministry in a particular place. Pastors are, of necessity, the "chief administrators," since they especially are responsible for all that happens in the life of congregations.

Pastors known for their ability to recruit and equip laity for ministry are good administrators. They use their organizational skills to build community among members. The colleague of one pastor known for his success at leading laity into ministry noted that: "He is good at delegating authority, at finding persons with the competency for a given task, and at letting them do the work of the church their own way." A lay leader in his congregation reported that he encourages members of a "diverse congregation to work together, not to become like each other, but rather to all live closer to the example of Jesus." Another member reported that her pastor's gifts in worship leadership and preaching are "unequalled." There is unusually high morale in the congregation. This seems to come from the combination of a ministry focused on leading laity into ministry, the gift of preaching and worship leadership, and personal example as a style of ministry.[1] This congregation—and its pastor—are an exception rather than the rule. This is an example of a church where there is a clear organizational structure; the pastor and church staff, lay leaders and members of the congregation are comfortable with their respective roles.

The Double Leadership Structure of Sunday School and Church

It is my thesis that lack of clarity about the legitimate leadership role of the pastor is related to a structural pattern that originated in American churches early in the nineteenth century. During the nineteenth century the Sunday school movement gradually became an institution as the school of the church. As an institution, and not just another organization, the Sunday school competed with other church-related organizations for the commitment, time, energy, and financial support of church members. As this occurred, the pastoral role as the teacher of the congregation was gradually replaced by the laity-led Sunday school.

In time, the laity-led Sunday school and the pastor-led church, representing two leadership structures and organizations, coexisted side by side. "The church" at worship in the sanctuary was led by a theologically educated and officially ordained pastor and elected officers. The Sunday school became a training laboratory for teachers and lay leaders. The importance of both institutions is evident wherever a congregation has erected a separate educational wing or building to house the Sunday school.

From the perspective of the Christian education movement the question of who leads the church can be seen in relation to the changing role of the Sunday school. While the Sunday school may not be quite as dead or bankrupt as some critics suggest, it is undeniable that the Sunday school no longer can be viewed as the sole educational agency in most churches. The role of the Sunday school in congregations was once more than education. In the past, the Sunday school provided not only study for all ages but also fellowship and mission outreach groups. In some churches the Sunday school may still have a separate budget that includes leadership training for teachers and staff members as well as stewardship and mission items.[2]

The Women's Association provided similar opportunities for education, mission, and leadership training for women. They, too, had their own budget and excelled at raising money for mission activities. The point is that for many generations there was a structure present in most congregations that did permit and encourage the nurture of lay leadership and lay ministry in the church. For the most part, pastors had no formal relationship to that structure. In the last twenty years, as the Sunday school has been incorporated into a unified church program structure, the natural connection between educational activities, mission activities, and leadership training has been severed. Because of the history of the two leadership structures, pastors have not been expected to give leadership to educational activities, mission activities, teacher training, or leadership training.

Before the advent of the unified church program structure, most activities in a congregation revolved aound an informal division of labor between the Sunday school and the church. Denominational judicatories and ecumenical agencies of the International Council of Religious Education sponsored training events. Sunday school teachers and staff were certified through lab schools. There were summer schools for mission, audio-visual workshops, Advent workshops, and so on. The other source of leadership training in congregations has been church officer training. In some cases, that too was sponsored on an annual basis by denominations.

During the last twenty years, as the balance of power between the Sunday school and the church began to shift, planners and leaders of denominational boards and agencies have attempted to reorganize the dual leadership and program structure into a unified approach. Ecumenical attention to teacher training for local churches diminished when the International Council of Religious Education was replaced by the mission oriented National Council of Churches.[3] Reorganized Boards of Christian Education in the mainline denominations shifted their attention away from teacher training to curriculum writing. Their research led to a substantial upgrading of the quality of published curriculum. However, this shift of attention away from teacher training at a local and judicatory level to curriculum writing at a national level was doomed to failure because the leaders and planners were out of touch with the reality of the local congregation.

There were not enough theologically sophisticated laity to teach the new curriculum. It did not matter how carefully the curriculum was introduced through well planned teacher workshops for that purpose. The curriculum was not written in the language of the persons for whom it was intended. The Presbyterian curriculum, *Christian Faith and Life,* was beautifully designed and well-written. It represented a notable attempt to unify and explain the meaning of the church through learning and instruction. It died the death of a foreigner in a strange land. For many of the teachers of that curriculum, the great biblical themes were strange. They did not experience "the Covenant" as connected to their lives, or to their experience of the church.

There have been other attempts to unify the programs of the congregation so that Sunday school teachers would become a part of the total church leadership structure. In many United Methodist congregations there is still a clear division of labor between the leaders of the Sunday school and the leaders of the church. Pastors reported that they would not interfere with the laity-led Sunday school as long as it did not create problems for them. Yet, United Methodist denominational leaders introduced guidelines for local program organization in which education is a program with the same status as worship, stewardship, mission, church and society, evangelism, and religion and race programs. There are nineteen work areas from which to choose the particular emphases for programs in a congregation. A Council of Ministries is to coordinate the work areas. Theoretically this seems like a good idea. Yet, research indicates that the pastor is the only person in a typical church who knows anything about most of the work areas.

Laity are not aware of the existence of many of the work areas. Most do not know if a given area is the work of the pastor, of laity, or both. They do agree that "church and society" is of interest only to the pastor and that teaching is the work of laity.[4]

The unified budget may have succeeded in bringing some coherence to the program structure of a congregation in a way that has not yet changed the informal power of the ethos (meaning, the distinguishing character and tone) of the Sunday school. The abortive efforts to upgrade learning in the church through better curriculum, to reorganize the program structure from above have not come to terms with the sociological truth that the programs of a congregation are themselves a curriculum. The life of a congregation is a curriculum that teaches a content all its own about what a Christian is and does. To be sure, the learning in this "school" is informal and unstated, but powerful. It carries the force of years of tradition.

Members of a congregation learn the attitudes, values, and behaviors of the most powerful people in the learning environment. An hour of formal study once a week cannot begin to compete with the ethos of a vital organization. Participating in Sunday school or "church" means that the participants are learning a religious tradition by what they say and what they do when they gather corporately. The informal curriculum, as it teaches a way of life in a congregation, is a form of religious socialization.

Persons who have experienced the "opening exercises" of the Sunday school have experienced an ethos. They have been given an identity as part of that ethos. The Sunday school has been an institution in its own right, with its own staff, its own budget, and its own worship. In many congregations it represents the evangelistic wing of the congregation and may support its own missionaries. The Sunday school has had its own informal worship tradition with its own Sunday school songs. In some congregations the Sunday school has been a laity-led "church" competing for members with the pastor-led church. There often has been a difference in the spirituality, beliefs, and language used in the worship of the Sunday school and the worship of the church. Pastors sometimes feel as if they are competing with a "Sunday school theology" in their attempts to lead a congregation.

While the Sunday school has had an ethos concerning teacher training, the church has an ethos of leadership training. "Leadership training" often is used to designate only church officers. It often is noted how difficult it is for a pastor to mobilize an army of volunteers for ministry. The double structure of Sunday school leaders and teachers and of church officers as the leaders of the church can convey the idea that the ministry of the laity consists only of being a teacher or an officer of the church or a church-related organization. Too little attention has been given to the way pastors recruit and equip laity for their ministry. Most pastors have not been educated to think of themselves as teachers, or as teachers of teachers. Laity do not seem to expect pastors to lead or equip other leaders in the church.

Leadership recruitment in many churches consists of little more than finding persons to "fill" offices in existing organizations. It should not surprise pastors if lay leaders in church organizations lack enthusiasm or skills for positions they have accepted. If they have been "drafted," chances are not very high that persons recruited under these conditions will think of themselves as participating in the ministry of the laity.

Because of the history of the two leadership structures, it is unusual to find a congregation where there is evidence that the recruitment, training, and support of many forms of lay ministry is important to anyone. It is more usual to find that where there now is a unified budget, the Sunday school openly competes with mission and social concern groups for financial support. It is as rare to find a church budget item for leadership training as it is to find a church agency that offers training to support the ministry of the laity.

For lack of better options, the pastor usually is responsible for church officer training. Even if the pastor interprets the leadership role as a servant ministry for the welfare of the congregation, many laity may see holding office as a sign of

power and status in the "church." In most congregations laity
regard some offices as better than others, including the office
of the pastoral leader. If lay leadership roles are seen as step-
ping stones in a power structure this is a sure sign that "church
work" is not being experienced as the service of persons gifted
by God for particular ministries.

Every Christian has the potential to grow spiritually
through ministry, or service, given to others. But where church
leadership is not experienced as valid ministry there is likely
to be conflict around power and authority issues between laity,
between pastors and laity, and between pastors and staff
members.

Careless patterns of leadership recruitment do not give
enough attention to the ability of persons to carry out particular
ministries. This is an insult to the human spirit that can hardly
be dignified by calling it "ministry" or "service." There is a
desperate lack of reality to discussions about "the ministry of
the laity" because so few laity have experienced their "church
work" as a time of spiritual growth and development. Like
overworked pastors, overworked lay leaders in congregations
also "burn out." Some drop out. Although this situation has not
been created by pastors, clergy should not use this as evidence
that laity are not really interested in participating in the ministry of the church.

The Pastor as a Teacher

Role conflict between laity and clergy is not new. The
history of leadership in the Christian tradition is that of an
unsteady balance of power and authority related to the basic
paradox of the Christian life—that a Christian becomes a leader
only as a consequence of being a follower of Jesus. Every Christian who is a serious disciple, or follower of Jesus, becomes a
"teacher" of the Christian life through personal example of
word and deed. Some followers also will have specific gifts for
ministry as church leaders.

Ordained leaders are "called out" or set aside by the
church to devote their lives to being both leaders of leaders

and teachers of teachers. Too often "ministry" is used to mean that only full-time pastors are "in ministry," or that "the minister" is the only leader in the congregation. All Christians are "in ministry" insofar as ministry is a way of life which teaches others what a Christian is and does. Beyond that, any Christian with knowledge and skills to perform one or several of the tasks associated with the role of pastors should be a church leader. Ordained leaders are distinguished from non-ordained church members as the persons in a congregation who are set aside to see that "the Christ" is embodied in the corporate life of the people so that the church can be the body of Christ in the world.

There has been much talk about "the ministry of the laity" in recent years but not much realization of the gifts given to every baptized Christian to be used in service to the church and the world. In fact, most congregations are now organized with a leadership structure in place that virtually insures that the present functions of the pastor and of the people will stay the same. The present division of labor in the church, and the way leaders are recruited to maintain existing programs and organizations, implies that only clergy are *really* in ministry, as if only pastors really have gifts for ministry.

Letty Russell questions the meaning of the ministry of all Christians in *The Future of Partnership*. "Ministry itself is a problem because it has become identified with clergy status and lost its essential connection to the diakonia as the work of the whole people of God. It is the whole people of God who carry out the One Ministry of the One who came to serve and to give his life a ransom for many" (Mark 10:45).[5] Russell argues that the reason for partnership between pastors and the whole people of God in ministry together is "for service, not for subordination."

However clearly theologians may state the problem, unless there is a change in both the way ministry is conceptualized and the way ministry is organized in a congregation, the ministry of the laity will continue to seem like a second-class ministry. As long as laity think of themselves as church members who do church work, as recipients of services performed by

pastors, or as consumers of pastoral services, there will be no
valid ministry of all of the people of God.

The time is ripe for new styles of pastoral leadership
that will invite all Christians to enjoy their own valid ministries. Every Christian is said to be "gifted" for ministry. The
biblical view of all Christians as "gifted" means that each one
has potential for spiritual growth through participation in the
worship, study, friendly associations, and mission of the church.
The service given by the pastoral leader to the whole people of
God is to see that the work of the church is done by all the
people of God. Otherwise, the people of God will be spiritually
deprived.

If there is anti-clerical sentiment in churches today, it
may be the attempt of lay people to express an intuition that
clergy, by virtue of the work they do, have access to spiritual
formation through ministry in a way that is not available to
laity. There are lay people who yearn to be engaged in some
form of ministry that is more satisfying than what seems like
doing the usual busy work of the church. Laity cannot realize
their potential for growth through ministry if pastors perform
most of the "services" associated with living the Christian life.

There is another facet to the role conflict between laity
and clergy. Some pastors suspect that there are laity who wish
to usurp their valid role as worship leader and preacher. They
are correct. This is not just a desire for more power and authority as a church leader, although it can be only that. It is
also a desire for spiritual power. There are laity who experience
a very basic need to know about themselves and the church by
studying the Scriptures, who want to experience God's presence
as a reality in their lives, and who want to know how to pray.
Some are so hungry for knowledge about the life of the spirit
that they enroll in seminary courses to learn about their own
religious tradition. This hunger is a clear indication that a
laity-led teaching ministry has not been spiritually satisfying.
The spiritual disciplines once considered essential to growth
in the Christian life through knowing, hearing, and doing God's
will have been lost to the memory of many who are the church
today.

The Bible as the Book of the Church

The point has been made that the language and character of the Sunday school may be more powerful than the pastor in shaping belief and role expectations in some churches. Any reorganization of roles in a congregation must account for the various kinds of power that can reside in the informal, or hidden, curriculum. The assumed way of life in a congregation invisibly communicates what it means to be a Christian in this particular congregation. The Sunday school ethos has been a major formative influence in the way laity understand the use of the Bible in the church.

Many pastors know intuitively that there is a great gulf between their own knowledge and interpretation of the Bible and that of most laity. The current popularity of various styles of Bible study—Bethel, Kerygma, Walter Wink's method, and a host of others—and the formation of ecumenical or parachurch Bible study groups is evidence that church members want to know and understand the Scriptures of the Christian tradition.

There is a marked difference between the traditional affirmation that "the Bible is the book of the church" and the way the Bible has been introduced to most church members as a part of the Sunday school instructional program. The style of teaching in Sunday school classes may teach laity only to consume the Bible as it is presented in the curriculum. This tradition has taught many adults that the class objective is to "get through the lesson for the day." This may mean little more than reading the curriculum together. This kind of study can proceed without ever opening a Bible. It may not be an exaggeration to say that many adults in the church today have not experienced group Bible study that is spiritually satisfying. Church members who seek other avenues for Bible study are expressing a genuine spiritual hunger to know and understand the Word of God.

Bruce Birch (see his essay elsewhere in this volume) accuses clergy of "preserving clear-cut arenas of clerical authority" by fostering or allowing laity to believe that "serious appropriation of Scripture and tradition requires skills that are principally available to the pastor or other church professionals with seminary training." It is true that biblical interpretation is surrounded by a certain mystique. Some laity believe that it is the pastor's ability to read the Bible in the original languages that distinguishes clergy roles from the work of other Christians. As surprising as that may seem to pastors, it is indicative of the fact that laity sense a great difference in attitudes about Scripture between pastors and laity.

Pastors have been influenced by the power of the Sunday school tradition as much as anyone else in the church. They may be shocked at the biblical illiteracy of adults in the church. Yet many of them would not think of becoming a teacher of Scripture as an essential part of their service to a congregation. If the Bible is really to be the book of the church—rather than the book of the Sunday school—the pastor will have to become a teacher of Scripture. If pastors do not learn how to teach faithful and intelligent interpretation of Scripture as Bible study leaders in the church, the Bible is likely to continue to be the book of the Sunday school.

To many laity, the spiritual insights of Scripture are shrouded in mystery; the culture and thought forms of the Bible are strange to modern readers. Bible study does require some familiarity with biblical scholarship in order to grasp the way in which Scripture speaks to life in the world today. Serious appropriation of Scripture does require skills that are made available principally to pastors in seminary courses. Exegesis (that is, critical explanation of Scripture) is not a skill to be appropriated only by pastors for the purpose of preaching. Anyone, including older children, can learn simple exegetical principles that are assumed by most pastors and unknown to most laity. Laity need their pastors to proclaim the Word of God to them. They also need their pastors to teach them how to read the Bible lest the book of the church remain closed to them.

In the past the Bible has shaped the consciousness of Christians as the source of their corporate identity. It also has been the source of language that shaped and expressed the experiences common to living the Christian life together. The corporate identity of the church and the unique identity of individual Christians depend on grasping the meaning of basic biblical themes. This requires familiarity with the Bible—even immersion in Scripture—as well as understanding of the meaning of "the Book." This kind of familiarity with Scripture will not occur if church members have little or no contact with the Bible other than as it is used in weekly worship.

Sociologist and theologian James Gustafson, concerned with the weak corporate characteristics of many churches, has concluded that "The church's social continuity and identity is dependent upon the use of the Bible as the source of its language." Where a church has two languages, that of the Sunday school and that of "the church," a coherent corporate character is weakened. Gustafson warns against using the language of other communities, such as the language of psychoanalysis, so much that the uniqueness of the language of the church is confused with the helping character of the psychoanalytic community.

> Although it is difficult precisely to designate and locate, there is a pattern of meaning and life that characterizes the Church, and which in turn is reflected in the outlook of its members. The language of the Bible, the liturgy, the hymns, and the testimonies of personal religious experience all impress meanings in persons. The pattern of a person's life and thought are conditioned by the symbols of communication in the church.[6]

Perhaps the most spiritually destructive consequence of the double leadership structure of Sunday school and the church is the way in which teaching the Bible and preaching have been institutionally separated. The secret of a unified corporate character is relatively simple. The Bible is the only language Christians have in common. Members of a congregation live in the several different language worlds of home, work, and church. When they are not gathered as the church they speak the language of their other worlds. If "the pattern of meaning and life that characterizes the Church" is to transfer into "the pattern of a person's life and thought," the Bible will have to become the book of the whole people of God.

Where a pastor intentionally provides focus and consistency for a congregation by using biblical language and images in liturgy, preaching, study, sharing, and mission groups, a foundation for leading laity into ministry is established. But it is not enough that church members hear and speak the same language. If laity are not able to search the Scriptures for themselves, it is not likely that the Bible will become the pattern for their life and thought. If pastors do not claim responsibility for teaching other Christians how to search the Scriptures, it is not likely that contemporary misunderstandings of ministry and the church will change.

Mobilizing for Ministry: Leadership Training as Corporate Spiritual Formation

Looking at leadership in the church in light of the power of the congregation to form and transform yields a different angle of vision about the pastoral task. Among the books available in a new literature about the analysis of congregations, Don Smith's *Congregations Alive* is especially pertinent to this discussion. In research designed to learn about the characteristics of congregations that are effective in mission and ministry, Smith defined the basic function of ordained ministry as that of leading laity into ministry.

> Equipping members for their ministries is the principal task of both pastors and elders. Of course, this is corollary to the conviction that ministry is the work of all the people. If indeed it is true that the basic responsibility for ministry rests upon every baptized Christian, then the clear responsibility of leadership in the church is to help members identify their gifts, develop those gifts, and make use of them in ministry.[7]

In testing this definition of ministry, Smith discovered that where the pastor gives opportunities to laity to discover and use their gifts through mutual ministry to each other, they are more likely to see that the whole world is in need of their ministry. A congregation in mission is first of all a caring community where persons can grow through relationships.

Similar information comes from the research of Kennon Callahan who writes that one key to an effective church is "pastoral and lay visitation." He links regular weekly visits with the unchurched, newcomers, constituents, and members by both clergy and laity to "concrete missional objectives" and "corporate, dynamic worship" as key elements in congregations that are spiritually alive. Depending on location, these congregations may or may not be growing numerically. The point is that there is a difference between a ministry that is a success measured in numbers and a ministry where spiritual formation and growth of all the people of God is the criterion for effective pastoral leadership.

Callahan describes "satisfied" congregations as having "a stronger sense of intentionality and wellbeing about their life in mission; they possess a sense of their own strength and a responsible hope that they can accomplish the mission to which God has called them."[8] The key to Callahan's distinction between "satisfied" and "successful" congregations lies in the definition of "satisfied" as people who are "working on a mission to which God calls them." He means that members of a missional congregation are spiritually satisfied people.

It has been claimed that the loss of the teaching function historically associated with clergy leadership in the church has led to confusion about the distinctive nature of pastoral ministry, resentment of clergy power by laity, and a suspicion among pastors that laity want to usurp their role in the church. Contemporary lack of clarity about what it means to be the "whole people of God" has been attributed to the overlapping and sometimes competing leadership structures of the Sunday school and the church.

The divorce of teaching functions from preaching responsibilities of the clergy is related to the extent to which the Bible has become the Book of the Sunday school. The question has been raised as to whether pastors can give adequate spiritual direction to a congregation if they are not teachers as well as preachers. Evidence suggests that if members of a congregation are to have a common understanding about ministry, they must be familiar with biblical stories, language, and images as a part of their corporate identity. It is clear that a biblically grounded character of the whole people of God in ministry is necessary if the church is to be "the body of Christ" in the world.

Mobilizing for Ministry as Paideia in a New Key

The pattern of faith transmission known to the ancient church was a Christian form of "paideia," which is a Greek concept related to classical educational instruction and nurture of young people. Pastors who organize the congregation's life around intentions to enable the ministry of the laity are engaging in a modern form of "paideia," or of "paideia in a new key."

We should note that the writer of one of the Pastoral Epistles used the Greek word "paideia" to describe how Timothy was nurtured and instructed in Christian faith (II Tim. 3:10–17). The writer refers both to the persons who nurtured Timothy in patterns of Christian life and thought and to Scripture as formative: "All Scripture is inspired by God and is useful for teaching the faith and correcting error, for resetting the direction of a [person's] life and training [her or him] in good living" (II Tim. 3:16). That modified J. B. Phillips translation captures the essence of the writer's intention to emphasize a style of Christian education in which the objective is to form the consciousness of the learner in such a way that attitudes and behavior flow from this central biblical perspective as a way of life.

The effectiveness of a Christian "paideia" depends on the convergence of two powerful forms of spiritual formation. The first is the influence of positive role models, persons who live in a way that demonstrates the Christian life. The second is Scripture as the source of knowledge, self-knowledge, and interpretation of life. The Bible traditionally has been used as the script for the life of Christians . . . telling them who they are and what God wants of them. It has been the curriculum of the church as the center of formal instruction. It also has been the informal curriculum, giving shape to the lives of persons who followed the promptings of the script. The written Word comes alive in the church as Christians embody the Word in their lives, giving form to what they say they believe by reaching out to each other, and to God's world, in service. That is, they re-present the Word in their own word and deed. Scripture must be known and studied in order to be lived.

A pastor who models a servant style of ministry inspires laity to engage in servant ministry. That is why clergy leadership has been defined as the spiritual direction of a congregation through preaching, teaching, worship leadership, and as a role model for servant ministry. Where pastors succeed at leading laity into ministry, they have permitted and encouraged members of a congregation to give and receive ministry from each other. There is good evidence that mutual ministry functions as a form of leadership training that leads to ministries by the same people to their community. The key to engaging laity in ministry seems to be learning "how to free people to express caring love in ways that flow naturally out of their concerns and that fulfill their potential for ministry."[9]

A slightly different way to look at the research about mutual ministry is to interpret mutual ministry as a form of spiritual formation. Some Protestants resist using the language of "spirituality" and "spiritual formation." Perhaps the vocabulary is uncomfortable because it challenges the Protestant tradition at a vulnerable point, the tendency to religious individualism. "Spirituality" as used here means that every person has the potential to experience and respond to God. Christian spirituality is formed as persons experience God's grace through Scripture, sacrament, and prayer. Worship is a form of corporate spiritual formation.

Participation in ministry is also a form of spiritual formation. Experience in ministry is a way of learning to live the Christian life as a response to God's love. That is why mutual ministry is known to lead laity into other forms of ministry. Insofar as the experience of laity in offering caring love to others is a form of spiritual formation, then a pastor's recruiting and equipping laity for ministry contributes to the spiritual formation of other Christians in a positive way. It can be said that whenever any Christian offers caring love as a service to someone else, this is on-the-job training in Christianity.

The following outline suggests how a pastor can provide spiritual direction for a congregation by engaging laity in ministry. The suggestions represent an intentional effort to guide the ability of members of a congregation to experience and respond to God's love. This kind of corporate spiritual formation is "paideia in a new key."

1. Provide a coherent vision of the whole people of God in ministry to each other and to God's world through consistent use of biblical images that convey the attractiveness and power of this vision of the church. This usually occurs through the quality of the worship experience and the extent to which the preaching helps the people understand the lives they live, both corporately and individually.

2. Provide for teaching/learning experience with Bible study and prayer so that laity experience this as the normal activity of Christians who want to "love and serve God."

3. Provide for training in whatever skills are needed to equip laity for ministry, especially in the areas of teaching, pastoral care, evangelism, and mission.

4. Provide leadership through oversight of all church programs, so that all leaders of groups can begin to claim the vision of lay ministry articulated by the pastor as their own. This means that the purpose of church administration is to free and equip laity for ministry.

5. Structure present church programs so that participants are able to learn from and encourage each other in living the Christian life. This is a way to support laity in ministry through their nurture of each other in mutual ministry.

6. Provide a model for servant ministry by practicing partnership with staff and with lay leaders and by delegating as much work and authority as possible so that the ministry potential of others is called out in positive ways.

The leadership style of the pastor communicates volumes about whether the pastor is free enough to be able to permit and encourage the ministry of the laity. When a pastor engages a congregation in ministry, the life of the people becomes more important than the administration of the corporation. Ministry for, to, and through the laity redefines and challenges the spiritual authenticity of identifying pastoral leadership of a congregation with skills in management, pastoral care, or social activism. In this style of ministry, the pastor is both a model of faithful servant ministry to the congregation and the teacher charged with calling out the potential for faithful ministry in others. A pastor who gives this kind of spiritual direction to a congregation is like a midwife who helps to bring forth the potential for new life in the people of God.

Smith's research about lively congregations shows that a pastor can be both a strong leader who guides the direction of the life of the congregation and a sensitive partner in ministry who knows how to get out of the way so laity can exercise their proper ministries. But the pastor who functions well as both the leader of the congregation and an enabler of lay ministries has made a choice to see that ministry becomes the work of the whole people of God.

Leadership Training as Spiritual Formation

It has been suggested that four of the tasks usually associated singularly with clergy leadership—most of the teaching, pastoral care, evangelism, and mission activities—also belong to the ministry of the laity. This does not mean that pastors no longer visit the sick and the bereaved or counsel the spiritually troubled. It does mean that much more visiting and caring between members of a congregation should be encouraged by a pastor. It could mean that the pastor will organize formal training and a support group for persons with gifts for visitation and calling of all kinds. Decisions about who becomes responsible for various ministries of the congregation will depend on the ability of the pastor and professional staff to recognize the potential of laity for particular forms of ministry. The criteria for attempting to restore legitimate ministry to laity is to delegate as much work and authority as is possible so that the potential of others is called out in positive ways.

This style of ministry—with enabling of the ministry of the laity as its objective—integrates teaching into the role of the pastor as a way of leading laity into ministry. The teaching role of the pastor requires attention to two kinds of learning. Ministry is learned through formal instruction and through the experience of learning to express love in caring ways. Leadership training in the church means helping other Christians learn to express their faith. In congregations where this has occurred, the Bible is both studied and lived. The Sunday school is not the school of the church. Rather, the church is "a school of service to the Lord."[10]

The pastor's responsibility for leadership training should not be misconstrued as an attempt to establish "professional" standards for lay ministry. Ministry is not a profession. It is a way of life. Leadership training in a church setting means to teach other Christians how pastoral care, teaching, evangelism, and missional tasks can be an expression of God's love to others in and through their lives. Training for particular tasks is then planned with reference to the present knowledge, prior experience, and skill of the learners. In some cases this would require the pastor to plan, train, evaluate, and provide ongoing support for a group, such as an evangelism team. In other cases, experienced lay leaders may need no additional training by the pastor. They can be recruited to organize and train other laity in a particular area of ministry.

This is a model like the training laboratories and teacher workshops which have been sponsored by and for professional Christian educators, teachers, and apprentice teachers. This system of extending networks of persons with the capacity to train others for a particular kind of ministry is a way of acknowledging that church members have gifts for leadership in the church. Although a pastor indirectly trains laity for ministry by the way he or she carries out teaching and pastoral care, the formal responsibility for training laity suggested here means that the pastor makes intentional provisions for training laity for ministry. The intention is not to add another task called leadership training to the list of pastoral tasks. This method of organizing a congregation for ministry is more like equipping and employing "the whole people of God" than the present practices of securing last-minute volunteers in an emergency.

Who is in charge of groups in a congregation? Do these groups convey positive experiences of God's love through mutual ministry, through the work they do, by what they do when they gather? Are official boards, planning groups, the choirs, and classes of the church aware that whenever they gather they do so "in Jesus' name?" What distinguishes the way they do the work of the church from the work of any other task-oriented group?

Group Bible study and prayer is a way to learn about and experience God's love. This way of deepening faith through reflecting together about the meaning of Scripture can be learned as an integral part of the normal practice of Christians whenever they gather to plan for and evaluate their common work. People make a statement about what is really important to them by the nature of their corporate gatherings. When church groups gather and never read the Bible together, or refer to the Book of the church, or pray about their common interests and concerns, that makes a statement about the nature of their group identity. Yet, in many church gatherings the group is so intent on getting through an agenda, on doing business as usual, that members feel they do not have time for Bible study and prayer too. This is a matter of priorities and group ethos. People do whatever they have learned to believe is important to the ongoing identity of the group.

Bible study and prayer are often separated from the "work of the church." That is because it has been a part of the character of the Sunday school to teach the Bible in isolation from all other church-related activities. The Bible has been studied as an end in itself, as if totally unrelated to the experience church members have of being the church together. This means that most groups in the church may not see Bible study and prayer as an integral part of their work together ... or even as related to the nature of their gathering. This separation of Bible study from the life of the church robs the groups of the church of spiritual resources that would give meaning and support to the work they do.

Church officers and committees, Sunday school teachers, and members of service groups can all learn to see themselves as doing work to which they have been called by God if reflection about their work is guided through Bible study and prayer. The Bible will continue to be divorced from the life of the church, unless pastors make intentional efforts for helping to assure the practice of seeking spiritual direction through reflection on Scripture when the groups of the church meet. This simple, but crucial, aspect of the teaching role of the clergy is not difficult to carry out. The pastor, by example, teaches others how to lead a group in Bible study related to their lives and work together. As needed, the pastor also teaches leaders of various groups in the church to become responsible for leadership of informal worship by forming groups in which church members learn Bible study skills and prayer.

If this kind of integration into the life of the people does not occur, the Bible and Bible study will be only the work of the Sunday school. Lacking a biblical perspective on the ministry of the laity, other work will be only church work. The Bible will become the Book of the church when it becomes the script for every aspect of the corporate life and work of the church. A pastor can help to teach people to seek God's will through Scripture and to pray about what is real and important to them through leading this kind of informal worship.

Finally, a discussion of leadership roles in the church raises the question of the purpose of the church. The first definition of "leader" in Webster's dictionary is "a guide." If a leader is "a guide," or "an office holder" or a "person with commanding authority or influence," the ordained leader in the church is all of this and more. As a representative of the church universal in a particular congregation, a pastor is the spiritual leader of that part of "the whole people of God."

Ideally, the church is a group of people among whom the "body of Christ" is taking form. It is this alone that distinguishes the church from all other human enterprises. And it is this responsibility for giving spiritual direction and support to a congregation which distinguishes the clergy or pastoral leader from all other Christians as part of the whole people of God.

Communicating: Informal Conversation in the Congregation's Education

CHARLES R. FOSTER
Scarritt Graduate School

The task of maintaining a community across the passage of time is not simple. Even as it seeks to transmit the visions, values, and patterns of behavior that give it a distinctive identity and purpose to succeeding generations, it is bombarded by alternative visions for its future and assailed by both internal and external forces threatening its strength and vitality. The fragility of a community is typical of small groups, like a church youth group, and of large complex organizations, like a denomination. It is evident in the adult Sunday school class or congregation facing a limited future because it has not attended to the continuing task of incorporating new members into its life. It also is to be found in the experience of many older church members who no longer recognize their contribution to the congregation's heritage in contemporary programs and activities. A study of a community of any size reveals a variety of political, economic, religious, and educational structures and strategies concerned with sustaining and extending the integrity of the community's life. It is in the urgency with which a community seeks to incorporate succeeding generations into its life that we discover its concern for and commitment to education.

The educational task of a community, however, is not simple. Walter Brueggemann has observed that it requires a functional balance between those efforts designed to sustain the continuity of a people's identity and those designated to introduce enough novelty and freedom to help a community adapt to new situations and circumstances. The result is to be found in the attention given to the structuring of a community's resources for what Edward Farley recently has called "ordered learning." It is reflected in Lawrence Cremin's definition of education as the "systematic and sustained effort to transmit, evoke, or acquire knowledge, attitudes, values, skills, or sensibilities, as well as any outcomes of that effort."[1] In the church, we are familiar with the results of this intentional, systematic, and sustained effort in the classes making up the Sunday, day, and pre schools. The recruitment and training of teachers, the development of curricular resources for all ages and a wide range of interests, and the organization of bureaucratic and economic superstructures all reveal our commitment to the task of handing on the faith we have received to the next generation. We see in them the possibilities for the continued liveliness of the church's faith and witness.

Curricular Undercurrents
in the Congregation's Education

In spite of the intentionality in our approaches to Christian religious education in both denominations and congregations, equally wilful processes influence the vision, values, and attitudes of the people in any community. Why do students, for example, so quickly and completely "forget" certain things that they have been deliberately and systematically "taught" in school or church? I first encountered this question in my field education assignment in seminary. As a teacher of junior high youths in a local church, I was intrigued by their lack of familiarity with the person or thought of the Apostle Paul. My curiosity was piqued when I discovered that this same group of young people had had a previous study of Paul in the sixth grade with one of the most creative teaching teams I have ever observed. Why did not the values and ideas of that experience have lasting power for these young people?

The question may be asked in reverse as well. How and why do a people accept values and beliefs which are not conveyed through formally structured educational processes? I recently have encountered variations on the following experience in several Protestant congregations. The prevailing view in these congregations was that children did not belong in worship. The organization of congregational life reinforced this view. Sunday school classes for children met during the worship hour. If children did attend worship, they never partook of the communion elements until they were confirmed. The belief that a person first shared in the eucharistic event at the time of confirmation was conveyed in teaching sessions for all ages. A small number of parents, however, insisted upon their children being present in the worship service with them. They also lobbied for the rescheduling of the Sunday school and worship hours to eliminate the conflict they experienced between them. Although the denomination held workshops espousing the presence and participation of children in worship, and a number of articles on the subject had appeared in denominational publications, most members of these congregations had little direct contact with those events or resources.

At some indeterminate point, other families began bringing their children to worship. Eventually the Sunday morning schedule was changed to make it easier for people to participate in both worship service and Sunday school. The stated reason, however, was usually to make it more possible for parents to participate in adult study classes. One Sunday morning, in keeping with the congregation's custom, the parents in one family came forward to the communion rail to receive the elements—bringing their children with them. The pastor served the elements to the entire family. During the next communion service other families included their children in the eucharist. This scenario eventually culminated in a policy statement by the congregational officers urging the inclusion of children in worship.

If we were to examine these two incidents carefully, it is my contention we would discover curricular undercurrents were as influential in the education of the people involved as were the conscious efforts institutionalized in the Sunday schools of the congregations, their curricular resources, and teachers. These curricular currents usually exist beneath the surface of congregational life. They may be found on the margins of congregational activity. At times they carry, with apparent ease and success, the intentional and planned efforts of teachers, pastors, and congregational leaders. At other times they hinder, divert, or set up patterns of resistance which effectively block the most careful plans of teachers and leaders.

The power and influence of "undercurrents" were impressed upon me at an early age. We lived close to one of the largest rivers in the United States. On a quiet day, the surface of the river appeared calm and the water appeared to move slowly. Underneath that placid surface, however, the "undercurrent" surged toward the ocean. The contrast was visible in the occasional sloughs where the lack of "undercurrent" meant the water did not flow with the river and stagnated instead until the next spring flood.

The informal conversation of a congregation often functions similarly as an "undercurrent" to its formal educational and program life. In the classroom, curricular resources and teaching plans reveal the "surface" or obvious features of congregational education. But the influence of these intentional efforts is due, *in part,* to the vitality of the conversations on the edges, underneath, and around these formal educational activities. These conversations beneath the surface can reinforce and carry the formal dialogical interaction of teacher and learner, of priest or preacher and worshipper, or of committee chairperson and committee member. They also can hinder and block those efforts. The intent of informal conversation, in other words, is also educational in that it helps to shape the vision, values, and actions of its participants. It is for this reason that an exploration of the educational character of informal conversation is appropriate.[2]

Informal Conversation as an Educational Activity

Informal conversation contributes to the congregation's education in at least three ways. The first involves people in the quest to think, explore, and understand. It is concerned with meaning and purpose. The second may be traced to our human quest for relationships that nurture, support, and sustain us. The third is located in our efforts to engage in actions to create something new or to accomplish the tasks we undertake. In each case, informal conversation helps to structure and reinforce our learning.

Conversations of Thinking. In a formal academic definition of conversation, David Tracy observes that the Platonic dialogue is the classical model for conversation in the Western tradition. Its structure involves a back-and-forth movement which entails "an ability to listen, to reflect, to correct, to speak to the point."[3] Tracy limits his analysis of conversation, however, to the cognitive aspects of human experience, as if mind, inductive or deductive analyses, and schools or academic contexts provide the primary occasions for conversation. He attends to conversations that formally shape the intellectual process in actions of thinking and moments of understanding. Hence Plato's dialogues provide an appropriate model for the quest for truth and the illumination of mind. At its deepest and most profound level, participants in such a conversation lose a sense of self-consciousness when they "allow the question, the subject matter, to assume primacy." Such conversation is not limited to academic settings. We also experience it in pastoral situations when questions of life and death, or of vocation and purpose, dominate our attention and energy. Conversations of thinking involve an element of risk. They lead us to the edges of our knowledge and dare us to explore the unknown. They lead us to the boundaries of our present understandings and heighten our frustrations with the inability of our knowledge to illumine our deepest questions. Tracy points out that real conversations of thinking and understanding are rare, because our fears about our self-image die as "we are carried along, and sometimes away, by the subject matter."[4] When they do occur, conversations for thinking embody both a sense of direction, because they are purposeful, and the experience of spontaneity and freedom, because they are open-ended. In the process they may lead us to new ways of understanding ourselves in relationship to God, the church, and the community in which we live. They may lead us into a deeper understanding of the content of our religious experience. Although they begin with cognitive activity, they involve the totality of emotion and physical attentiveness to the interaction. In the continued pursuit of the question or subject matter, participants obviously engage in an educational activity.

Conversations of Belonging. Psychologically, conversation also serves the human quest for belonging. Perhaps Jung's concept of participation is useful at this point because it helps us to understand the processes by which people are gathered up into corporate identities around certain events, values, and ideals that are deeply rooted in the past—perhaps a past of which we are unaware—and to extend that past into the future through our commitments to its deeply rooted visions and values. A major concern of conversations of belonging has to do with our sense of identification with the traditions that locate us in the history of humankind, bind us to the corporate experience of "our people"—whether that people be family, church, region, culture, or nation—and reveal a sense of our common future. The entry point into conversation for belonging may be with a question, as it is in the Jewish Passover tradition when a young boy asks the questions that prompt the re-telling of the story of liberation from Egypt. Yet the question has little to do with subject matter or conceptual truth. It is concerned with relationships that reveal the historical and corporate content of one's identity. It opens up and intensifies the connections between one's present experience and the roots of that experience in the past.

Conversations for belonging often have a narrative quality. I am reminded of the hours I have spent listening to the conversations in my grandfather's home. A topic might come up, but before it would be engaged, the events and people identified with it first had to be placed in context. Stories would be told about some of the people, revealing their character and commitments. Certain values integral to those stories would be reinforced. The content of the topic became included with the relationship of the narrators to the people and events involved. These conversations of belonging created a web of relationships that established for me a sense of my own connectedness to certain people and events in the past, to specific places from East Tennessee to Maine, Oregon, and Washington, and to certain expectations of what it meant to be identified with those relationships in my own life. I discovered in the process something of my own humanness in the collaborative recollections of my family heritage.

In a congregation, similar conversations of belonging occur during social events or the gathering of persons for baptisms, weddings, or funerals. They intensify our sense of belonging to each other and help link us to the dreams, struggles, and accomplishments that distinguish our social identities from those of other congregations and denominations.

Conversations of Creating and Doing. A third form of conversation has to do with action and competence. In this pattern of conversation, we are caught up in the quest for creating or doing. Its method is exploratory and involves the testing of possibilities and limits. Perhaps it may be most fully described in the dialogical process that occurs in John Dewey's methodology for thinking—actually a process of problem solving. It focuses the attention of participants upon a problem rather than upon subject matter, as in conversations of thinking and understanding, or upon relationships, as in conversations of belonging. Lively congregations are filled with problem-solving conversations. We hear them in committee meetings, where the planning of some program or project is taking place. We hear them as people engage in some ministry task. I think of groups preparing a church supper, engaging in a mission project, decorating the place of worship for one of the liturgical seasons, or learning a new skill in Bible study. These conversations are characterized by the raising of alternatives and the testing of hypotheses. They engage persons in experimentation and the evaluation of their efforts. They combine mental and manual skills, as well as verbal and non-verbal patterns of communication in the rhythmic interplay of words and actions.

Informal conversation, in other words, is an educational activity. It may facilitate thinking, belonging, and the solving of specific problems. If informal conversation is valued, it also may serve to support and reinforce the formal educational activities and programs of the congregation. The anticipation of the potential in a learning event can be heightened by the conversation preceding it. The teachings or lessons of that event may be more readily appropriated if people have an opportunity, after the experience, to continue to explore, test, and decide what to do with any new information they may have encountered or skill they have developed. Perhaps at this point we can identify a clue to the "forgetting" by the junior high youths of their previous encounter with the life and teachings of Paul. Little conversation outside the classroom in their families, in the congregation, or in the community supported and reinforced the values of those lessons. Similarly, the change in the attitudes of a congregation toward children in worship may be traced, in part, to informal conversations among parents, clergy, and lay leaders on this topic.

Informal conversation significantly enhances and enriches the formal educational efforts in a congregation. Informal conversation sanctions the quest for thinking and understanding, belonging, problem solving, and doing. It provides a safe context for people to consider alternatives and new possibilities, because it usually occurs outside the formal settings of congregational or parish life. It extends the range of opportunities for people to test, clarify, and decide how to relate to new information, attitudes, expectations, or skills. It exists in places where people are not restricted by formal rules governing the communication of persons or by official positions of status or authority.

Informal conversation also may limit and inhibit the formal educational efforts of a congregation. The boundaries establishing a corporate consensus regarding what is important or appropriate in formal educational activities are usually set and reinforced in the informal conversation of congregational leaders. We may discuss a wide range of issues and ideas in the classroom, for example, but in the informal conversation that follows, it soon becomes apparent which ideas will be taken seriously and which will be discarded as irrelevant, too idealistic, or contrary to the group's values. Church officials may develop a program to reach persons in the neighborhood who do not participate in the life of a given congregation. But the acceptance of that program will be revealed in the informal conversations of church members. Informal conversation often censors classroom discussions, sermon ideas, or committee plans. In these instances, the conclusions reached in the informal conversation of people circumscribe the options available for the public work of the congregation. The character and quality of the informal conversation in a congregation or parish, in other words, significantly influence, either positively or negatively, the disposition of its members to its intentional, systematic, and sustained educational efforts.

Characteristics of Informal Conversation

A close examination of informal conversation may reveal at least four characteristics that illuminate its educative potential. *The first of these is the experience of mutuality* among participants. When two or more people are caught up in conversation they engage in an activity of giving and receiving. Cooperation is enhanced. The possibility of mutual influence is accepted. A certain willingness to suspend prior commitments and views is granted, with the expectation that one might undergo some change in understanding, relationship, or skill growing out of an exchange with another person.

The patterns of mutuality in conversation can be quite diverse. Herve Varenne explores one such pattern in his study of the use of the concept "everybody" by people in a midwestern community. "Everybody" is that referent to those who make up "my group or people." It serves as an external boundary to the range of conversation, identifying that which is considered to be acceptable or not-acceptable to those included within its bounds.[5] I have experienced such conversation in the informal, yet ritualistic, interaction of people clarifying for others what it means to be Methodist, Mormon, or Baptist, or what is required of those who live within the boundaries of a particular neighborhood or social class. The educational patterns at work involve clarification, identification, and reinforcement. They focus upon the quest for identity and commonality.

Such conversation is essentially integrative, by clarifying norms of membership in the group or congregation, and segregative by making visible the lines that separate insiders from outsiders. It gathers its participants into common submission to the authority of group norms and values as the source of their shared identity. It tends to emphasize conversations of belonging to the exclusion of conversations of thinking and understanding. Such conversations obviously can lead to a rich interpersonal common life, but if limited to the experience of the immediate group, they also can contribute to the bigotry and prejudice of its members toward people whom they consider outsiders.

Even in the formal conversations of an academic community, this element of mutuality is present. David Tracy, for example, points to the open-endedness that is possible when participants in conversations concerned with the quest for truth or meaning submit themselves to the authority of the question(s) they ask. They are caught up in the mutual quest and experience of "thinking" and "understanding." This dynamic is characteristic of conversations of belonging as well. The openness of participants to a sense of mutuality is governed partially by their acceptance of the bond of a common tradition. In problem-solving conversations, participants accept the authority of the disciplines of cooperative interdependence in actions of creating or doing. In all three forms of conversation, the submission of participants to the authority of the quest may lead them to changes in their lives which exceed or transcend the limits of both their context or place and the content, experience, or skills with which they have familiarity.

In formal organizations like the congregation or parish, informal conversations tend to occur at the edges of the common life. Hence, *marginality is a second characteristic* of the educational potential in informal conversation. Arnold Van Gennep and Victor Turner, in their study of the rites of passage of people, point to the intensity and power of the experiences people have between the structures of organized life.[6] There is a freedom and spontaneity evident at these "times between" which simply is not found in the rituals of worship, classroom, business meeting, or planned activity. Note, for example, where conversation often occurs: in the church entry, on the steps, in the hallways, in the kitchen. Note when it occurs: during the prelude to worship, prior to and after any planned activity, during the ride between the place where a group gathers and its destination, during chance meetings of church members in the community, or when small groups gather for social occasions in each other's homes.

When I teach—both in the congregation and in the theological school—I always am intrigued by the burst of conversational activity after a class session. It usually is more lively and dynamic than during class time. Especially is this true when conversation during class has been vital and deep. Students with the most profoundly moving questions often wait until the formal class session is over to pursue them with a teacher. Subconsciously at least, these students may recognize that their peers often are not caught up in their question—at least not in a way that enhances the mutuality of their quest. To ask such a question in the public environment of the classroom reveals a vulnerability, an openness to risk and change which often is not sanctioned at a given moment in the academic classroom or in the church study group environment. So these students turn to the safety of the time at the margins of the class session to explore the question on their minds with peers or teachers.

Most clergy recognize a similar pattern. If conversation is valued in a congregation, during the week a pastor will be engaged by parishioners in an exploration of a statement or theme from the previous Sunday's sermon. This usually does not occur in the public settings of sanctuary or while greeting people at the door. It takes place in a visit to the office or home, or through a telephone call. In these activities between the formal times of congregational life there is a freedom to risk, to play with and to test ideas, relationships, and skills outside public view. It is in this freedom, at the margins of a congregation's programmatic experience, that we may discern a unique openness to learning.

A third characteristic of informal conversation is located in its urgency. People cannot wait until the next class session to discuss an issue or until the next meeting to explore an agenda item. Instead, they feel compelled to address the question, topic, or problem immediately. This sense of urgency occurs most often in challenges to familiar ways of knowing, relating, and doing. It is experienced as a collision between past commitments that give order and security to our lives and threatening alternatives. A clue to the sources for this experience may be found in Peter Berger's analysis of modernization. He points to the toll on our lives created by the pluralism of options and the demand for change which characterize our contemporary experience. These dynamics confront us with making choices among the many ideas, values, or beliefs available to us. Displacement, insecurity, and confusion are often common consequences of this encounter. For example, for many people biblical criticism has made biblical authority relative. For many Roman Catholics, the vernacular reduced and fragmented the mystery of God. For many others, the insights of historical theology have proliferated the content of faith. The resulting optional views and experiences in our religious heritage confront us with the task of choosing among the interpretations available to us.

The voluntary principle of social organization provides us, as well, with the opportunity of associating with people we like and respect, but it also requires us to make that choice. In our inevitable confrontation with similar options, conversation is essential. In spite of our longing for the apparent simplicity which we associate with what Peter Berger has called a pre-modern consciousness of the structures of our existence,[7] we are faced with the necessity of choosing. First, however, we must clarify the meanings and test the implications of the options we encounter to reduce the ambiguity and confusion we often experience. As a teacher, I usually know when the content of my teaching has disrupted the familiar and accepted worlds of my students. With an unusual sense of urgency they either will interrupt my plans, by insisting upon pursuing and exploring the issues at hand, or will pursue their questions immediately after the class session has been dismissed. In this sense preaching, liturgy, and teaching may intensify the urgency of informal conversation to clarify options of faith, action, or relationship among congregational members. They become catalysts to the educational activity of clarifying options for faith, action, or relationship in the informal conversation among congregational members.

A fourth characteristic of informal conversation as an educational activity locates participants in the middle of the exercise of interpretation or making meaning, of creating identity or of shaping one's world. These interpretive tasks engage participants in the exercise of thinking and reflection in the pursuit of understanding, commitment, and identification in the pursuit of belonging, or making and implementing which are integral to the pursuit of creating and doing. As an interpretive activity, conversation is not neutral. It alters the lives of its participants by restructuring their sense of reality. When conversation occurs at the juncture of making meaning, it illumines the disparities between old beliefs, values, and skills and the possibilities and demands of the new upon our lives. This characteristic builds on the previous one. It moves people beyond the task of clarifying options to that of transforming prior knowledge, relationships, and skills with the content of new information, perceptions, abilities. Much of this task of appropriating the new into the way we think, relate, and act occurs in the give and take of informal conversation because it provides a relatively safe environment where public opinion and values can be set aside in a mutual quest for appropriating the implications of our new understandings, sense of belonging, or skill.

In summary, the mutuality of informal conversation engages people in an openness to the possibility of learning and change. The marginality of informal conversation provides a relatively unrestricted environment for the consideration of issues, ideas, and alternative modes of action. The urgency in much informal conversation undergirds the momentum that leads to the decisions culminating in new interpretations, new commitments to others, and new or refined skills.

Facilitating Informal Conversation as a Christian Education Activity

Few congregations or parishes consciously nurture informal conversation. It can be done however. It can be enhanced and enlivened. Where it does occur, it typically emphasizes the quest for relationship or community that is integral to the sense of belonging. Often a congregation creates structures to facilitate informal opportunities for people to become acquainted and to develop deeper relationships. The time-honored tradition of potluck or covered dish dinner is one example. It is more common, however, for congregational programs to hinder or limit the efforts of its members to engage in conversation. In many congregations, members see each other only when they meet for some official activity. Many people, if not most, do not know each other well enough to risk the mutuality that undergirds conversation. Church activities tend to engage people in institutional rather than interpersonal agendas. Schedules tend to eliminate the spaces and times at the margins of congregational programs which are the typical settings for informal conversation. Professional staff are so busy with their managerial and pastoral activities that they do not model the value of conversation.

Perhaps in the majority of congregations and parishes, "to meet" has become an organizational term. It has little to do with an older view: coming together as if of one mind. The result is a loss of the psychological content in the patterns of reaching out and receiving which are integral to conversation. To meet is to commune with one another, to participate in community. In contrast, church meetings may efficiently facilitate program decisions, but they usually do not include the discussions integral to the gathering of people into a corporate commitment to those decisions. They limit and fragment the processes of thinking and understanding to the pros and cons of a given proposal. And they often hand over the interaction of doing, which underlies a congregation's ministry, to those with special training.

In his study of an orthodox Jewish congregation, Samuel Heilman observed that much of what I am calling informal conversation occurs in specific spots or places of sociability.[8] In that phrase we may begin to discern several clues to enhance the quality of the conversation at the edges of congregational life. A first step has to do with *legitimating times and places for conversation.* I have a pastor friend who believes that one can ascertain the vitality of congregational life, at least in part, by the length of time people stand around talking with each other after a service of worship. This congregational activity usually points to the strength of the sense of corporate identity among church members. In some instances it also may reveal a shared commitment to critical reflection as a response to the preaching and celebrating they have just experienced.

The Sunday morning schedule in all too many places prevents such times for gathering. Fifteen minutes are allotted for moving from Sunday school to worship. If a congregation has more than one service of worship they are scheduled so as to leave just enough time for one group of people to leave before the next begins to arrive. Custodians hang around church doors sending only slightly veiled messages to people to leave. Lights are turned out and the pastoral leadership disappears after shaking the last hand in the rituals of departure—all indicators that this event has concluded and that those who remain are both hindering the work of people and exceeding the accepted bounds of the stated schedule.

Church buildings, moreover, are designed for the most part to inhibit conversation. Hallways are for greeting and moving, not meeting people. Foyers are to provide space for people to remove coats and to create barriers against street noises. The "lounges" churches build are designed for formal social and celebrative events, not conversation. Classrooms both gather and divide people. It was not until I began writing this essay that it occurred to me how often in one congregation certain friends and I had retreated to the church kitchen when we were caught up in conversation. It was the one place where we could pull up stools to be with each other, did not feel rushed by our internal time clock or the church's schedule, and did not sense that we were in the way of some group or program.

The possibility of conversation is enhanced, in other words, when places and times for conversation are seen as legitimate. This step involves a close look at schedules in order to make room for informal conversation around planned activities and an effort to create places that enhance the excitement and reduce the risk inherent in the mutuality of conversation. It is a step that should be considered in both the planning of new programs and the designing of new church buildings. Do the programs and buildings encourage or hinder the meeting of people that nurtures conversation? It is a step that can be taken as well by sanctioning existing places of sociability. In one congregation, for example, someone noticed that between the worship service and Sunday school hours, a number of adults gathered and talked at a point where two hallways intersected—usually blocking traffic. A coffee pot was set up in the classroom at the point of the intersection. The double doorways were left open. No other group was scheduled into that room in order not to create a sense that people were invading someone else's turf. Church staff members dropped by for a cup of coffee and stayed to talk with persons in the room. It is now a major gathering place for people from all over the church building. Much of the talk may not be deep or profound, but that place conveys the message that "meeting" and conversation are valued.

Creating times and places for informal conversation is not enough. *It also must be encouraged and stimulated.* This is not an easy task. Evidence of resistance to the open-endedness of conversation is overwhelming. Many adult Bible study classes concentrate their energies upon the acquisition of biblical information while rejecting at the same time any attempts by class members to raise questions both inside and outside class time that might disturb commonly assumed values and beliefs. Preaching that challenges the status quo often is viewed as a threat rather than an invitation to conversation between preacher and parishioner or among parishioners. Concern for social justice frequently is limited to church legislation rather than to activities engaging people at the point of the diversity of their views and fears. The homogeneity of many contemporary congregations may be traced partially to the lack of time taken for diverse peoples to meet each other. The mission of the congregation generally has been domesticated by management objectives. In such congregations or parishes cohesiveness and efficiency usually have supplanted the quest of their members for increased understanding, a deeper sense of commitment and belonging, and a more relevant engagement in the mission of the church.

This resistance is located, in part, in the tendency of people to limit their understanding of Christian education to what happens in the classroom, to confine their expectations of church relationships to the potluck supper, and to view worship as a release from the routines and pressures of the week. There is another way. The activities of the church can be seen as a catalyst to the learning, worship, sense of community, and mission of the congregation.

The task of stimulating informal conversation usually

is achieved through the creation of events and experiences offered simply for the mutual reflection of people whenever and wherever they might gather. Some examples are commonplace: the provocative sermon title posted on the church signboard; a visiting lecturer who introduces new ideas not tied to any member or program of the congregation; a drama presented by the youth revealing new ways of viewing familiar biblical narratives; a painting or art print displayed for a special occasion or season. I think of a worship service in which the Scripture lesson was first read and then dramatized. People were still talking about it a week later. I think of work camps and retreats, of lay leaders visiting mission sites, and of an occasional column in the church newsletter. Each prompted informal conversations among congregational members. In some instances these conversations worked their way into formal classes, and administrative and worship settings. In the process, they enriched and extended the life and mission of the congregation. They contributed directly to a sense of excitement and vitality. The task of stimulating informal conversation consequently should be among the priorities in the work of congregational leaders and professional staff.

These events promote informal conversation especially when pastors and other church staff, officers, and teachers initiate both formal and informal conversation. When congregational leaders value conversation, they take the time to listen and enter into a discussion with church members after a meeting, class, or worship service, thereby encouraging people to share their thoughts and concerns. When they include time in a class session or a meeting for people to explore optional ways to look at an issue, they promote conversation. When they respect the insights and questions of people, they give them permission to probe beyond the safety of the familiar. When they view differences of opinion as an occasion to explore an issue more deeply, rather than as an obstacle to completing an agenda, they nurture the open-endedness of conversation. Informal conversation is encouraged when leaders model its importance for the life and work of the congregation; and it is stimulated by the quality of their listening, the provocative character of their questions, and the depth of their own contribution to the conversation of congregational members.

A third way to facilitate informal conversation is *to create explicit places of sociability*. Such settings encourage movement beyond the small talk and rituals of social intensification found in the ways we usually greet each other, inquire after each other's children, briefly describe how busy we are, how the weather is affecting us, or how the local athletic team is faring.

In my own pastoral experience these sociable places generally have been located on the margins of the organized life of the congregation. They usually were found in the special studies sponsored by women, and in the maverick Sunday school class that expressed frustration with many of the curricular resources. Occasionally, these sociable places also could be found in the special Lenten study series that gathered people into an intensified experience of the journey through the events of Holy Week, or in the work camp setting where, in giving ourselves to others, we might experience the freedom to examine cherished beliefs and values.

There have been many organized efforts over the past several years to restructure congregational life in such a way that informal conversation would be enhanced as an educational activity. Few have been granted legitimacy by congregational leaders or by the officials in denominational program agencies, however, because they correctly surmised that such efforts usually brought some kind of organic change to congregational life. One of the more recent attempts toward making sociability legitimate may be located in the *Koinonia* movement of the late 1950s and early 1960s.[9] This movement emphasized the necessity of strong corporate identity reflected in the commitment to making short-term covenants with a small group of other persons for the purposes of study, prayer, and mission. The title of one of the popular books of the movement, *The Miracle of Dialogue*, by Reuel Howe, reflects the movement's primary educational strategy. Its emphasis upon interdependence and mutuality is seen in the title of another popular study book of the movement, Martin Buber's *I and Thou*. This conversational structure emphasized, initially, the processes of belonging and identification. At the same time it generally prompted an openness to the consequences of thinking and the possibilities for change in one's life through some form of witness or mission. Some years later a curricular design by John and Adrienne Carr, entitled "An Experiment in Practical Christianity," built on the themes of this movement by providing participants with structured practice in the sociability that leads to conversation toward commitment, thinking, and doing.[10] In these formal educational activities, informal conversation is sanctioned as an appropriate methodology for teaching and learning. It is prompted and enriched by more traditional teaching activities, but it is made possible by creating time and space for it.

Conclusion

In the modern congregation, places of sociability are increasingly limited. A major consequence is to be found in the decreasing possibilities for the informal conversation that serves as context, catalyst, and agent of much of the church's educational program and activity. The irony of attempting to explore its contribution to the education of the congregation at this point in time should not be lost on us. For the contemporary congregation to affirm the value of the educational potential in informal conversation, its members may have to experience some profound changes in their relationship to each other as well as in the way they organize their common life. And yet, as I conclude this essay, I am convinced of the necessary interdependence of the intentional educational structures designed to educate people and of the curricular undercurrents that enrich, shape, and extend that education. Informal conversation is a major element in the congregation's education. In the fragmented experience of the modern world, its significance may become even more obvious as we seek for ways together to maintain and renew the life of the church as a community of faith for and with the next generation.

Teaching:
Forming
and
Transforming
Grace

MARIA HARRIS
Fordham University

One of the greatest myths in the Christian church is that we must do it alone. No matter what the "it" is, when issues or problems face us, the characteristic response—too often—is along the lines of "But what shall I do?" In that question lies a threefold reaction: (1) it is up to *me* to solve things; (2) the solution lies in some *action*; (3) the task at hand is to arrive at techniques and procedures for carrying out the particular action.

In this chapter, where we look at teaching as forming and transforming grace in the congregation, I wish to set that perennial question aside, not because it is unimportant, but because, surely, it is never the first question. If we are ever to understand the hows and whys of teaching, we must begin somewhere else. And so, in the place of "But what shall I do?" I want to suggest a different initial question: "Who calls?" Reflecting upon that question may not lead us to new ones, but it might suggest a different order for the familiar ones and provide a broader framework for the questions we do ask. And then, from the examination of the call to teach, we can move more easily to the curriculum which calls us and then to the realization we do not have to work alone. Our context is the congregation, a communion of people gathered together. We are gifted with persons whose vocation is to be catalysts—our pastors. And when we do teach, we do it as colleagues: as companions with one another, with our students, with the wider community of our church, and with the Creator God, in whose commonwealth it is our privilege to serve. Thus the design of this chapter forms a pattern in five parts:

1. The Call
2. The Curriculum
3. The Context
4. The Catalyst
5. The Colleagues

Put another way, I will be suggesting that any congregation examining its own teaching does so best by following a process of five questions, which may lead to new beginnings. These questions are:

1. Who calls us to teach?
2. What are we to teach?
3. What is our setting, our environment, our context?
4. On whom do we depend for support?
5. (And now finally) But what shall we do?

The Call

"There lies the dearest freshness deep down things," wrote Hopkins, "And though the last lights off the black west went,/ Oh, morning at the brown brink eastward springs/ Because the Holy Ghost over the bent/ World broods with warm breast, and with/ Ah! bright wings." When we contemplate the terrible things of our times, the tragedy and horror of our world, we cannot be faulted for missing the dearest freshness deep at the core of reality. The fissures of evil crossing our century; Holocaust, war, and apartheid can freeze us in apathy and can rob us of compassion. Nevertheless, we are a people of Creation. The creed of the Christian church begins with the affirmation: I believe in God the Creator. The Creator broods over and in and with the Creation, each morning, calling us to begin anew.

Teaching is the particular call we consider in this chapter. By reason of our Creator's summons, we have found ourselves Christians, members of the church of Jesus the Christ. As Christians, we find ourselves in possession of a heritage that has been preserved not only through words, but through the lives and blood of martyrs, apostles, and prophets. We are bearers of a gift, and if that gift is to be handed on in turn, then some activity must address it directly. And so we have the activity of teaching, or in more religious language, the grace of teaching. Often we think of grace as a static reality, a commodity, a thing we earn or acquire. But theology teaches us that in actuality grace is a living, pulsing, dynamic life; the awesome Reality of the Living God present in the body of the Christ, forming and transforming that body into the Divine Image. If we examine it, we see the activity of teaching as a form through which this living grace is made manifest. The teaching of the heritage is a *forming* grace, since it offers an identity within a community, and can enable the discovery of who we are spiritually. It can give us our selves. But history shows teaching is also a *transforming* grace, with a dynamic and a power within it to reshape and recreate the earth, to forge new structures for peace, for justice, and for the understanding which can lead to a world where all may be one.

The particular issue we face today is not whether teaching is near death, but whether the forms we have used for our teaching (Bible classes, the Sunday school, graded curricula) are appropriate to us, particularly as agents of grace. We sense the presence of wider issues which our old forms often keep us from facing. And we are right. The contemporary world is incredibly complex and calls for complex responses. What might the doctrine of the Creator Spirit, calling us as a people, suggest? Are there other ways to talk about and to examine teaching in the church?

I am convinced of an affirmative answer to this question, found through our responding to the threefold call we have received in baptism: to the imitation of the Christ who is priest, who is prophet, who is *kyrios* or sovereign. We who are made in the image of the Creator Spirit, and who are sisters and brothers of Jesus, have received a call to continue the ministry of our Brother as a priestly, a prophetic, a political people. Moreover, each of the church's activities participates in this threefold call or triple office. Along with worship, community, outreach, and the proclaimed word, teaching is a *priestly, prophetic, and political* ministry, and the shapes for this ministry in today's church begin with this threefold office, call, or vocation. How is this so?

1. Teaching is a priestly act. The priestly character of teaching can be described as living fully in the present out of the past. Here is the dimension of teaching which makes sure we attend to, and *tend* to, heritage, story, the received tradition, with intelligence, critical thought, and care-full reflection. Here is the dimension of teaching which insists that the lives of the saints and the martyrs be preserved. Here is the dimension of teaching preserved in liturgy and sacrament and in our instruction and reflection upon them. This grace-full activity can occur in Bible classes and Sunday school, of course, but it cannot transform unless it is rooted in the conviction that to be respondents to the call of our Creator, we must be engaged in the priestly activity of reengaging the past. We must be involved in the presentation and handing on of our story, with all its anguish and sin as well as its wonder and glory. We must *remember*. We must say "Yes" to those from whom we have come. But this is not enough.

2. Teaching is a prophetic act. The prophetic character of teaching can be described as living fully in the present out of the future. The prophetic is an essential element in the grace of teaching because Jesus was not only priest, he was prophet.

Following upon this, the vocation or call of the Creator Spirit to carry on Jesus' work is the reminder that in teaching we must take the heritage or tradition and do two things. First, we must use it as a measuring stick, a norm, a guide to church and world; we must draw on the Gospel as critical source. Second and more difficult: in our teaching, we also must examine the tradition itself, which paradoxically calls us to examine it, to see if our teaching and our telling of the Gospel must be revised in the light of present reality. We need to address the Scriptures themselves, to discover where even they might fall short of the call of the Creator God. Looking at the present conditions of our world, especially those such as hunger, racism, poverty, political oppression, and sexism, teaching must be a grace of criticism. It must take the realities of our world and complicate the thinking of church members even to the point of calling the Gospel to account. For the prophetic dimension in teaching is the grace to say "No! Never! Never again!" to whatever destroys, to whatever falls short of the radical demand of the Creator Spirit: "Come, follow me."

3. Teaching is a political act. The political character of teaching can be described as living fully in the present out of the forms and structures which embody our lives together: our order, polity, ways of coming together, ways of sharing authority and power, and ways of engaging in "wise rule." For Jesus is priest and prophet, but he is also sovereign—a perhaps outmoded but nevertheless political title which reminds us that both in the church and beyond, the body of the Christ is in the form of a body politic. Within, we are the body of the Christ, and members one of another. Without, we are called to see the presence of God in all our brothers and sisters: I was hungry . . . I was naked . . . I was in prison. We are intertwined with one another and the original commandment has not changed: we must love one another; we must love one another or die.

The political character of the grace of teaching impels us to study how we might create structures, forms, and systems—political bodies—which can make church life more Christian and human life more human. In other words, we must hand on the heritage, we must say the "Yes" of our priesthood.

But this is not enough. We must develop critical capacities and think things through, especially around the presence of evil. We must say the "No" of prophecy. But this is not enough. In tandem with both of these, we must create forms both in and for our teaching which can bring a new way of being-together as people—a new *polis*—into being, where we can say of all creation the word of a graced polity: "We." The Creator Spirit calls us, pushes us, and thus brings us to the brink of the next question: "If our vocation is a way of participating in the Christian call to be priestly, prophetic, and political, what are we to teach?"

The Curriculum

The question, "What are we to teach?" is the question of the choice of forms we make, forms which if used might become agents of transforming grace. Traditionally, the avenue for answering this question has been to select from an overabundance of materials a particular set of knowledge resources, put together in a particular way, and then to use them as the basic "stuff" which is presented to students or learners. Such "stuff" is called by the term: curriculum. In *The Educational Imagination,* Elliot Eisner suggests a set of insights into curriculum which enables a far richer understanding of curricular forms as starting point. He points out that all institutions teach not one, but *three* curricula, a distinction enabling us to see a much broader range of forms for our teaching. These three curricula, taught in every church, are the following: (1) the explicit curriculum; (2) the implicit curriculum; and (3) the null curriculum.

1. The explicit curriculum. The explicit curriculum is equivalent to the knowledge resources, the particular topics, ideas, courses, themes, and units of study to be explored. Iris Cully has surveyed the range of options people use here by naming four ways in which the forms of explicit curriculum are chosen. First is the choice of a graded set of lessons, where a particular published course of study is followed throughout a church school. This makes for consistency and ease, although it tends not to challenge creativity. Second is the choice of a *theme* by a church, followed by the selection of published materials which will enable all teachers to be concerned with that same theme. A third could kindly be called the "independent" approach, where individual teachers follow their own lights, or less kindly, the "hit or miss" approach where people choose to work with whatever materials they like, at times choosing not to use suggested resources. And fourth is the design of a curriculum which fits the local situation and comes out of the life of the local parish. Cully says the major trend in curriculum development today lies in the increasing initiative being taken at the parish level. She goes on to suggest this trend is encouraged by the systems approach which alerts planners to the interaction among factors in the educational program. Some of these factors are understanding assumptions, development of goals, teacher development, and common ownership by the congregation. All of these, however, are only one form of curriculum: the explicit. Two others remain.

    2. The implicit curriculum. In the church, the implicit curriculum would refer to such elements as the patterns of organization or authority; the attitudes of persons toward one another; the ways power is shared; the freedom to speak (who does speak, and perhaps more subtly, who gets heard); and the kinds of physical setting in which teaching happens (what goes on in what goes on). We can discover some of the most powerful dynamisms within the implicit curriculum, for example, by examining the way students and teachers talk to each other. We can reflect carefully on the informal conversations in the teaching situation, drawing on the suggestions of Charles Foster's essay elsewhere in this volume. We can look at the ways teachers choose to shape subject matter—an excellent topic for teacher supervision and teacher conferences. If the procedures are caring, dialogical, and concerned with truth and understanding (as they are in many places), one message is received. If procedures are authoritarian, condescending, uncaring, or sloppy (despite what is said in the explicit curriculum), something else is taught. Basically, the implicit curriculum is an illustration of the following notion of John Dewey. "Perhaps the greatest of all pedagogical fallacies," he wrote, "is the notion that [people] learn only the particular thing [they] are studying at the time."[1]

3. The null curriculum. The null curriculum is a paradox. This is the curriculum that exists because it does not exist. It refers to areas left out and procedures left out. And the point of naming it and including it here is critical: ignorance is not neutral. Not being educated in something skews our perceptions, limits our alternatives, narrows our options. Failure to study Christian attitudes toward Judaism since the time of Jesus (the so-called "teaching of contempt" which either ignored the presence of Jews in the world, or held them responsible for the death of Jesus) is one example. Silence on the church's involvement in sexual and racial bias is another. Attending only to the church's inner life without also attending to mission, outreach, and the planet itself is another. Failure to teach the ministry of the whole people of God is another. Citing only white, or middle class, or middle aged, or North American, or European clergymen as authors or authorities are other examples. But procedures, processes, and ways of doing things are part of the null curriculum too: the absence, for example, of drama, art, dance, or sculpting as ways of learning; and the ignorance of procedures such as case study, open classroom, or journal keeping are others.

If we examine the three curricula as they exist in our local settings, interesting questions arise. Although these are questions only the individual congregation can answer, the asking is nonetheless pertinent. We can ask, for example, which of the four approaches to forming the explicit curriculum is the one we are choosing and why. Have we chosen in order to *transform* or to shore up the status quo? Do we believe teaching is a forming and transforming grace, and if so, have we looked carefully at the possibilities we have for devising our own curricula? With reference to creating our own, do we believe that "it won't work," or has that been made more difficult than it is in actuality? In the United States and Canada, Christian education scholars and teachers have been offering resources to do this for many years. For example, to name only a few: from the regular publications of *Christian Education: Shared Approaches* and Joint Educational Development, to the continuing freshness in the suggestions of John Westerhoff, to Walter Wink's proposals for transforming Bible Study, to Norma Everist's *Education Ministry in the Congregation* (see the end of this chapter for more suggestions).

Basic Christian communities in Latin America and in many parts of Europe have taught us that for people to come together prayerfully to read the gospel, to reflect, and then to decide on action does not require fancy, expensive materials, although it does require the often painful decisions of making choices of some issues, some material, and some criteria, and of discarding others. Such questions as these, as well as others we might reflect upon, push us to discover, as a community of people, what in our heritage we wish to be sure to hand on. They enlighten us on our own framing of the three curricula. And they enable us to realize the truth of Ellis Nelson's comment that whatever the written curriculum, or whatever the intention, the deliberate words and actions that people use in all kinds of specific events and the quality of the corporate life of the believers *are* the curriculum.

We see, then, that in actuality absence of attention to the community's life together is tied inevitably to all three curricula and thus raises further questions. For the explicit curriculum is the form we have chosen in which to say: here is the heritage we wish to hand on; these are the things which make us *us*. The implicit curriculum is the set of forms, the procedures and processes of our living together as a body politic, which are teaching us. And the null curriculum becomes the prophetic voice, reminding us of what we have left out, often to our detriment as a people.

If we look at these three curricula with fresh eyes, we might find clues to understand either how our forms of teaching are keeping us from transformation, or how our being together as a congregation is transforming not only ourselves as individuals but also this graced, embodied, and communal unit of

Christ's body which we call the congregation. It is to the congregation's role in teaching we now need to turn.

The Context

I have argued thus far that teaching is a forming and transforming grace to which a calling exists. The basic forms which can transform our teaching are found in the curriculum. However, if the grace of teaching is to be made visible and to become incarnate, it must be born in a particular setting, environment, or context, which is itself part of the world as a whole. In the Christian church, this context is the church, the gathered, corporate, communal body of the Christ.

Pascal suggested long ago that one Christian is no Christian; paraphrasing him, we need to realize that one teacher is no teacher. For when we examine it, we find the grace of teaching does not rise out of an individual's right or even duty to teach. It arises out of the nature of the church in its gathered form as the seat and source of the teaching ministry. This ministry is never *my* ministry; it is *ours*. Despite appearances to the contrary, ministry—especially the teaching ministry—is the least individualistic of the church's acts.

If this is true, then the starting point for teaching cannot be the individual teacher, or as noted above, the Bible study, or Sunday school. Rather, the starting point must be the people, the corporate body from which the teacher comes, and for whom the teacher acts. It seems to me this point is critical, and often abused in practice. Teachers volunteer or are drafted to teach not because they have a personal or private desire (although these can exist), but because a larger community, which understands itself to be graced, wishes to instruct, form, and transform. This community needs some members who will be agents of forming and transforming grace as delegates of the wider community. The activity is not taken on for oneself; it is always a congregational office, where one is essentially a representative and a presenter as well—for, with, in, and to the entire people. And this suggests that the congregation's role will take at least four forms. These forms are not disparate activities. Instead, they are moments in a rhythm, moments each of which leads to the next, in which the members of the congregation are involved in a kind of moving pattern, or churchly dance. The moments are receptivity, responsibility, embodiment, and ritual.

1. *Receptivity.* At the beginning of this chapter, in commenting on the "What shall I do?" question, I raised the issue of assuming the first step is action. I return now to that issue. To do so, allow me to share an anecdote. The story is told of the World Council of Churches meeting in Sydney, Australia in 1980. Whenever a question arose, it is said, national groups tended to react in characteristic ways, in keeping with their regional characters. The Latin Americans could be relied on to address the question with passion and compassion; they were the symbols for the life of feeling being brought to the fore. The Africans almost always would respond in terms of the meaning of the issue for the community. The Asians would respond with periods of contemplative, silent reflection. And the North Americans, especially those from the United States, would ask immediately: "But what are we going to do, and how?" Progress and procedures continue to be our most important products; we continue to be a can-do people; it is our national character.

Nevertheless, the point of the story is to remind us that in the face of any profound reality, we need first to be still, to be silent, to contemplate, and to listen. We need to be receptive: to Being most essentially, and to the address of the One who calls us by name. We need to be receptive to the situation; to hear all the sides. We need to be comfortable with poking around, getting to know what is involved, finding out where the tough and the rough spots are, before we plunge into actual engagement with the teaching activity as it goes on in the church. In practice this would be reflected in such processes as beginning congregational meetings with ten or fifteen minutes of silence or meditation, along lines such as those suggested elsewhere in this volume by Mary Elizabeth Moore; in concrete and corporate tending to the spirituality of the congregation; in retreats for vestry and board members which have long stretches of silence.

One church, for example, conducted a retreat for its leaders with no other agenda than silent listening in the presence of one another; another church places in its job description the requirement that all of its ministers spend an hour of silent prayer daily. The outcome of such activity is the realization that teaching begins when we are still, when we take time to listen, and not when the first words are spoken. Perhaps it is true that all of the great troubles of the world have come from the inability to sit still in a room. Certainly, the congregation which has learned how to listen is in less danger of making foolish mistakes. Further, grace lies in such moments, which are themselves instances of forming and transforming. And if such receptivity does occur, then it pulses toward a second moment in the congregation's teaching involvement: responsibility.

2. *Responsibility.* All in the congregation may not be able to center regularly upon this creative receptivity. Thus it becomes a necessity in the congregation that a group of people, again representing the larger group, be delegated as Partners or Companions to the teaching office. Such people would be a team or a board or a committee whose responsibility would be to listen, especially to students and teachers, incorporating into their listening the silence just described; to serve, again especially those who are in the teaching role in terms of material needs (for chalk, for books, for heat and light, for baby sitters, and so on); to act as liaison for the congregation to the teaching staff, and as liaison for the staff to the congregation. Genuine conflict can arise in any congregation, of course, and such a board might be called upon to assist in such a circumstance. Of far more importance, however, is the need volunteer teachers have for someone or some group in the congregation to act in the role of advocate, partisan, or trouble-shooter. Such a group might sub-divide into smaller groups concerned with

The Rhythm of Congregational Involvement in Teaching

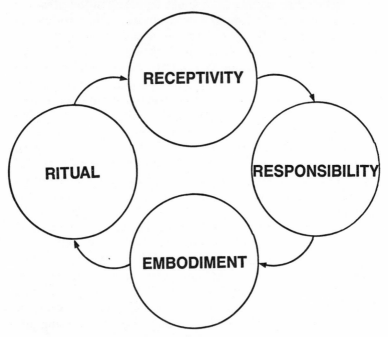

specific areas, either of subject matter (Scripture, church history, justice), or of human concerns in teaching (children of divorced parents, handicapped church members, young married people), or of teaching environment (appreciation, payment, awareness).

It is a sad comment, but one which must be made, that at times a congregation can be seen as ignorant of, or worse as adversary to its own teaching staff. The presence of a group which anticipates needs, which solicits comments, which follows up requests, and which acts as partner and ally is a sacred symbol for the reality of the larger body of the Christ. The work of responsibility would not extend only to the teachers, however; the same face would be turned toward the congregation as a whole, reminding *it* of *its* participation in the teaching office of the church. Thus, a third moment would emerge: embodiment.

3. Embodiment. Embodiment is a way of naming the truth that the congregation as a whole has its characteristic ways of participating in the triple office of the Christ; its ways of being priestly, prophetic, and political. And although these are not direct and intentional teaching roles, it must be said (A) the roles are essential to the actual teaching activities since the life of the congregation is the context of this teaching; and (B) the congregation as a body is implicitly teaching through each of these forms of communal life. And what are the forms of communal life through which the congregation embodies (incarnates, demonstrates in perceptible form) what it believes? What are the forms through which the congregation teaches?

Traditionally, four have been named. The first two are *leiturgia*, which is the church at prayer, the church at worship; the church acting through its sacramental forms of baptism and Lord's Supper; and *kerygma*, which is the church speaking, proclaiming the Word. We find these illuminated in the doctrine that the church can be found where the gospel is preached and the sacraments duly administered. The third is *koinonia*, the church gathered in community and communion, striving to create forms for the body politic to live in; searching for avenues of healing and wholeness. The fourth is *diakonia*, the church reaching out in service, in help, and in healing to a bruised world. The point to be made here is that these four, along with *didache*, or the church teaching as forming and transforming grace, are the church's characteristic ways of teaching what it is like to live the Christian life. No word said in a classroom or a study group will be able to take flesh in learners' lives unless a demonstration community exists as the fulfillment, or at least the attempted (even though flawed and faulty) embodiment, of the words the teacher speaks, and towards which the teacher can point. And once again, if this form is seriously

tended, it will lead the church to find corporate ways to embody
its concern; in other words, it will precipitate to a final, new
moment: the moment of ritual.

  4. Ritual. Perhaps the richest way the congregation can
fulfill its responsibilities to be partners and companions to the
teaching act is through ritual. Traditionally, the church knows
how to conduct rituals: ceremonial acts of a religious, often
sacred nature. Baptism and confirmation are among these rites,
which are certainly among the richest graces we possess for
forming and transforming. We are deeply faithful to our baptism and confirmation when they lead us to the creation of
other rituals. I would advocate the congregation drawing on
its knowledge and experience of ritual in order to affirm the
lives and work of those who are its delegates in the teaching
office. Certainly, commissioning and affirming ceremonies, at
the beginning and the end of each school year, are ways of
doing this, and already a given in many local churches.

  Beyond these, however, which sometimes can become
deadened through overuse or routine, congregations might add
several other ceremonies: for teachers of particular ages or
groups (the handicapped, older adults, the retarded, the pre-
schoolers, the pregnant, the choir) in the middle of the year,
perhaps at Thanksgiving; at Labor Day, to lift up and affirm
this work; on the Baptism day of each teacher, remembering
their initial call. As an act of gracious gratitude, the congregation also might host celebrations for departing teachers, who
are moving elsewhere or not returning. Additionally, the congregation might prepare at least one worship service each year
as a direct exploration of the teaching ministry, or it might
design a teacher awards night with a dinner or banquet where
the appreciation and affection of the community can be shown.
Rituals which address the darker side of teaching might also
be devised, to lift up our moments of hesitation, mourning,
failure, and regret. In addition, creative and imaginative congregations might even conceive and develop a ritual that acknowledges and affirms the sacramental nature of teaching.
Such rituals, as forming graces, might then be understood as

transforming graces as well—manifestations of the presence in the midst of the congregation of the Creator, the Christ and the Spirit in whose names the ministry of teaching is performed.

The Catalyst

What is everyone's job is nobody's job; therefore, the reality of the situation demands a particular office in the church as a whole where the responsibility for calling the congregation to its work as the body of the Christ resides. This is, of course, the pastoral office, which is held most often by an ordained minister, pastor, or priest, and which sometimes is enlarged to include a Minister of Education or Director of Education. Although the office is situated in the center of the community, indeed, although the office belongs to the community as a whole, it is held by one or two, but certainly no more than three or four, persons who have been formally ordained or commissioned to *teach*, and following upon that, to be overseer, guide, and first among equals in being the church as it teaches. Such persons have many other duties besides teaching in the church— they are concerned with worship, outreach, community, and Gospel as well. Indeed, the life of the church is their full-time work.

Nevertheless, as pastors or ministers, they do have certain roles which only they can perform, in part by reason of both office and expertise. The term "catalyst," indicating one who precipitates a process or event, one who is in a position to create the circumstances which lead to transformation, is the one I have chosen for the pastor, minister, or DCE. This person is the one who precipitates the teaching grace, who stays with teachers as a living organism, or catalyst, always available; and who does so through inspiration, envisioning, and presence.

1. Inspiration. One of the more difficult responsibilities of any pastor is the task of inspiration—of being and doing in such a way that others are touched by the Spirit. The major place for doing this, among most pastors, is in the pulpit, through the preached word, and with reference to teachers, through words which speak directly and eloquently of the importance of the teaching role. But the pastor also inspires by being a facilitator and a mentor. Facilitating is making things easier— the "oiling," the removing of obstacles, and the setting up of environments where teaching can be accomplished in a structure of care, where teachers know they are thought about and wanted. To know, as a church school teacher, that your pastor is your aide, that your DRE or DCE is especially commissioned to be with you, that advocacy for you and your concerns is always present is an extraordinary but possible source of inspiration.

But inspiration also is accomplished by the pastor who is a mentor: who is familiar herself or himself with teaching, and who provides in the pastor's class, or weekly Bible study, or monthly congregation conference, a model of teaching and care for teaching. As mentor, the pastor is one who can be relied upon to assist as a reliable guide; one who knows the terrain and can point out both rocky hillsides and lovely paths; one who—most of all—is available for conversation about teaching in the face of questions on the part of the teaching staff.

2. *Envisioning.* The work of envisioning might have been placed among the forms for the congregation's activity in Part 3, and individual churches may find it more feasible to do so. But at some point, it is necessary to designate someone as responsible for inviting those who will envision the form and nature of the church teaching, those who will do the designing and choosing of procedures for decision making which will bring about graced teaching in the congregation. Generally, the pastor or the Minister of Education will be the most appropriate and educationally prepared person for this work. As such, the pastor will help the congregation examine formats for teaching, discover resources to assist planning, and take responsibility for inviting and calling teachers.

Envisioning will include the question of what forms the teaching ministry of the church is to take. Together with the congregational board or committee, the pastor will assist in examining present practices and generating alternate or additional ones. Does the church wish to have, or continue, graded

Sunday school? Does the teaching program exist only for children? Where adults are involved, will the teaching be in classes or through retreats, or in home discussion, or in some other form?

Practically speaking, innumerable resources exist to help a group in asking such questions. Patterns such as AAAR (Awareness, Analysis, Action, Reflection); as EIAG (Experience, Identify, Analyze, Generalize); and Setting Goals and Objectives, Outlining Tasks, Naming Processes, Citing Resources, and Planning for Feedback are three of the best known. Iris Cully's *Planning and Selecting Curriculum for Christian Education,* with its counsels on putting it all together, is another. Norma Everist's distinction between presentation, worship, discussion, inductive study, individualized learning, confrontation, experiential learning, and journals is yet another. Many more could be cited (note the list at the end of this essay); but the point of naming these is to remind the pastor and congregation that they are not alone in their planning: their task is to come together, with the help of resources, in order to do some dreaming and to make some decisions.

Having done this, and having worked together with the congregation in shaping the program it wants, the pastor can then facilitate the important work of inviting and calling teachers. Who will they be, and **how** will they be invited or selected to participate? Again, this task is never started from scratch, but it should not begin until the congregation, through and with its pastor, has envisioned and decided upon the forms for teaching in that church.

3. Presence. Once the basic issues of formats, processes, and invitation are addressed (and those are at least yearly works), the pastor's ongoing role as a catalyst remains. The critical center of this ongoing role is the work of presence. Because of her or his office, the pastor/minister/DCE is looked to for support, for confirmation, for assistance, and, most of all, for *being there.* The dominant form of this presence will come by way not only of teacher training and provision of materials, but also of ongoing instruction, convening, worshiping, out-

The Three Teaching Agents

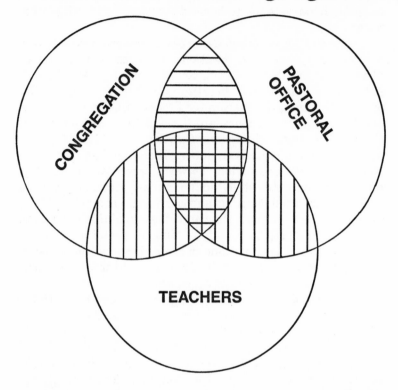

reach, and discussion—the five forms of ministry now directed to those called to teach. Often teacher training will occur on a weekly or monthly basis, but it needs to be undergirded with encouragement for attendance at regional or national conferences, and at the very least by one annual weekend retreat. It also will be manifested through rituals such as those mentioned in section three. One of the rituals the congregation might design is one of Promise, where, as teachers begin their yearly work, the pastor or minister, in the name of the congregation (or better the congregation itself), pledges this supportive presence, and the teachers express acceptance of it. And there might be a ritual of Partnership or Companionship, where those who have been called to teach are invited to take the position of colleagues; not only in the sense of associates in the profession of teaching or in the sense of associates of the gospel, but also in the sense of agents of grace for the church as a whole, through whom the forming and transforming grace and power of teaching may be offered.

The Colleagues

The first agent of teaching in the church is the congregation. The second agent of teaching in the church is the pastor. The third agent of teaching in the church is the person recruited to be a delegate for the first two, who stands in the role of a colleague: with the entire church body, with the pastor, with other colleagues, with students, and with subject matter. When we come to the work of the colleagues, the people called out of the congregation to teach, we come home: we finally touch teaching as it is put into actual practice. In this final part of the paper, I come to the question with which we began: "But what are we to do?" As we engage in the work of teaching, what forms have the capacity to lead to transformation?

I believe there are three levels to the response. At the deepest level, and in primary position: we are to transmit the heritage, to make it accessible to our students, and to discover how that heritage can make us aware of our world and can teach us how to act in our world. Formal, intended, direct teaching must hold on to both these poles at the same time: aware of the inheritance we have received, of the forms of church life we have received, not only helping us to give an account of the faith that is in us, true, but also using our critical intelligence to make that inheritance a touchstone for the transformation, indeed the re-creation of the world.

At a second level, and more specifically, we as teachers are to incarnate, that is, give form to subject matter. We are to shape, design, and re-form subject matter in such a way that our students come to moments of revelation—moments where the subject matter appears before them as a possibility to be chosen, an "Existence Possibility," in Kierkegaard's terms. In other words, the incarnation of subject matter must be accomplished by teachers in such a way that their students discover meaning in what is being offered, and experience moments of genuine discovery, coming upon the material fresh and new, as if it is seen for the first time.

Such moments of revelation, if they are accompanied by the student's genuine ownership of the material, will lead to a recognition on the part of the learner of his or her own power, of his or her own capacities face-to-face with the subject matter: to consider it, to discuss it, to play with it, to make new connections with it, perhaps even to discard it. The subject matter will not be "out there," it will instead be taken in and become part of the self and as such—especially as new knowledge—be a source of empowerment or transformation. My own favorite rendering of this activity comes in a poem of Christopher Logue:

> Appollinaire said, "Come to the edge."
> "It's too high."
>
> "Come to the edge."
> "We might fall."
>
> "COME TO THE EDGE."
> And they came.
>
> And she pushed them.
> And they flew.[2]

The teacher is one who incarnates subject matter in such a way that it leads to the revelation of subject matter, the greatest revelation being of one's own power, or in Paulo Freire's terms, the discovery of one's "ontological vocation to be a Subject."[3] When that discovery is made, the individual subjects, in communion with one another know that they have come to the moment where it is their vocation to use this revelation and power in the service of the world, lessening injustice certainly, but perhaps also contributing to recreation.

The third level is the everyday level, the practical level, and the one which consumes most of our attention and interest as teachers. This is the level of choosing the particular forms for our incarnation or embodiment of subject matter. And, given the extraordinary range of subject matter in the sense of content, as well as the extraordinary range of styles of learning in the human subjects, the basic rule for all teachers is that they will need to have an extensive repertoire of forms for their teaching.

These forms will be neither offered nor attained all at once, since teachers in every congregation will surely be at or in-between at least four different stages. Some will be at a level best named *survival*, and so their range of forms may be small. Others will have reached a place of *basic competence*, and their range or repertoire thus may be extended—like a pianist learning to play with two hands. A third will be at a place of *broad experience*, and they will be able to call on many possibilities. And last will be those who feel themselves moving either toward *boredom*, because their range is not expanding, or increased *creativity*, because their repertoire still is growing. The congregation, pastor, and colleagues together must make allowances for teachers being at these different places, and thus plan accordingly.[4]

In making plans for assisting the teaching colleagues to develop their repertoire of teaching forms, the congregation and pastor once again can depend on an overabundance of resources: from congregational consultants to printed materials to the presence of highly skilled lead teachers. Whichever they choose, however, the nature of the Christian church and the dynamics of the Christian message demand at least the following five: a repertoire which includes verbal forms, earth forms, embodied forms, art forms, and forms for discovery. I will give a brief one-paragraph description of each of these, followed by a short list of examples of the form. The examples are meant to be provocative, not exhaustive, and can serve as a mode of planning for an individual church.

Verbal forms. The normal vehicle for teaching is through words. Teaching is a verbal activity. Indeed, our existence is so founded on words that we live in language as fish live in the sea. Sometimes the words are discursive, and their form is one that encapsulates thought and ideas, concepts and doctrines, the foundations of our faith. At other times the words are more poetic, as we strive to get to layers of meaning underneath the words themselves. In teaching, words may be shaped in innumerable ways: the teacher's task is to work to make them fresh, accurate, appropriate, and inviting. Among these ways are:

- discourse/lecture
- journal keeping
- psalm recitation
- mock courtroom
- making up questions
- case studies

- rewriting parables
- choral speaking
- completing phrases
- interviewing:
  "Telling a Life"

Earth forms. Beyond words, we can use matter to tell its story. I think, for example, of Jerome Berryman leading a class of six-year-olds to the church and then saying three words. They walked to the Baptistry, he pointed and said, "Water." They then walked to the altar, where things were laid out for communion, lifted the cup and poured, and said, "Water." They then walked to the stained-glass window of Jesus calming the sea. And he said, "Water." Nothing else was needed: the water taught. Some other examples, where air, earth, and fire are included are:

- candle lighting
- fires lighted for warmth
- tending a lawn for older persons
- washing babies
- molding clay

- petition burning
- breathing exercises for prayer
- making weather vanes
- simulated baptisms
- growing a garden

Embodied Forms. These forms are twofold. The first refers to how the learners come together (in straight lines, in circles, in easy chairs, as listeners, as participants) and to how this coming together draws on the local setting. Are they a university church, an inner city church, a multi-racial church, a house church, a woman church? The second refers to teaching in ways which actually use the body in teaching, such as drama, charades, and demonstration. Other examples are:

- being a Bible character
- pantomime
- cooking meals
- blindfolded trust walks
- reading to the visually impaired
- games, especially New Games
- giving blessings
- services of healing, anointing
- walks for peace
- hiking in prayerful silence

Art forms. Here, although overlapping with the previous three, teaching occurs in such a way that capacities beyond logical discourse are drawn upon in order to probe the subject matter more deeply, whether that subject matter is the story of the Exodus or the critical consideration of racism in our time. I think, for example, of an exercise where people are asked to take the time to mold in clay something they fear. Given time, people make symbols or representations of caves, wasps, snakes, swords. After some conversation they then are asked to work in silence and to remold their symbol of fear into a symbol of hope. Amazingly, a cave becomes a crèche; a wasp becomes a dove; snakes are turned into a traditional staff symbolizing medicine or a physician; swords become plowshares. Other examples of art forms are:

- film making
- play writing
- portrait painting
- choreography
- video tape recording of current events
- liturgical or community dance
- clowning
- song
- museum field trip
- silk screening

Forms for dis-covery. In one sense, these forms are found in the midst of the first four; and the first four, in turn, are necessary to dis-covery forms as well. Their distinguishing characteristic, however, is that they are generally activities or actions, planned in such a way that the outcome is unknown. What is known, however, is that when people take part, they will learn something new and, with a skillful wedding with verbal forms, make connections to the Christian life based on the gospel. Forms for dis-covery are risky; they can change one's life. They are particularly appropriate for the investigation of areas of justice and peace. Some examples are:

- Spend three days in town with no money in your purse or pocket.

- Spend the entire two hours of a class session in silence.

- Pretend you are a Martian, and have been told this place is a church. Report what you see and hear over a Saturday and Sunday.

- Trade work places with someone in your congregation for a day.

- Pretend for a day you have been born in the first century.

- Exchange church roles for a day: pastor/sexton/teacher/child.

- Change families for a week (especially for teenagers).

- Build a home for those without one, through Habitat for Humanity.

- Participate in a sanctuary church for Latin Americans.

Conclusion

This chapter has surveyed some of the possibilities for teaching in the congregation. The basic premises have been simple, indeed perhaps are reducible to the old adage: "The congregation does not have a Christian education program; it is one." But beyond that, the chapter has been an appeal to see teaching in the local church as a religious activity: an activity characterized as graced, where the ministry of teaching is itself both forming and transforming grace. Finally, it has been an appeal to see teaching, not as the work of one agent—the harried and hapless person who volunteers and then is left on his (or more usually) *her* own, with the fourth grade. Instead, it has been a brief for the three agents of teaching: the congregation, the pastor, and the teacher who is their colleague; for the three curricula: the implicit, the explicit, and the null; for the threefold office which is the Christian vocation; and for the One Creator God, who also is Three, and in whose name we have responded to the Gospel command: "Go and teach." In responding to that command, let us be convicted of the charge that we have discovered and dwelt in the grace that we have come to know as teaching.

Resources

Cully, Iris. "Changing Patterns of Protestant Curriculum." In Marvin J. Taylor (ed.) *Changing Patterns of Religious Education.* Nashville: Abingdon, 1984, 220–233. Cully gives a number of additional resources, including several from Joint Educational Development.

———. *Planning and Selecting Curriculum for Christian Education.* Valley Forge: Judson, 1983.

Downs, Thomas. *The Parish as Learning Community.* Ramsey, NJ: Paulist, 1979.

Eisner, Elliot. *The Educational Imagination.* New York: Macmillan, 1979.

Everist, Norma. *Education Ministry in the Congregation.* Minneapolis: Augsburg, 1983.

Fagan, Harry. *Empowerment: Skills for Parish Social Action.* Ramsey, NJ: Paulist, 1979.

Fenton, Thomas (ed.) *Education for Justice: A Resource Manual.* Maryknoll, NY: Orbis, 1975.

Griggs, Donald. *Teaching Teachers to Teach.* Nashville: Abingdon, 1976. All of the materials prepared and published as Griggs Educational Resources by Abingdon, and prepared by Donald and Patricia Griggs, are well worth consideration.

Harris, Maria. *Teaching and Religious Imagination.* San Francisco: Harper and Row, 1986.

Little, Sara. *To Set One's Heart. Belief and Teaching in the Church.* Atlanta: John Knox, 1983.

McCollough, Charles. *Heads of Heaven, Feet of Clay.* New York: Pilgrim, 1983.

McGinnis, James, et al. *Educating for Peace and Justice: Religious Dimensions*. St. Louis: Institute for Peace and Justice, 1984.

Rusbuldt, Richard. *Basic Teacher Skills*. Valley Forge: Judson, 1981.

Westerhoff, John. *Living the Faith Community*. Minneapolis: Winston, 1985.

Wingeier, Douglas. *Working Out Your Own Beliefs*. Nashville: Abingdon, 1980.

Notes

WHY THIS BOOK ON
CONGREGATIONS?
C. Ellis Nelson

1. Robert N. Bellah, et al., *Habits of the Heart* (Berkeley: University of California, 1985).

2. Elinore Pruitt Steward, *Letters of a Woman Homesteader* (Lincoln: University of Nebraska, 1961). See also John McPhee, "Annals of the Former World," *The New Yorker* February 24, March 3, and March 10, 1986.

3. Robert W. Lynn and Elliott Wright, *The Big Little School* (New York: Harper and Row, 1971), pages 17–39, 56–77. See also Robert W. Lynn, *Protestant Strategies in Education* (New York: Association, 1964) 65.

4. C. Ellis Nelson, *Where Faith Begins* (Atlanta: John Knox, 1967). This book provides a general explanation of how congregations through their life and work "form" the lifestyle of their members. The possibility of "transformation" by the same process is recognized but not given the practical attention you will find in this book.

5. Jackson W. Carroll, Carl S. Dudley, and William McKinney, *Handbook for Congregational Studies* (Nashville: Abingdon, 1986). This is an excellent guide for a congregation seeking self-understanding. It also provides practical guidance for a group of leaders to study the history, location, and mission of a congregation.

MEMORY IN
CONGREGATIONAL LIFE
Bruce C. Birch

1. This same dual quality is discussed as being and doing aspects of Christian life in Bruce C. Birch and Larry L. Rasmussen, *Bible and Ethics in the Christian Life* (Minneapolis: Augsburg, 1976).

2. The images are suggested by Jürgen Moltmann, "Christian Theology Today," *New World Outlook,* LXII, 1972, 483.

3. Recent thinking about biblical community as alternative community may be found in Walter Brueggemann, *The Prophetic Imagination* (Philadelphia: Fortress, 1978) ch. 1; and in Bruce C. Birch, *What Does the Lord Require? The Old Testament Call to Social Witness* (Philadelphia: Westminster, 1985) ch. 3.

4. Recent Protestant work in theology and ethics has given new emphasis to the formation of character in the life of the church. See Stanley M. Hauerwas, *Vision and Virtue* (Notre Dame, IN: Fides, 1974); and *Character and the Christian Life* (San Antonio, TX: Trinity University, 1975).

5. For a fuller discussion of questions of biblical authority see Birch and Rasmussen, *Bible and Ethics,* ch. 5.

6. For a complete discussion of the issue of the canon in biblical theology and in the life of the church see my article "Biblical Theology: Issues in Authority and Hermeneutics," *Wesleyan Theology Today* (Nashville: Kingswood, 1985).

7. Brevard Childs, *Biblical Theology in Crisis* (Philadelphia: Westminster, 1970) 105.

8. Ernesto Cardenal, *The Gospel in Solentiname* (Maryknoll, NY: Orbis, 1976). See also Robert McAfee Brown, *Unexpected News: Reading the Bible with Third World Eyes* (Philadelphia: Westminster, 1984).

9. The notion that the Bible was not to be taught to children except in brief verses was characteristic of the liberal theology that influenced many Protestant denominations after WWI. In recent times a good deal of Protestant and Roman Catholic curriculum has reflected the work of Ronald J. Goldman on teaching the Bible to children [*Religious Thinking from Childhood to Adolescence* and *Readiness for Religion* (London: Routledge and Kegan Paul, 1964 and 1965)]. His work gave new impetus to the notion that the Bible was to be regarded as an adult book by grounding that notion in his own assessment of Piaget's theories and his own

testing of biblical material with children. Even a cursory glance at his understandings of the Bible by someone conversant with recent discussions in the biblical field would quickly give evidence of a simplistic, reductionist, and Marcionite (that is, rejecting the Old Testament as Scripture) understanding of the Bible and its development. Yet, his work has deeply influenced many Christian educators and educational curriculum material. Robin Maas has written a recent dissertation for Catholic University of America which critically analyzes Goldman's work and its influence and suggests the importance of moving beyond Goldman ("New Foundations for Biblical Education with Children: A Challenge to Goldman," 1985). See also Robin Maas, "Biblical Catechesis and Religious Development: The Goldman Project Twenty Years Later," *Living Light,* 22, January 1986, 124–144.

10. For a detailed and helpful treatment of this process of equipping adults for Bible study see Robin Maas, *Church Bible Study Handbook* (Nashville: Abingdon, 1982).

THE CONGREGATION AS CHAMELEON
Jackson W. Carroll

1. Others have also used the "chameleon" metaphor for the church. See, for example, James M. Gustafson, *Treasure in Earthen Vessels* (New York: Harper and Brothers, 1961), 112.

2. The research is a pilot study by economist John Hiller for Hartford Seminary's Center for Social and Religious Research. A follow-up study of a sample of 650 congregations is currently underway to test further the pilot findings and to discover how internal factors in congregations interact with community changes.

3. H. Paul Douglass and Edmund deS. Brunner, *The Protestant Church as a Social Institution* (New York: Russell and Russell, 1935), 237.

4. For a discussion of social worlds and methods for studying them, see Jackson W. Carroll, Carl S. Dudley, and William McKinney, eds., *Handbook for Congregational Studies* (Nashville: Abingdon, 1986), 51–54.

5. For a helpful summary, see Michael Argyle and Benjamin Beit-Hallahmi, *The Social Psychology of Religion* (London: Routledge and Kegan Paul, 1975).

6. *From Max Weber: Essays in Sociology,* translated, edited and with an Introduction by H. H. Gerth and C. Wright Mills. (New York: Oxford University, Galaxy Book, 1958), 63.

270 Congregations: Their Power to Form and Transform

7. An especially helpful summary of research on this issue is in Keith A. Roberts, *Religion in Sociological Perspective* (Homewood, IL.: Dorsey, 1984), 269–323.

8. Wayne A. Meeks, *The First Urban Christians: The Social World of the Apostle Paul* (New Haven: Yale University, 1982).

9. David C. Leege and Thomas A. Trozzolo, "Participation in Catholic Parish Life: Religious Activities in the 1980s," Report No. 3 of the Notre Dame Study of Catholic Parish Life, April 1985, 2. (Emphasis in the original.)

10. Ibid.

11. David A. Roozen, William McKinney, and Jackson W. Carroll, *Varieties of Religious Presence* (New York: Pilgrim, 1984).

12. Ibid., 261 ff.

13. For an interesting discussion of regional differences in one denomination, see Robert L. Wilson and William H. Willimon, *The Seven Churches of Methodism* (Durham, N.C.: The Ormand Center at Duke University, 1985).

14. See Douglas Alan Walrath, "Sizing Up a Congregation" *Alban Institute Action Information* (May—June 1985): 7–9.

15. Irenaeus, *Against Heresies,* 5, Pref.

16. Andrew M. Greeley and Mary Greeley Durkin, *How to Save the Catholic Church* (New York: Viking, 1984), 166.

17. A congregation in a highly mobile community, where there is constant member turnover, probably will not have as strong a sense of a shared identity as will a congregation in which there is some continuity of membership over a period of time. A pastor in one such congregation, in a highly mobile community (adjacent to a military base), also noted that it is difficult for a congregation of that kind to generate much excitement about its future.

18. Orrin E. Klapp, *Models of Social Order* (Palo Alto, CA.: National, 1973), 296.

19. Gerth and Mills, eds., *From Max Weber,* 280.

20. George A. Lindbeck, *The Nature of Doctrine* (Philadelphia: Westminster Press, 1984). See especially 32 ff.

21. For a fuller discussion of congregational identity and methods for studying it, see Carroll, Dudley and McKinney, eds., *Handbook for Congregational Studies,* Chapter 2. Also, the discussion of "corporate cultures" by organizational researchers and consultants is akin to what I mean by congregational identity. A helpful

summary of this perspective can be found in Edgar H. Schein, "Corporate Culture: What It Is and How to Change It," Address delivered to the 1983 Convocation of the Society of Sloan Fellows, Massachusetts Institute of Technology, Cambridge, MA, October 14, 1983.

22. See, for example, Lyle Schaller, "A Practitioner's Perspective," in *Building Effective Ministry*, edited by Carl S. Dudley (San Francisco: Harper and Row, 1983), 162–164; and Kennon Callahan *Twelve Keys to an Effective Church* (San Francisco: Harper and Row, 1983), xii.

23. A guide to gaining strategic knowledge about a congregation's context is found in Carroll, Dudley, and McKinney (eds.), *Handbook for Congregational Studies*, Chapter 3.

24. Cited in Alan K. Waltz, *Images of the Future* (Nashville: Abingdon, 1980), 15.

25. James MacGregor Burns, *Leadership* (New York: Harper and Row, 1978), 19. (Emphasis in the original.)

26. Douglass and Brunner, *Protestant Church as a Social Institution*, 254.

27. Roozen, McKinney, and Carroll, *Varieties of Religious Presence*, 272 ff.

28. Jackson W. Carroll, *Ministry As Reflective Practice* (Washington, D.C.: Alban Institute, 1986).

WHY DO PEOPLE
CONGREGATE?
David S. Steward

1. Sidney E. Mead, *The Lively Experiment: The Shaping of Christianity in America* (New York: Harper & Row, 1963).

2. Kenneth Scott Latourette, *A History of the Expansion of Christianity* (New York: Harper and Brothers, 1937–1945, 7v), IV, 424.

3. Mead, *The Lively Experiment*, 103.

4. George Santayana, *Character and Opinion in the United States* (New York: Charles Scribner's Sons, 1920), 168.

5. Alexis de Tocqueville, *Democracy in America*, trans. Henry Reeve, 4th ed. (New York: J. & H. G. Langley, 1841).

6. Emile Durkheim, *The Elementary Forms of the Religious Life* (New York: The Free Press, 1967), 61.

7. Ibid.

8. Ernst Troeltsch, *The Social Teaching of the Christian Churches* (Chicago: University of Chicago, 1931).

9. Ibid., 745.

10. Lauve Steenhuisen, *Determinants of Disaffiliation: Research into the Events and Motivations which Lead Persons to Leave Local Churches in the Northern Virginia Synod of the Lutheran Church in America,* Doctoral Dissertation (Ph.D.), Graduate Theological Union, 1984, 18–19.

11. Edward Rauff, *Why People Join the Church* (New York: Pilgrim, 1979), 15.

12. Andrew M. Greeley, *Crisis in the Church* (Chicago: Thomas More Press, 1979), 55–56.

13. David A. Roozen, *The Churched and the Unchurched in America: a Comparative Profile* (Washington, D.C.: Glenmary Research Center, 1978).

14. J. Russell Hale, *Who Are the Unchurched?* (San Francisco: Harper and Row, 1980), vi.

15. John Savage, *The Apathetic and Bored Church Member* (Pittsford, New York: Lead Consultants, 1976).

16. Jack L. Seymour develops a method for looking at history and purpose in "The Future of the Past: History and Policy Making in Religious Education," *Religious Education,* Vol. 81, No. 1, 1986, 113–133.

17. cf. Jack L. Seymour, Robert O'Gorman, and Charles R. Foster, *The Church in the Education of the Public* (Nashville: Abingdon, 1984), chap. 1.

18. cf. Jack L. Seymour, *From Sunday School to Church School: Continuities in Protestant Church Education in the United States, 1860–1929* (Washington, D.C.: University Press of America, 1982).

19. "Annual Message to Congress, December 1, 1861," in Abraham Lincoln, *The Life and Writings of Abraham Lincoln,* ed. by Philip Van Doren Stern (New York: Random House, 1940), 745. Cf. Mead, *The Lively Experiment,* chap. 5. For a current exploration of American life and values cf. Robert N. Bellah, et al., *Habits of the Heart: Individualism and Commitment in American Life* (Berkeley: University of California, 1985).

20. Roozen, *The Churched and the Unchurched,* 30.

21. Dean Hoge, *Converts, Dropouts, Returnees* (New York: Pilgrim, 1981).

22. Joseph H. Fichter, *Social Relations in the Urban Parish* (Chicago: University of Chicago, 1954).

23. Hale, *Who Are the Unchurched?*

24. Ibid., 186.

25. Steenhuisen, *Determinants of Disaffiliation,* 21.

26. Bruce Reinhart, *The Institutional Nature of Adult Christian Education* (Philadelphia: Westminster, 1962).

27. John H. Westerhoff III., *Living the Faith Community: The Church that Makes a Difference* (Minneapolis: Winston, 1985), 9.

28. Warren J. Hartman, *Membership Trends* (Nashville: Discipleship Resources, 1976), summarized in Steenhuisen, 34.

29. John Kotre, *The View from the Border* (Chicago: Aldine-Atherton, Inc., 1971), 91.

30. John Savage, *The Apathetic and Bored Church Member.*

31. Steenhuisen, *Determinants of Disaffiliation,* 11.

32. Ibid., 113.

33. Cf. Robert Stoll Armstrong, *Service Evangelism* (Philadelphia: Westminster, 1979).

USING CHURCH IMAGES
Carl S. Dudley

1. Paul S. Minear, *Images of the Church in the New Testament* (Philadelphia: Westminster, 1960).

2. Hans Küng, *The Church,* tr. Ray and Rosaleen Ockenden (New York: Sheed and Ward, 1967). See especially pages 107–260.

3. Lyle E. Schaller, *Parish Planning* (Nashville: Abingdon, 1971). Note that Schaller has returned to this theme in different perspectives in several books, especially: *Hey, That's Our Church* (1975), *Activating the Passive Church* (1981), and *Looking in the Mirror* (1984), all published by Abingdon.

4. This typology is most clearly defined in "Types of Small Churches and Their Implications for Planning" in *Small Churches Are Beautiful* (New York: Harper and Row, 1977), ed. Jackson W. Carroll. Programmatic applications of his typology can be seen in *Leading Churches Through Change* (Nashville: Abingdon, 1979), by Douglas A. Walrath. Procedures for determining social location are provided in Walrath's *Planning for Your Church* (Philadelphia: Westminster, 1984).

5. Ezra Earl Jones first published this in *Strategies for New Churches* (New York: Harper and Row, 1976). It was set in the context of other studies by James D. Anderson and Ezra Earl Jones in *The Management of Ministry* (New York: Harper and Row, 1978).

6. See especially: Ian G. Barbour, *Myths, Models and Paradigms* (New York: Harper and Row, 1974); Carl S. Dudley, *Where Have All Our People Gone?* (New York: Pilgrim, 1979); Ralph P. Martin, *The Family and the Fellowship: New Testament Images of the Church* (Grand Rapids: Eerdmans, 1980); Gaylord B. Noyce, *Survival and Mission for the City Church* (Philadelphia: Westminster, 1973); and Lyle E. Schaller, *Activating the Passive Church* (Nashville: Abingdon, 1981).

7. H. Richard Niebuhr, *Christ and Culture* (New York: Harper and Row, 1951).

8. David A. Roozen, William J. McKinney, and Jackson W. Carroll, *Varieties of Religious Presence* (New York: Pilgrim, 1984).

9. Avery Dulles, *Models of the Church* (Garden City, NY: Doubleday, 1974).

10. Dan Baumann, *All Originality Makes a Dull Church* (Santa Ana, CA: Vision House, 1976).

11. This particular set of images is based on teaching, consulting, and workshop research through McCormick Theological Seminary and the Center for Congregational Ministries. Its earliest formulation was published in the chapters on "Choice for Churches" and "Something That Works" in *Where Have All Our People Gone?* (New York: Pilgrim, 1979); and its most recent expression can be found in *The Christian Ministry*, "Seven Images of the Church" (Vol. 17, No. 6; January 1986). Images of the church are among the tools for congregational renewal through self-understanding which have been developed by the Center for Congregational Ministries of McCormick Theological Seminary.

12. Although these questions and images were written from responses among the laity of the congregations we work with, they clearly are informed by other authors and consultants. The emphasis on the relational dimensions of church participation is often mentioned but rarely used as a category of analysis. Ralph Martin (see footnote 6), in his study of images in the New Testament, makes a distinction between family and fellowship, which is similar to our distinction of old and new family. Curiously, the Apostle Paul provides much of our most vivid imagery for the continuity of family (e.g., in Eph. 2:19), while Jesus dramatically points to

the need for new beginnings in his functional definition of brothers and sisters in the family of God (Matt. 12:46–50). Other writers who use family or extended family images (e.g., Baumann, Dulles, and Noyce, as cited in footnotes 6, 9, and 10) either blur the distinctions we have found or emphasize one dimension to the exclusion of the others.

13. This concept of the sense of the sacred is very similar to the work of Avery Dulles (see footnote 9) who uses the image of church as sacrament to unite the church images of institution and mystical communion. The Old First Church image is one expression of emphasis on order and continuity (as found in Dulles' church as institution, in a sense of grand tradition found in Noyce's image of cathedral, and in a sense of authority found in Baumann's image of the church as teacher [see footnotes 6, 9, and 10]). The Christian Sanctuary is more a combination of Dulles' images of Sacrament and Mystical Communion. Our use of Sanctuary is significantly different from Roozen, et al. (see footnote 8), since we have not found that the sanctuary ideal leads only to withdrawal from the world. Sanctuary may be a more basic image of the vertical relationship between God and humanity carried in relationships with people and places. It may be the foundation for other images without being in the forefront of our consciousness at all times.

14. The relationship of the church to the community is more similar to the issue about which Niebuhr, Noyce, and Roozen, et al. have written. In our experience, the Roozen, et al. ideal of Civic Church finds expression in two forms which are parallel to Noyce's two images of Living Room/Forum and Servant, and similar to Niebuhr's distinction between "Christ above Culture" and "Christ and Culture in Paradox." Many writers (Baumann, Dulles, etc.) have noted the biblical and contemporary importance of the servant image in contrast with other categories (above) without noting the distinction between Citizen and Servant: the Christian Citizen ideal uses the church building to provide services for people who essentially are similar to themselves and living in a common community. The Christian Servant seeks to touch the lives of others who are in need, doing so either through the church building or, more frequently, through other agencies in the community. We have found a major difference between Citizen and Servant in the motivations of members and the programs they support in the local church.

15. Commitment to change is one of five basic images which Niebuhr developed. Similar to the research of Roozen, et al., we find the

motivation toward change in two broad expressions: Evangelistic and Social Activist. However, the image of the Christian Evangelist which we find is more similar to Dulles and Baumann than to Roozen, et al., who anchor their image in an emphasis on otherworldly salvation. The image of Evangelist we find in mainline churches sees worldly wealth as reward and as responsibility which is not inconsistent with their Christian calling. The image we find of Christian Prophet also is similar to Noyce's Revolutionary Cadre which, as he observes, may be more a subgroup within the church than the dominant image of the whole congregation.

CENTERS OF VISION
AND ENERGY
Donald Eugene Miller

1. The suggestions of this chapter are developed further in Donald Miller, *Story and Context: An Introduction to Christian Education* (Nashville: Abingdon, in press).

2. A dynamic interaction between conditioning and guiding factors derives from Max Weber, for example, *The Theory of Social and Economic Organization* (Glencoe, Illinois: The Free Press, 1947). Ernst Troeltsch, *The Social Teaching of the Christian Churches* (New York: Macmillan, 1956). Talcott Parsons and Edward Shils, *Toward a General Theory of Action* (New York: Harper and Row, 1962).

3. Max Stackhouse, *Ethics and the Urban Ethos* (Boston: Beacon, 1972), develops the idea of a functioning credo. For the way that belief functions as a link between individual and community see Sara Little, *To Set One's Heart* (Atlanta: John Knox, 1983).

4. A classic statement of this view is in Emile Durkheim, *The Elementary Forms of the Religious Life* (New York: Free Press, 1965).

5. An introduction to the relationship of formal and informal authority is to be found in Amitai Etzioni, *Modern Organizations* (Englewood Cliffs, New Jersey: Prentice-Hall, 1964).

6. Robert Worley, *A Gathering of Strangers: Understanding the Life of Your Church* (Philadelphia: Westminster Press, 1983), has useful suggestions for studying the relationship of formal and informal authority.

7. Sara Little, *To Set One's Heart.*

8. Contextual and other factors are discussed in Carl S. Dudley (ed.), *Building Effective Ministry: Theory and Practice in the Local Church* (San Francisco: Harper and Row, 1983).

9. The importance of story and narrative is emphasized in such works as Stanley Hauerwas, *A Community of Character: Toward a Constructive Christian Social Ethic* (Notre Dame, IN: University of Notre Dame, 1981); Craig Dykstra, *Vision and Character: A Christian Educator's Alternative to Kohlberg* (New York: Paulist, 1981); and Donald Miller, *Story and Context.*

10. The categories of comedy, tragedy, romance, and irony are taken from James Hopewell. See Carl Dudley, *Building Effective Ministry,* ch. 5.

11. The method given here is a variant of that developed in James Poling and Donald Miller, *Foundations for a Practical Theology of Ministry* (Nashville: Abingdon, 1985). Compare the method found in Thomas Groome, *Christian Religious Education,* (New York: Harper and Row, 1980). For a practical application of Groome's approach, see his chapter on "Experience/Story/Vision" in *Beautiful upon the Mountains: A Handbook for Church Education in Appalachia,* ed. D. Campbell Wyckoff and Henrietta T. Wilkinson (Memphis, TN: Board of Christian Education of the Cumberland Presbyterian Church, 1984), 101–122. Compare also James Whitehead and Evelyn Whitehead, *Method in Ministry* (New York: Seabury, 1980).

12. Principal among them are John H. Westerhoff and William H. Willimon, *Liturgy and Learning Through the Life Cycle* (New York: Seabury, 1980); and Robert L. Browning and Roy A. Reed, *The Sacraments in Religious Education and Liturgy* (Birmingham, Alabama: Religious Education Press, 1985).

13. A well-known statement of the management type is James D. Anderson and Ezra Earl Jones, *The Management of Ministry* (San Francisco: Harper and Row, 1978).

14. A fine description of the small church as a primary group is given by Carl Dudley, *Making the Small Church Effective* (Nashville: Abingdon, 1978).

15. A description of the growth and development type is given in Jack Seymour and Donald Miller, *Contemporary Approaches to Christian Education* (Nashville: Abingdon, 1982), ch. 4.

16. For a discussion of the prophetic type of congregation see James M. Gustafson, *The Church as Moral Decision Maker* (Boston: Pilgrim, 1970).

17. Amitai Etzioni, *Modern Organizations.*

18. Though primarily directed to theological education, Edward Farley, *Theologia* (Philadelphia: Fortress, 1983), implies that con-

gregations should be centers of interpretation. See also Seymour
and Miller, *Contemporary Approaches to Christian Education*, ch. 6.

MEETING IN THE SILENCE
Mary Elizabeth Moore

1. World Council of Churches, *Jesus Christ—the Life of the World: Worship Book for the Sixth Assembly* (Geneva: World Council of Churches, 1983), 94. This prayer is translated from the German.

2. Thomas Merton maintains the historical distinction between infused (or passive) contemplation and active contemplation. The former is completely given by God and involves no acts of will on the part of the contemplative. Active contemplation, however, does involve intentional acts of will to help one focus on God. Merton understands infused contemplation to be the vocation of mystics and active contemplation to be part of the calling of all Christians. See: Thomas Merton, *Spiritual Direction and Meditation* and *What Is Contemplation?* (Wheathampstead, Hertfordshire, England: Anthony Clark Books, 1975, 1950), 95–98.

3. Ibid., 85.

4. Ibid., 90.

5. Ibid., 77.

6. Ibid., 78.

7. Ibid., 63–64.

8. These different aspects of reflection are developed more fully in: Mary Elizabeth Moore, *Education for Continuity and Change* (Nashville: Abingdon, 1983), 130–131.

9. Charles Foster, *Teaching in the Community of Faith* (Nashville: Abingdon, 1982), 93, 100–101.

10. Phenix considers wonder, awe, and reverence together as one cluster of dispositions. He also includes hope, creativity, awareness, and doubt and faith in his listing. See: Philip Phenix, "Transcendence and the Curriculum," in William Pinar, ed., *Curriculum Theorizing: The Reconceptualists* (Berkeley: McCutchan, 1975), 328–333.

11. Ibid., 332.

12. Richard J. Foster, *Celebration of Discipline: The Path to Spiritual Growth* (San Francisco: Harper & Row, 1978), 13.

13. Paulo Freire, *Pedagogy of the Oppressed,* tr. Myra B. Ramos (New York: Herder & Herder, 1972), 28–29.

14. See particularly: Elisabeth Schüssler Fiorenza, *In Memory of Her: A Feminist Theological Reconstruction of Christian Origins* (New York: Crossland, 1983); *Bread Not Stone: The Challenge of Feminist Biblical Interpretation* (Boston: Beacon, 1984).

15. Jack L. Seymour and Donald E. Miller, *Contemporary Approaches to Christian Education* (Nashville: Abingdon, 1982). This book offered an insightful review of the contemporary approaches, and the failure to include a category for meditative approaches seems to reflect accurately the field rather than the editors' blindness.

16. Thomas Merton, *Contemplation in a World of Action* (Garden City, N.Y.: Doubleday & Co., Inc., 1973 [1965]), 179.

17. Ibid., 173–174.

18. Merton, *Spiritual Direction and Meditation,* 54–62.

19. Merton, *Contemplation in a World of Action,* 175. See also: Merton, *Spiritual Direction and Meditation,* 74.

20. Merton, *Contemplation in a World of Action,* 176–177.

21. Stephen Verney, *Fire in Coventry* (London: Hodder and Stoughton Ltd., 1964), 13.

22. Ibid., 13–14.

23. Ibid., 15. Reprinted by permission of Hodder and Stoughton Ltd.

24. Ibid., 16–17.

25. Ibid., 19–22.

26. Ibid., 35.

27. Ibid., 56–57.

28. Ibid., 61–66.

29. Ibid., 72.

30. See particularly: Dorothee Soelle, *The Inward Road and the Way Back,* tr. David L. Scheidt (London: Darton, Longman & Todd, 1978, 1975); and J. B. Libanio, *Spiritual Discernment and Politics: Guidelines for Religious Communities,* tr. Theodore Morrow (Maryknoll, N.Y.: Orbis, 1982, 1977).

31. Francis X. Meehan, *A Contemporary Social Spirituality* (Maryknoll, N.Y.: Orbis, 1982). Meehan discusses what he calls "three levels of spiritual living, namely, the intrapersonal, the interpersonal and the structural" (see page 7). These are similar to what is being proposed in the first and third dimensions here, but Meehan puts somewhat more emphasis on society as the recipient

of our service and less on listening to and critiquing the voices of society in order to discern and meet God there. The similarities are probably far more important than the differences of emphasis.

32. Moore, *Education for Continuity,* 169.

33. Some of these are already included in these notes. See: Thomas Merton, *Spiritual Direction and Meditation & What Is Contemplation?*; Richard Foster, *Celebration of Discipline*; Dorothee Soelle, *The Inward Road and the Way Back*; J. B. Libanio, *Spiritual Discernment and Politics*; Francis X. Meehan, *A Contemporary Social Spirituality.*
   Other resources include: Tilden Edwards, *Spiritual Friend* (New York: Paulist, 1980); Matthew Fox, *On Becoming a Musical Mystical Bear* (New York: Paulist, 1976); or Hallie Iglehart, *Womanspirit: A Guide to Women's Wisdom* (San Francisco: Harper & Row, 1983).

BELONGING
Robert L. Browning

1. Søren Kierkegaard, *Attack Upon "Christendom",* translated by Walter Lowrie (Boston: Beacon, 1956), 218.

2. Karl Barth, *The Teaching of the Church Regarding Baptism* (London: SCM, 1948), 49.

3. Ibid., 54.

4. See Oscar Cullmann, *Baptism in the New Testament* (Philadelphia: Westminster, 1950).

5. See *The Rites of the Catholic Church* (New York: Pueblo Publishing Co., 1976).

6. See Aidan Kavanagh, *The Shape of Baptism: The Rite of Christian Initiation* (New York: Pueblo Publishing Co., 1978).

7. Elizabeth O'Connor, *Call to Commitment: The Story of the Church of the Saviour* (New York: Harper and Row, 1963), 104.

8. Alexander Schmemann, *For the Life of the World* (Crestwood: New York: St. Vladimir's Seminary, 1973), 8–16.

9. Paul Tillich, in *The Future of Religions,* ed. by Jerald Brauer (New York: Harper and Row, 1966), 87.

10. Karl Rahner, *Theological Investigations,* XIV (London: Darton, Longman & Todd, 1976), 166.

11. See Robert L. Browning and Roy A. Reed, *The Sacraments in Religious Education and Liturgy: An Ecumenical Model.* (Birmingham, AL: Religious Education Press, 1985), Part I.

12. Edward Schillebeeckx, *The Mission of the Church* (New York: Seabury, 1973), 48.

13. Browning and Reed, *The Sacraments in Religious Education and Liturgy.*

14. Louis Bouyer, *Rite and Man: Natural Sacredness and Christian Liturgy* (Notre Dame, IN: University of Notre Dame, 1963), 196.

15. Erik Erikson, *Toys and Reasons: Stages in the Ritualization of Experience* (New York: W. W. Norton, 1977), 89–90.

16. See James W. Fowler, *Stages of Faith* (New York: Harper and Row, 1981).

17. See Browning and Reed, *The Sacraments in Religious Education and Liturgy,* Part III, 119–300.

18. See Bernard Cooke, *Sacraments and Sacramentality* (Mystic, CT: Twenty-Third Publications, 1983). He sees the sacrament of marriage as a primary model of what sacraments are all about in terms of theology and human development.

19. Geoffrey Wainwright, *Christian Initiation* (Richmond, VA: John Knox, 1969), 40.

20. For resources see William J. Bausch, *A New Look at the Sacraments* (Notre Dame, IN: Fides/Claretian, 1977), a Roman Catholic resource.
James F. White, *Sacraments as God's Self-Giving* (Nashville: Abingdon, 1982), a United Methodist resource.
Anthony M. Coniaris, *These Are the Sacraments: The Life-Giving Mysteries of the Orthodox Church* (Minneapolis, MN: Light and Life Publishing Co., 1981), an Orthodox resource with a full description of the drama of infant baptism, using the "unified initiation" approach.

21. See Edward Yarnold, *The Awe-Inspiring Rites of Initiation: Baptismal Homilies of the Fourth Century* (Slough, England: St. Paul Publication, 1971).

22. See *Rites of the Catholic Church.*

23. See James B. Dunning, *New Wine, New Wine Skins: Pastoral Implications of the Rite of Initiation of Adults* (Sadlier, 1981); and Kenneth Bayack, *A Parish Guide to Adult Initiation* (New York: Paulist, 1979).

24. See *A Service of Baptism, Confirmation, and Renewal.* (Nashville: The United Methodist Publishing House, 1980), revised edition.

25. Geoffrey Wainwright, *Eucharist and Eschatology* (London: Epworth, 1971), 141.

26. See John H. Westerhoff and William H. Willimon, *Liturgy and Learning Through the Life Cycle* (New York: Seabury, 1980).

27. See James F. White, *The Sacraments as God's Self-Giving.*

28. Max Thurian, *Consecration of the Layman* (Baltimore: Helicon, 1963) 84.

29. Erik Erikson, "Identity and the Life Cycle," in *Psychological Issues.* 1 (New York: International University, 1959), 142.

LEADING
Janet F. Fishburn

1. Janet F. Fishburn and Neill Q. Hamilton, *Effectiveness in Ministry Research Report* (Forthcoming), Part III, 7.

2. Robert W. Lynn and Elliott Wright, *The Big Little School* (New York: Harper and Row, 1971).

3. Philip H. Lotz, ed., *Orientation in Religious Education* (Nashville: Abingdon-Cokesbury, 1950), 396–397.

4. Fishburn and Hamilton, *Effectiveness in Ministry,* Part V.

5. Letty M. Russell, *The Future of Partnership* (Philadelphia: Westminster, 1979).

6. James M. Gustafson, *Treasure in Earthen Vessels* (New York: Harper and Brothers, 1961), 51–52.

7. Donald P. Smith, *Congregations Alive* (Philadelphia: Westminster, 1981), 112.

8. Kennon L. Callahan, *Twelve Keys to an Effective Church* (New York: Harper and Row, 1983), xiii.

9. Donald P. Smith, *Congregations Alive,* 109.

10. This inspired phrase comes from the Benedictine Rule as developed by St. Benedict of Nursia (c. 480—c. 547) for the Roman Catholic order and monastery at Monte Cassino in Italy.

COMMUNICATING
Charles R. Foster

1. The emphasis upon the intentionality of the systematic efforts of a people to maintain structures for teaching and learning over time dominates most discussions of education; cf. Walter Brueggemann, *The Creative Word: Canon as a Model for Biblical Education* (Philadelphia: Fortress, 1982), 1; Edward O. Farley, "Can Church Education Be Theological Education?" *Theology Today,*

July 1985, 158; Lawrence A. Cremin, *Traditions of American Education* (New York: Basic Books, 1976), viii; as well as in the works of such educators as Maxine Greene, *Teacher as Stranger.* (Belmont, CA.: Wadsworth Publishing Co., 1973), 69–71; Thomas H. Groome, *Christian Religious Education* (New York: Harper and Row, 1980), 4–12; and my own *Teaching in the Community of Faith* (Nashville: Abingdon, 1982), 109–117.

2. I am distinguishing "informal conversation" as a pattern of communication from several other patterns which could also be analyzed for their contribution to the education of a people. Gossip, for example, is a major source of the information critical to the formation, maintenance, and revitalization of group or community life. For a discussion of the function of gossip see James W. Fowler, *Becoming Adult, Becoming Christian: Adult Development and Christian Faith* (New York: Harper and Row, 1984), 15–17; and especially Samuel C. Heilman, *Synagogue Life: A Study in Symbolic Interaction* (Chicago: The University of Chicago, 1976), 151–92. The contribution of small talk to the corporate task of sustaining group cohesion and solidarity over time and the relationship of the rhythm of the talk of the people of some cultures to their work productivity could also be examined for their contribution to the learning of people.

3. David Tracy, *The Analogical Imagination: Christian Theology and the Culture of Pluralism* (New York: Crossroad Publishing, 1981), 101.

4. Ibid.

5. Herve Varenne. *Americans Together: Structured Diversity in a Midwestern Town* (New York: Teachers College, 1977), 92–95.

6. Arnold Van Gennep. *The Rites of Passage* (Chicago: University of Chicago, 1960) and Victor Turner. *The Ritual Process: Structure and Anti-Structure* (Ithaca, NY: Cornell Paperbacks, 1977), 125ff.

7. Peter L. Berger, *The Heretical Imperative: Contemporary Possibilities of Religious Affirmation* (Garden City, NY: Doubleday, 1970), 2.

8. See Samuel C. Heilman, *Synagogue Life: A Study in Symbolic Interaction,* 135.

9. Many books have described this movement. Among the most influential are John L. Casteel, ed., *Spiritual Renewal Through Personal Groups* (New York: Association Press, 1957); Elizabeth O'Connor, *Call to Commitment: the Story of the Church of the*

Saviour, Washington, D.C. (New York: Harper and Row, 1963); Robert A. Raines, *New Life in the Church* (New York: Harper, 1961).

10. Adrienne and John Carr, *An Experiment in Practical Christianity* (Nashville: Discipleship Resources, 1985), revised edition.

TEACHING
Maria Harris

1. John Dewey, *Experience and Education* (New York: Collier, 1938), 48.

2. Christopher Logue, "Ode to the Dodo" in *Collected Poems 1953–1987* (London: Turret Books, 1987), 96. Poem reprinted by permission of the author.

3. Paulo Freire, *Pedagogy of the Oppressed,* tr. Myra B. Ramos (New York: Herder & Herder, 1972), passim.

4. Frank Proctor, "Matching Training to a Teacher's Level of Experience," *JED SHARE,* Vol. 11, No. 3, Fall 1982, 20–21. Note: Proctor's article is based on Lillian G. Katz, *Talk to Teachers* (Washington, D.C.: National Association for the Education of Young Children, 1977).

Notes on Contributors

BRUCE C. BIRCH is Professor of Old Testament at Wesley Theological Seminary in Washington, D.C. He is an ordained member of the Baltimore Annual Conference of the United Methodist Church and serves on the denomination's General Board of Church and Society. He is the author of *What Does the Lord Require?* and, with Larry Rasmussen, co-author of *Bible and Ethics in the Christian Life* and *The Predicament of the Prosperous.*

ROBERT L. BROWNING is the William A. Chryst Professor of Christian Education at The Methodist Theological School in Ohio. He is author of or contributor to several books and self-instruction tape series. His most recent book, with Roy Reed, is *The Sacraments in Religious Education and Liturgy: An Ecumenical Model.* His current projects are a book on pastoral leadership in religious education, and research on the communications revolution and religious education in the future.

JACKSON W. CARROLL is Professor of Religion and Society, and Director of Research, at Hartford Seminary. An ordained United Methodist minister, he served as a local church and university pastor and taught at Emory University before joining the Hartford Seminary faculty in 1974. He is author or co-author of several books, including *Too Many Pastors?*, *Women of the Cloth*, *Varieties of Religious Presence*, and *Ministry as Reflective Practice.* He is co-editor of *Handbook for Congregational Studies.*

CARL S. DUDLEY is Professor of Church and Community at McCormick Theological Seminary, and Director of the Center for Congregation Ministries, in Chicago, Illinois. He has specialized in the study of congregations, including small churches, church growth, churches in changing communities, and the issues of evangelism, stewardship, social service, and justice ministries of the church. He has written *Making the Small Church Effective* and *Where Have All Our People Gone?*, edited *Building Effective Ministry,* and co-authored *Handbook for Congregational Studies.*

JANET F. FISHBURN is Associate Professor of Teaching Ministry and American Church History in the Theological School and the Graduate School of Drew University in Madison, New Jersey. She brings a historical and theological perspective to the theory of Christian education and the teaching role of pastors in the church. She is the author of *The Fatherhood of God and the Victorian Family: The Social Gospel in America* (1982) and numerous articles about educational ministry. Her most recent research, for the United Methodist Board of Higher Education and Ministry, includes a sociological study of the characteristics of effective ministry. A book about the respective roles of family and church in the spiritual formation process is forthcoming.

CHARLES R. FOSTER is Professor of Christian Education at Scarritt Graduate School. He has been a member of the Christian education faculty and served as acting dean of the Methodist Theological School in Ohio. Recent publications include *The Ministry of the Volunteer Teacher, Teaching in the Community of Faith, The Church in the Education of the Public: Refocusing the Task of Religious Education,* and *The Black Christian Education Journey.*

MARIA HARRIS is Visiting Professor of Religious Education in the School of Religion and Religious Education, Fordham University, New York City Previously she served as Howard Professor of Religious Education at Andover Newton Theological School in Massachusetts. She is author of over fifty articles and six books: among them are *The D.R.E. Reader,*

Portrait of Youth Ministry, and most recently, *Teaching and Religious Imagination* (Harper and Row).

DONALD EUGENE MILLER is Brightbill Professor of Ministry at Bethany Theological Seminary, Oak Brook, Illinois, where he has been teaching for the past twenty-four years. He teaches in the area of Christian Education and ethics, and he is also director of the Doctor of Ministry Program. Don spent his last sabbatical leave teaching at the Theological College of Northern Nigeria. He is a member of the Church of the Brethren and is a graduate of Bethany Seminary, The University of Chicago, and Harvard University.

MARY ELIZABETH MOORE is Associate Professor of Christian Education and Theology at the School of Theology at Claremont, California. She is author of *Education for Continuity and Change* and has written and taught in areas of educational ministry, feminist theology, and theology of spirituality. Her church work has been focused in youth ministry and in denominational and ecumenical boards related to education and ministry. She is married to Allen Moore, and they have five children.

C. ELLIS NELSON is Visiting Professor of Christian Education at Austin Presbyterian Theological Seminary. Previously he served as Skinner and McAlpin Professor of Practical Theology at Union Seminary in New York and as President and Professor of Louisville Presbyterian Theological Seminary. He is the author of *Where Faith Begins, Don't Let Your Conscience Be Your Guide, Conscience: Theological and Psychological Perspectives* (ed.), *Using Evaluation in Theological Education,* and essays on moral education.

DAVID S. STEWARD is Professor of Religious Education at Pacific School of Religion. He lives in Berkeley, California, which is a crossroad of cultures and religions. His research has focused on the experience people and their families have of cultural boundaries, and of how these are important in school and church settings. In the process, he has become aware of many of the patterns which make American culture, and of the independence which makes Americans pluralistic.